Blender 3D Incredible Models

A comprehensive guide to hard-surface modeling, procedural texturing, and rendering

Arijan Belec

BIRMINGHAM—MUMBAI

Blender 3D Incredible Models

Group Product Manager: Rohit Rajkumar
Publishing Product Manager: Kaustubh Manglurkar
Senior Editor: Hayden Edwards
Content Development Editor: Abhishek Jadhav
Technical Editor: Simran Udasi
Copy Editor: Safis Editing
Project Coordinator: Ajesh Devavaram
Proofreader: Safis Editing
Indexer: Pratik Shirodkar
Production Designer: Shankar Kalbhor
Marketing Coordinator: Teny Thomas

First published: August 2022

Production reference: 3080922

Published by Packt Publishing Ltd.
Livery Place
35 Livery Street
Birmingham
B3 2PB, UK.

ISBN 978-1-80181-781-3

www.packt.com

To Marijan and Nataša, for the greatest lesson one can learn.

– Arijan Belec

Contributors

About the author

Arijan Belec is a 3D artist and YouTuber specializing in hard-surface modeling. Since the age of 14, he has been developing and sharing advanced modeling techniques within the Blender community. With both online and face-to-face tutoring experience, Arijan has a growing YouTube presence with Blender tutorials suitable for an audience with varying skill levels.

His most successful YouTube videos and freelance projects are primarily related to tank modeling, which has led some to refer to him as the best tank modeler on YouTube.

About the reviewer

Steve Robinson worked as an Aerospace engineer for nearly 20 years, with 12 years specifically dedicated to working in the space industry. One of his most recent personal achievements was assisting in the construction of the ExoMars TGO spacecraft whilst living in Germany, the mission being to address the question of whether life has ever existed on Mars.

In early 2021, Steve resigned completely from his lifelong engineering career, to focus his energy on his obsession with computer games and becoming a competent self-taught 3D artist. He is currently employed as a volunteer at Cinder Interactive, working on a fan made recreation of TimeSplitters, where he contributes as an environment artist

I'd like to thank my parents, family, and friends who understand the time and commitment it takes to study and self-teach industry standard game art. I would also like to thank the growing online 3D community for their incredible help and the guys at Cinder Interactive for giving me an opportunity to work on an amazing project.

Table of Contents

Preface

Part 1: Introduction to Hard Surface Modeling

1

Introducing Hard Surface Modeling

Understanding hard-surface modeling	4	Edge loops	11
		Loose parts	13
Understanding organic modeling	5	Creating a simple hard-surface modeling workflow	14
Defining hard-surface objects in Blender	7	Reviewing the projects	17
Edges	8	Summary	19
Surfaces	9		

Part 2: Modeling an Assault Rifle

2

Creating Basic Shapes for an FN SCAR

Technical requirements	24	Modeling the upper receiver	34
Preparing references	24	Creating the stock	40
Separating the parts	27	Adding a handgrip shape	43
		Creating attachment rails	44
Modeling the lower receiver	28	Shaping the barrel	48
Loop cutting	30		
Shading the viewport	32		

Mirroring an object with a
Mirror modifier   50

Adding a simple magazine   54
Summary   58

3

Adding More Details with Polygon Modeling and Modifiers

Technical requirements   60
Introducing the 3D Cursor   60
Modeling the handgrip   61
Detailing the receiver   67
Simplifying detail creation   73
Modeling screws   75

Completing the rails with the
Array modifier   78
Finishing the stock   85
Modeling iron sights and
detailing the barrel   93
Summary   100

4

Texturing and Rendering the FN SCAR

Creating materials   102
Understanding Material Nodes   102
Combining nodes   105
Adding multiple materials   106

Generating an Edge Mask   109
Detecting edges   109
Baking an edge map   116

Creating edge wear   119

Separating materials   126
Copying nodes to other materials   129

Lighting and rendering   132
Lighting the scene   132
Rendering the scene   136

Summary   140

Part 3: Modeling a Sci-Fi Race Ship

5

Modeling a Sci-Fi Race Ship

Modeling basic shapes   144
Adding details   150
Modeling armor panels   157
Adding more parts   162

Creating smaller details   168

Finishing the model   171
Applying a MatCap   173

Summary   175

6
Texture Painting the Sci-Fi Race Ship

Baking a normal map	178	Painting decals	204
UV unwrapping	184	Painting normal decals	207
Baking a bevel map	189	Baking a normal decal	207
Texture painting the		Painting the decal	211
armor panels	193	Summary	215

Part 4: Modeling a T-72 Tank

7
Modeling the T-72 Tank: Basic Shapes

Modeling a hull	220	Adding wheels	232
Creating a skirt	226	Summary	236
Adding a simple turret	230		

8
Modeling the T-72 Tank Hull

Completing the front end	238	Creating exhaust grills with arrays	262
Detailing the lower plate	239		
Modeling the side armor	244	Finishing the rear end of the hull	268
Completing the hull front	249	Summary	272
Modeling the skirt	259		
Adding an exhaust pipe	261		

9
Modeling the T-72 Tank Turret

Modeling the commander's hatch	274	Finishing the gun	286
		Summary	291
Creating more turret details	280		

10
Modeling Tank Tracks

Creating the suspension and wheels	294	Modeling the front sprocket	307
Modeling the wheels	297	Creating the tracks	310
Modeling the rear sprocket	301	Finishing the tracks	314
		Summary	320

11
Rigging Tank Tracks

Adjusting the tracks	321	Rigging the wheels and sprockets	330
Rigging with constraints	325	Parenting the tracks	333
		Summary	339

12
Texturing the Tank

Texturing the turret	342	Texturing the tracks	354
Combining nodes	347	Summary	362

Index

Other Books You May Enjoy

Preface

Blender is a massively popular and powerful 3D program with a variety of versatile modeling abilities, which makes it a great way to enter the 3D modeling world.

Blender 3D Incredible Models is a comprehensive guide for those who are new to hard-surface modeling with Blender, helping you understand all the various tools and features on offer, and how to efficiently employ them to create realistic models. You'll be led through progressively more challenging modeling projects where you'll develop assault rifle, army tank, and sci-fi spaceship models and pick up all the skills you could need in Blender's vast ecosystem of features and functionality, ranging from procedural texturing, texture painting, and UV mapping to lighting, rendering, rigging, and beyond. Each engaging project builds upon the last until you're equipped with everything you need to tackle your own modeling challenges, whatever they may be.

By the end of this book, you won't just know how to create the models we guide you through, but you will be able to turn your own concepts and references into 3D Blender models too!

Who this book is for

This book is for aspiring 3D artists, animators, architectural visualizers, and game developers looking to learn hard-surface modeling, an essential skill in these creative industries. Readers will need a basic understanding of Blender and its interface, orienting in the 3D Viewport, creating and moving objects, and mesh editing is necessary to get started.

What this book covers

Chapter 1, *Introducing Hard Surface Modeling*, includes a briefing about the central concept learned in this book.

Chapter 2, *Creating Basic Shapes for an FN SCAR*, shows the beginning of the first modeling project.

Chapter 3, Adding More Details with Polygon Modeling and Modifiers, shows the second part of the assault rifle project, adding hard-surface details.

Chapter 4, Texturing and Rendering the FN SCAR, shows the third part of the assault rifle project, turning the plain clay model into a rendered image.

Chapter 5, Modeling a Sci-Fi Race Ship, helps us create a medium-poly game-optimized model.

Chapter 6, Texture Painting the Sci-Fi Race Ship, provides us with an introduction to painting custom textures and baking high-poly details into images.

Chapter 7, Modeling the T-72 Tank: Basic Shapes, covers the beginning of the final project by creating the foundation.

Chapter 8, Modeling the T-72 Tank Hull, demonstrates completing the body of the tank.

Chapter 9, Modeling the T-72 Tank Turret, shows how to complete the turret.

Chapter 10, Modeling Tank Tracks, the final modeling chapter of the book, shows how to add tracks to the tank.

Chapter 11, Rigging Tank Tracks, uses constraints to rig the tank tracks for animation.

Chapter 12, Texturing the Tank, uses procedural texturing to finalize the tank.

To get the most out of this book

Software/hardware covered in the book	Operating system requirements
Blender 3D	Windows, macOS, or Linux

Download the color images

We also provide a PDF file that has color images of the screenshots and diagrams used in this book. You can download it here: `https://packt.link/EPzJU`.

Conventions used

There are a number of text conventions used throughout this book.

`Code in text`: Indicates code words in text, database table names, folder names, filenames, file extensions, pathnames, dummy URLs, user input, and Twitter handles. Here is an example: "Set the value to something between `0.040` and `0.050` to get a circular shape."

Bold: Indicates a new term, an important word, or words that you see onscreen. For instance, words in menus or dialog boxes appear in **bold**. Here is an example: "The tool is activated by clicking on the **Proportional Editing Objects** button in the top middle of our screen in our 3D viewport window."

> **Tips or Important Notes**
> Appear like this.

Get in touch

Feedback from our readers is always welcome.

General feedback: If you have questions about any aspect of this book, email us at `customercare@packtpub.com` and mention the book title in the subject of your message.

Errata: Although we have taken every care to ensure the accuracy of our content, mistakes do happen. If you have found a mistake in this book, we would be grateful if you would report this to us. Please visit `www.packtpub.com/support/errata` and fill in the form.

Piracy: If you come across any illegal copies of our works in any form on the internet, we would be grateful if you would provide us with the location address or website name. Please contact us at `copyright@packt.com` with a link to the material.

If you are interested in becoming an author: If there is a topic that you have expertise in and you are interested in either writing or contributing to a book, please visit `authors.packtpub.com`.

Share Your Thoughts

Once you've read *Blender 3D Incredible Machines*, we'd love to hear your thoughts! Scan the QR code below to go straight to the Amazon review page for this book and share your feedback.

https://packt.link/r/1801817812

Your review is important to us and the tech community and will help us make sure we're delivering excellent quality content.

Part 1: Introduction to Hard Surface Modeling

This section elaborates on what hard surface modeling is, how it can be applied, and how it differs from other modeling styles. You will gain an understanding of why hard surface modeling is relevant and learn the basics of how a hard surface object is made.

We will cover the following chapter in this section:

- *Chapter 1, Introducing Hard Surface Modeling*

1

Introducing Hard Surface Modeling

Blender is becoming a massively popular and powerful 3D program. It is used by more than 6,000 companies worldwide, across various industries and companies, including Facebook, Ubisoft, and Lockheed Martin (`https://blenderbasecamp.com/home/which-global-companies-use-blender/`). Its modeling versatility makes it a great way to enter the 3D industry. Most 3D projects begin with a 3D model, which is then textured and prepared for further use in animation, VFX, scene rendering, and video games. Because of this, hard-surface modeling skills are fundamental and applicable in virtually all 3D disciplines.

This chapter introduces hard-surface modeling and how it is different from other modeling styles, namely organic modeling. You will learn about some basic principles that are commonly used in hard-surface modeling that we will later apply in the hands-on projects.

We will also cover the importance of hard-surface modeling skills and how they can be applied professionally in different areas, which will help you realize the potential benefits of what you will learn in this book.

By the end of this chapter, you'll be ready to begin creating complex 3D objects and prepare them for further use by creating materials and textures from scratch.

In this chapter, we will cover the following topics:

- Understanding hard-surface modeling
- Defining hard-surface objects in Blender
- Creating a simple hard-surface modeling workflow
- Reviewing the projects

Understanding hard-surface modeling

In this section, we will define hard-surface modeling by discussing some of its attributes and differentiating it from organic modeling.

Hard-surface modeling is a 3D modeling technique used to create machines, vehicles, weapons, and any non-living objects with hard and static surfaces. Most man-made objects in our everyday surroundings would be categorized as hard-surface objects. A typical computer is an example of a hard-surface object. It is made of hard and artificial materials; it cannot be bent or folded like a shirt.

In Blender, hard-surface objects are typically defined by more technical features such as sharp edges, flat surfaces, and separation between loose parts. They are rigid bodies or objects that are restricted in motion to a particular mechanical movement and do not deform. This will be discussed further in the next section, *Defining hard-surface objects*. Things such as clothes, creatures, and natural objects are not hard-surface objects because their surfaces are usually *soft* and non-static.

Figure 1.1 shows an electric guitar model, an example of a typical hard-surface object:

Figure 1.1 – Typical hard-surface model

The electric guitar has flat surfaces, lots of sharp edges, and separate parts. As with almost any complex model, some parts consist of some organic modeling features, but it is generally a hard-surface model.

Understanding organic modeling

Organic modeling is the opposite of hard-surface modeling, and it deals with things such as plants, animals, characters, and generally other living things, but also things such as clothes, statues, and car bodies. I know what you're thinking – those last two don't seem to fit in there at all.

Categorizing clothes as organic modeling makes some sense since they are soft and foldable, but cars and statues sounds silly. The reason these are in the same category is not because of the nature of the objects, but because of how they appear in a 3D modeling program. *Figure 1.2* shows an example of a typical organic model:

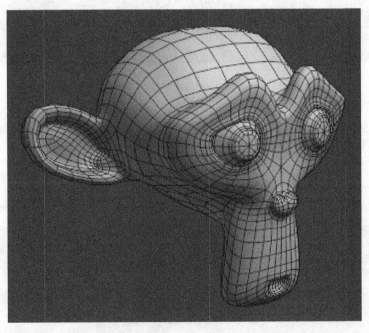

Figure 1.2 – "Suzanne," a typical organic model

The monkey in *Figure 1.2*, commonly referred to as Suzanne, has a different surface from the electric guitar. It appears much more intricate and there aren't any sharp edges or flat surfaces. Instead, the entire object is covered with a grid of polygons. To fully understand the difference between organic and hard-surface modeling, we must get a little more technical.

Some artists will argue that if a model is animated, it is organic and not hard-surface. A tank is a great example of a typical hard-surface model with a static surface, but it can still become partially organic. Do you remember that scene from *The Hulk*, where the Hulk bends the barrel of a tank backward and points it at the driver's head, as shown here?

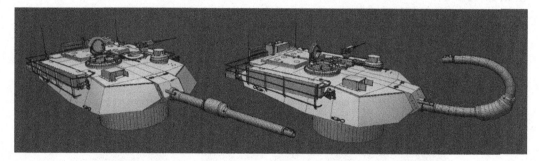

Figure 1.3 – A hard-surface object becomes organic

According to some artists, this type of animation will turn the hard-surface barrel of the tank into an organic model. This is because making an animation like that requires a model to have some features that are typical of organic modeling.

Understanding this argument can be a little difficult, so let's take a close look at a simple example to help us understand why a bending animation requires a model to become partially organic. Let's imagine an aluminum panel in two variations, as shown here:

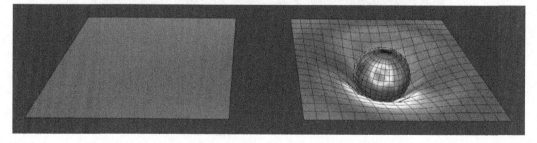

Figure 1.4 – Hard versus organic surface

In the first variation, it is completely straight and flat, like a typical *hard-surface* object. In the second variation, we dropped a heavy metal ball on it and bent the surface. To achieve this look, we need to subdivide the surface into many small faces, each of which is slightly angled. This creates a lattice-like pattern on the surface, which is typical of organic objects. Now, even though the metal surface is still hard to touch, it can be described as having an organic surface.

The conclusion, then, is that the most important aspect that makes the distinction between organic and hard-surface modeling is the geometry of the objects' surface. *Hard-surface objects generally have sharp and straight edges, flat faces, and static surfaces, while organic models generally have bumpy, deformed, bent, or irregular shapes and surfaces.*

Before we start creating some basic hard-surface objects, let me explain why it is important to distinguish between the two modeling styles in the first place and why we aren't just jumping straight into a modeling project. The main reason is that they use completely different modeling techniques and workflows.

This is something that needs to be considered because we cannot start a complex modeling project without doing some planning and preparation. How we begin our modeling process depends heavily on the style of modeling, so it's important to decide which style we are going to use beforehand.

Blender offers many different modeling tools, but some simply aren't suited for hard-surface modeling, while others aren't suitable for organic modeling. Again, this will be clearer when we start introducing some practical examples, but for now, it's important to understand that we're making this distinction because it will allow us to develop a workflow more easily.

In this section, we quickly reviewed the theory of hard-surface modeling and how it differs from organic modeling. We established that hard-surface modeling is mainly defined by the characteristics of an object's surfaces and its geometry. In the next section, we will determine what exactly all those characteristics look like on a 3D object in Blender.

Defining hard-surface objects in Blender

Now, it's time to jump into Blender and look at some examples. As we stated in the previous section, hard-surface modeling is typically defined by features such as flat surfaces, sharp and straight edges, and multiple loose parts.

We are going to focus on hard-surface modeling, but it is important to understand the differences between the two modeling styles, so let's go over those features one by one and compare them to organic modeling.

Edges

Figure 1.5 shows a side-by-side comparison of a hard-surface model (left) and an organic model (right):

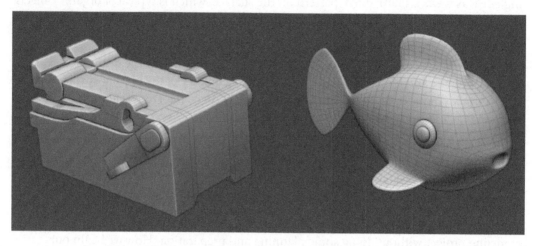

Figure 1.5 – A typical hard-surface model and an organic model

The first thing that identifies a hard-surface object is the sharpness of its edges. We don't see any sharp edges on the right-hand object. Instead, every edge appears to flow and bend smoothly. Most of the time, edges on hard-surface models will also have thin bevels.

A **bevel** is a slightly rounded edge that looks as though it has been sanded and smoothed. This adds a touch of realism since there are no perfectly sharp edges in real life. *Figure 1.6* shows an object with and without beveled edges:

Figure 1.6 – An object with and without beveled edges

Bevels are used to simulate real edges in 3D, and they also affect how light reflects from the edges to allow for realistic rendering. In game development, bevels are often avoided because they cost a lot, meaning that they add a lot of polygons to the model, which makes them harder to render.

Because of their high cost, bevels are often baked as normal maps so that they are visible on the surface, but they aren't part of the 3D model. Apart from realism, bevels can also be useful in many other ways, as we will see later in our modeling projects.

Surfaces

Unlike organic models, hard-surface models tend to have a lot of flat surfaces. This is different from organic models because most organic surfaces appear soft and curvy. Organic surfaces consist of many smaller faces with slight angular differences between them, which create the lattice-like pattern on the mesh. This lattice pattern is usually a dead giveaway of an organic-style surface.

Of course, this doesn't mean that we will never see a curvy surface on a hard-surface model. *Figure 1.7* shows a tank turret made with two different modeling styles:

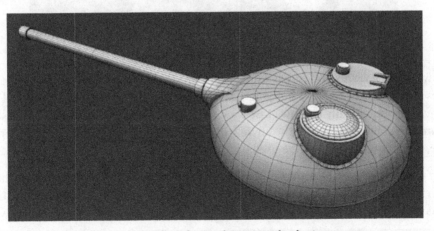

Figure 1.7 – A hard-surface tank turret with a lattice pattern

This tank turret is a good example of a hard-surface object with an organic-like surface. It is most definitely a hard-surface object, but the mesh pattern looks a lot like something you would see on an organic model. Because of this, when modeling the tank turret, we can use tools that we would normally use for organic modeling.

Proportional Editing is an example of a tool that's typically used in organic-style modeling because of how it changes the surface. It can also be used to model a hard-surface object, such as the tank turret in *Figure 1.7*. **Proportional Editing** is a polygon modeling tool that allows us to control how much an action influences polygons or objects around the one we selected. We can use it if we want to create a smooth bump on a surface, as shown here:

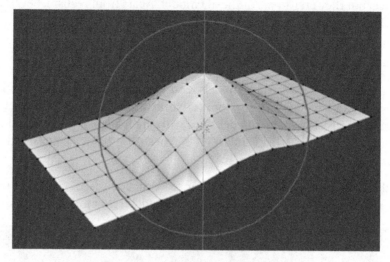

Figure 1.8 – Proportional Editing

When we select a vertex and move it up with **Proportional Editing** enabled, the other vertices around it will also move, but not as much as the one we selected. They will be influenced proportionally by how close they are to the center of the gray circle, as shown in *Figure 1.8*. Anything outside the circle will not be influenced. This looks like an organic surface, but let's see how it can be used on a hard-surface model.

We can use **Proportional Editing** if we want to deform the tank turret to make it slightly pointier in the front. The tool can be activated by clicking on the **Proportional Editing Objects** button in the top middle of our screen in our 3D viewport window, as shown here:

Figure 1.9 – Activating Proportional Editing

Then, we can select any vertex in the front of the turret and scale it down on the *Y axis*, as shown here:

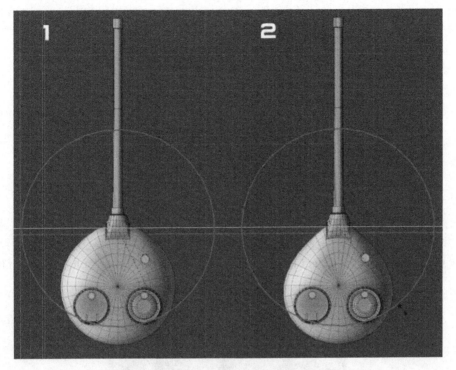

Figure 1.10 – Using Proportional Editing on a tank turret

This will cause other vertices around it to come closer and create a pointier shape. From this example, it is important to remember that while an object does have a *hard surface*, organic modeling tools can still be useful.

Edge loops

Another feature typical of hard-surface modeling that we haven't mentioned yet is the non-continuity of the **Edge Loops**. An Edge Loop is a generally continuous line of edges. In theory, loops should be connected end to end, but even when this is not the case, we can select a line of edges, vertices, or faces in the section where they are continuous.

This can be observed by using the **Select Loop** tool in Blender. We can select a loop by hovering over an edge and holding *Alt* while selecting it with the left mouse button. On a typical hard-surface model, most edge loops are going to be short and unconnected.

As shown in *Figure 1.11*, when we select a random edge loop, most of the time, only a few edges, vertices, or faces will be selected. At the end of the selection, the loop breaks down into different elements because of the sharp edges that are typical of hard-surface modeling:

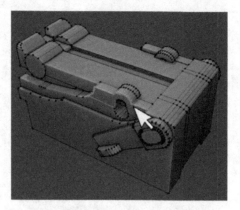

Figure 1.11 – Typical hard-surface edge loop

On an organic model, the **Select Loop** tool would give us different results, as shown here:

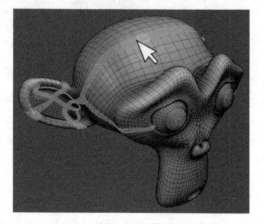

Figure 1.12 – Continuous edge loop

The selection is long and usually continuous, meaning that the selection has no beginning or end. Sometimes, the selection is surprisingly intricate, as you can see on the ear of the subdivided Suzanne.

Loose parts

Another interesting thing that is common to hard-surface objects (and less common on organic ones) is that most of the time, the object will consist of several **loose parts**. Loose parts are individual items with fully connected geometry. *Figure 1.13* shows an exploded view of a hard-surface object with all its loose parts separated:

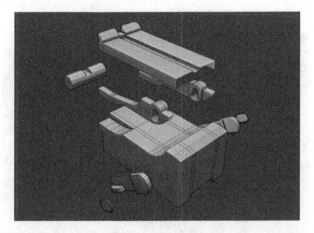

Figure 1.13 – Loose parts

If we select any face on an object and move it, the face will pull a few other connected faces with it. This will deform the mesh, creating an unwanted result, as shown here:

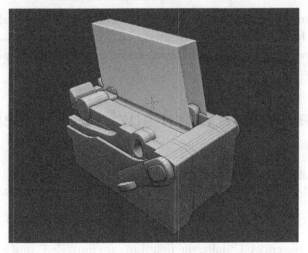

Figure 1.14 – Deformed mesh

To prevent this, we must select all the polygons that are connected so that nothing is deformed when we move the selection. This can be selected instantly by hovering over a vertex, edge, or face and pressing the *L* key in **Edit Mode**.

The letter *L* stands for *Linked* and commands the selection of all vertices, edges, and faces that are connected to the loose object. *Figure 1.15* shows a selected and separated loose part:

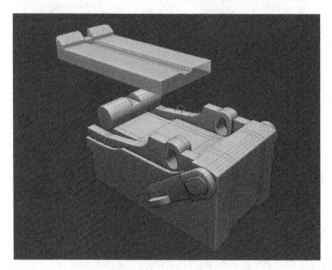

Figure 1.15 – Separating a loose part

With that, we've gone over some technical differences between hard-surface and organic modeling, and we have a clearer image of what exactly hard-surface modeling means. Now, let's learn how to start a hard-surface modeling project by developing a simple workflow template.

Creating a simple hard-surface modeling workflow

So, how do we create hard-surface objects in Blender? Let's make a simple four-step outline for a typical workflow, which we will later use when creating more sophisticated models.

In this example, we're going to look at the modeling workflow for this T-72 tank:

1. **Gathering references**: Usually, the first thing we must do is find a reference image to help guide us through a project. For a simple object, a single photo will be enough. But when creating a more detailed object, such as a vehicle, it's best to find a blueprint, as shown here:

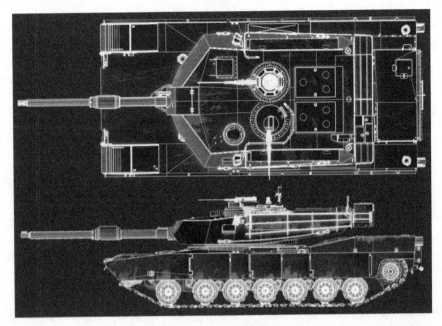

Figure 1.16 – Blueprint

We will cover the details of how to find a blueprint and set it up in Blender in *Chapter 2, Creating Basic Shapes for an FN SCAR.*

2. **Separating the parts**: We want to break the object down into separate components because this allows us to work step by step. It's important to do this because when working with complex objects, it's easy to become overwhelmed as to where to start working. This tank can be broken down into three major components: the hull, the turret, and the tracks/wheels, as shown here:

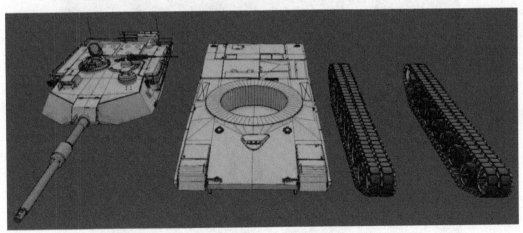

Figure 1.17 – Parts of a tank

3. **Creating the block-out model**: Now, we can begin creating the objects, starting with the *parent*. We always want to find a part of the model that everything else is attached is. This will act as a frame of reference and once we create that, we can just keep adding other things to it. In this case, the parent will be the hull because everything else is attached to it. Then, we can create a very simple version of all the major parts:

Figure 1.18 – Block-out

4. **Increasing detail**: Once we have created an outline for the rough shapes of the object, we can start creating the smaller and more detailed parts. In this case, we will start adding hatches, screws, armor panels, and similar. This is what makes the model look more intricate and complete. Most of the work is done in this step:

Figure 1.19 – Details

We now have a basic four-step workflow structure to follow when creating a 3D model. We will follow these steps in our upcoming three projects, which we will quickly go over in the next section.

Reviewing the projects

This section briefly outlines the contents of this book.

In the first part, we will create a high-poly FN SCAR assault rifle. Here, we will carefully introduce some essential modeling tools and techniques, while elaborating on the four-step workflow we just covered. This project will be covered over three chapters:

- *Chapter 2, Creating Basic Shapes for an FN SCAR*
- *Chapter 3, Adding More Details with Polygon Modeling and Modifiers*
- *Chapter 4, Texturing and Rendering the FN SCAR*

Figure 1.20 shows what you will be creating:

Figure 1.20 – FN SCAR project

In the second project, we will design and model a sci-fi race ship without using any blueprints. We will use some of the tools we will have learned about in the first project and improvise our way through a medium-poly model. Once the model is complete, we will use some interesting texturing techniques to make the model appear more detailed and realistic. The second project will be covered over two chapters:

- *Chapter 5, Modeling a Sci-Fi Race Ship*

- *Chapter 6, Texture Painting the Sci-Fi Race Ship*

    Figure 1.21 shows what you will be creating:

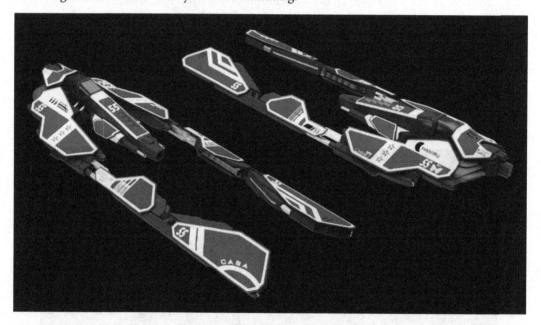

Figure 1.21 – Sci-fi race ship project

Our final and most advanced project will involve creating a T-72 tank. Here, we will use everything we've learned so far, as well as some new methods, to create a highly detailed top-quality modeling project. After modeling and texturing, we will use constraints to rig the tracks, which will make animation possible. This is the skill and quality level that's typically expected from professionals in the 3D modeling industry. This project will consist of six chapters:

- *Chapter 7, Modeling the T-72 Tank: Basic Shapes*

- *Chapter 8, Modeling the T-72 Tank Hull*

- *Chapter 9, Modeling the T-72 Tank Turret*

- *Chapter 10, Modeling Tank Tracks*
- *Chapter 11, Rigging Tank Tracks*
- *Chapter 12, Texturing the Tank*

Figure 1.22 shows what you will be creating:

Figure 1.22 – T-72 tank project

Every model will be textured and rendered, which allows for better presentation in a portfolio. By the end of this book, you will be able to model, texture, and present mechanical hard-surface models at virtually any level of complexity.

Summary

In this chapter, we defined hard-surface modeling and reviewed some features common to this style. We established that hard-surface objects typically have sharp edges, flat surfaces, and non-continuous edge loops and are usually separated by parts. We also developed a basic four-step workflow that we are going to use for our projects in the coming chapters.

In the next chapter, we will follow the first three steps of our workflow structure to create a simple version of an FN SCAR assault rifle. You will learn how to use some essential modeling tools that will later be used in more advanced modeling techniques.

Part 2: Modeling an Assault Rifle

This section leads you through the entire process of modeling a high-poly assault rifle. You will learn about the tools and features that are essential for any other hard surface modeling project.

We will cover the following chapters in this section:

- *Chapter 2, Creating Basic Shapes for an FN SCAR*
- *Chapter 3, Adding More Details with Polygon Modeling and Modifiers*
- *Chapter 4, Texturing and Rendering the FN SCAR*

2
Creating Basic Shapes for an FN SCAR

In this chapter, we will begin working on our first project and applying some principles from the previous chapter, such as the modeling workflow.

First, we will prepare references and learn to correctly set them up in Blender, which will make it much easier to create a model with realistic measurements and proportions.

After we prepare our references, we will start modeling by using some essential modeling tools and creating the basic shapes of the model. The basic shapes serve as an outline, which we will later fill in with more details in *Chapter 3, Adding More Details with Polygon Modeling and Modifiers*.

By the end of this chapter, we will have a simple version of an FN SCAR assault rifle and a good grip of some essential modeling tools and techniques.

The main topics of this chapter are as follows:

- Preparing references
- Modeling the lower receiver

- Modeling the upper receiver
- Creating the stock
- Adding a handgrip shape
- Creating attachment rails
- Shaping the barrel
- Mirroring an object with a **Mirror** modifier
- Adding a simple magazine

Technical requirements

This chapter requires you to have access to Blender and the internet, as well as a basic understanding of Blender controls such as orientation in 3D view.

Preparing references

This section covers the first two steps of the modeling workflow from *Chapter 1, Introducing Hard Surface Modeling*. In the first two steps, we will find and prepare references, before breaking down our projects into parts in the second step. This will allow us to keep our work organized.

References are photos or images used as a basis for 3D modeling. We use references to look at and copy from when we try to create a model. References are important for proportions and dimensions, but they also help us place details correctly. If we work from memory and without a reference, we will soon run out of ideas, and our model will look different from how we intended it.

References can be real-life photos, diagrams, blueprints, or any images that help us imagine what we are trying to create. Blueprints are usually highly accurate and help us create realistic proportions, but real-life photos help us understand some shapes that are difficult to see in 2D images such as blueprints. For most models, references can be found by conducting an image search on an internet browser. For this project, we need a side view reference of an FN SCAR assault rifle.

Tip

Adding keywords such as `side`, `top`, or `blueprint` to a Google search can be helpful for finding specific images. There are also plenty of blueprint sites that can easily be found online and are free for personal use.

It is best to always have a reference showing the model from the side, top, and front/back view. This shows us exactly what a model looks like from every side without perspective distortion. It can be difficult to find a high-quality blueprint, but any image of the object that appears to be in **orthographic projection** will suffice. Orthographic projection is, in simple terms, a 2D representation of a 3D object created by illustrating the object directly from the front, top, or side.

Figure 2.1 is an example of an object in orthographic projection:

Figure 2.1 – Orthographic projection

It shows a simple object in 3D view and in orthographic projection from each side. An object can look very different from other perspectives. References showing all sides help us understand and create a shape in Blender.

For the sake of simplicity, we will only use one reference image in this project. To set up an image as a reference in Blender, we must follow three simple steps:

1. Enter **Side View** by pressing *1* on the Numpad.

2.   Add a reference from the **Image** section of the **Add** menu (shortcut *Shift + A*):

Figure 2.2 – Adding a reference

3.   Navigate to the folder with our downloaded image and open it. The result should look something like this:

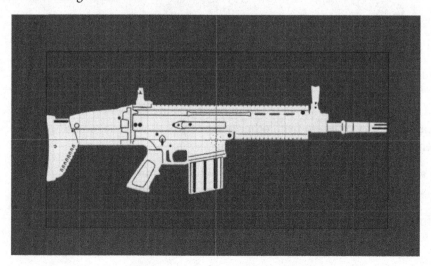

Figure 2.3 – Reference in Blender

> **Tip**
>
> Numpad numbers *1*, *3*, and *7* are used for switching between the front, right, and top orthographic view. *9* switches the view to the opposite side of the current one. Holding *Ctrl* when pressing *1*, *3*, or *7* will switch to the back, left, and bottom view, respectively.

Sometimes, references in Blender are a little too bright or irritating to the eye. We can fix this by making the image slightly transparent. To do this, select the reference image and navigate to the **Image Properties** tab on the right side, and check **Opacity**. Then, simply drag the slider down:

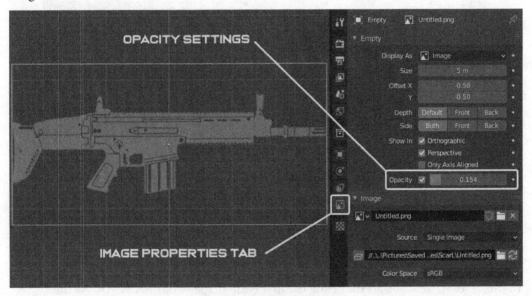

Figure 2.4 – Reference opacity

Now, the reference is ready for use. This entire process can be repeated multiple times with references from different sides, so it will look like the earlier *Figure 2.1*. Doing so makes it easier to imagine an object from every angle, but it is not a requirement. In this case, using multiple background references isn't necessary, and the side view image is the most important reference.

Separating the parts

Now, let's figure out how we can separate the parts of this object. There are many different components in the design, but we can simplify the object by breaking it down into five main parts: the body, the stock, the handgrip, the magazine, and the barrel. We can also include the sights as part of the barrel because of their similar placement and level of detail.

In a different example, we would also consider attachments such as scopes or grenade launchers as a separate component, but we won't do that here. *Figure 2.5* shows the separate parts of the assault rifle:

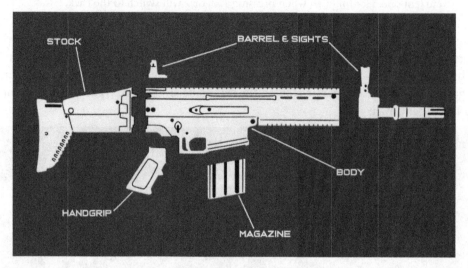

Figure 2.5 – FN SCAR separated into parts

We have now prepared a reference image that will help us correctly model the proportions of our FN SCAR and remind us of some details. We also broke down the model into different parts that we will create one by one. Next, we will begin our modeling process.

Modeling the lower receiver

In this section, we will start modeling the first basic shape of our FN SCAR. As the workflow model from the previous chapter suggests, we will begin by modeling the largest part of the object first, which is the body of the gun. This consists of the handguard and the lower and upper receiver. Let's start by modeling the lower part of the receiver in five steps:

1. Add a cube from the **Add** menu and align it with our view, so we can use it to shape the lower receiver:

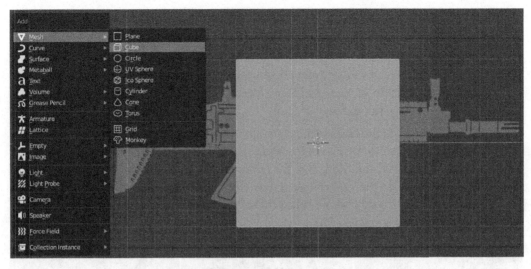

Figure 2.6 – Adding a cube

2. Use this cube to create the shape of the lower receiver. First, scale the cube down using the *S* key. When you have the correct size, click the left mouse button once to confirm the action. Then, drag it to a corner by pressing the *G* key and clicking the left mouse button to confirm. Let's put it at the back of the receiver so we can start working from there:

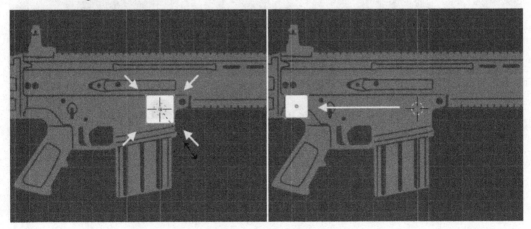

Figure 2.7 – Scaling (left) and moving (right)

3. Once our cube is in place, we can start **polygon modeling**. To enable polygon modeling (that is, manually manipulating vertices, edges, and faces), we must enter **Edit Mode** by pressing the *Tab* key with the object selected.

4. We will then switch to **Edge Select** by pressing *2*. This allows us to select individual edges, as opposed to vertices and faces. **Vertex Select** and **Face Select** are accessed with keys *1* and *3*, respectively.

5. Select and extrude the face on the right along the *x* axis. Press *E* to extrude and *X* to limit the extrusion to the *x* axis. We want to push the edge all the way to the front part of the receiver, and then click the left mouse button when we want to leave it in place. When we do this, we will get a new edge at the bottom, which we will extrude down the *z* axis. To do this, we select that edge, press *E* and *Z*, and then click the left mouse button to apply the extrusion.

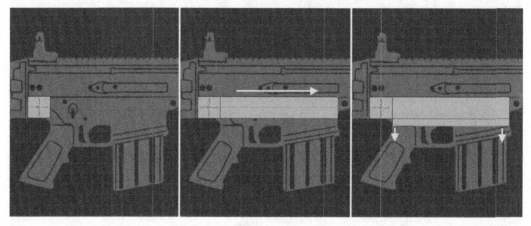

Figure 2.8 – Extruding edges

To create the next part of this shape, we need to use a tool called **Loop Cut**. Let's quickly learn how to use this tool with a simple example.

Loop cutting

Loop cutting is used for creating a new **edge loop**. It creates a set of new polygons that we can use for modeling. The shortcut for activating the **Loop Cut** tool is *Ctrl + R*. With the tool activated, hover the cursor over an edge where you want to create the loop cut. You can control the number of loop cuts by scrolling the mouse wheel up or down. *Figure 2.9* is an example of loop cutting a default cube:

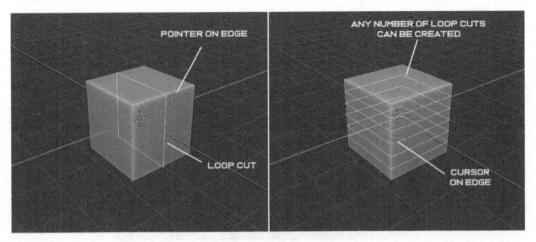

Figure 2.9 – Loop cutting

After using *Ctrl + R*, click the left mouse button once to create the loop cut. Now, you can slide the loop along the edge with the mouse cursor. Click the left mouse button again to apply the loop cut. Here's how we will use this tool on our FN SCAR:

1. Press *Ctrl + R* to create a loop cut and hover the mouse cursor over the mesh, as shown in *Figure 2.10* (left). In our case, a vertical loop cut separates the two side faces into four. We can use a face from the bottom to extrude the magazine holder down, as shown in *Figure 2.10* (right).

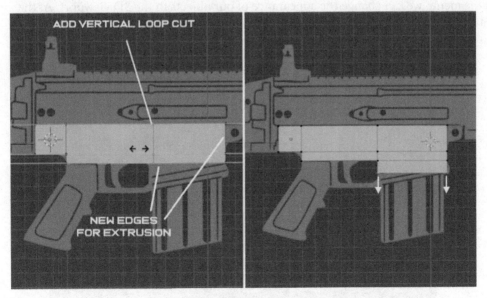

Figure 2.10 – Loop cut (left) and extruding edges (right)

2. Move vertices individually in **Vertex Select** mode, which is enabled by pressing *3*. This lets us create the angled bottom of the magazine holder and the small shape sticking out on the right side:

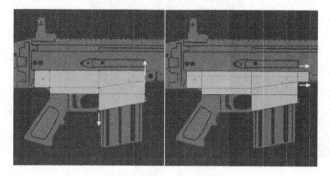

Figure 2.11 – Moving vertices (left) and extruding (right)

Now, we have finished modeling our first basic shape, but we will add a few more details later.

Shading the viewport

Before we continue modeling, let me show you a cool way to make our meshes look nicer as we're working. In the top right of the screen, there is a menu called **Viewport Shading**. In the menu, we can change the appearance of our objects in the 3D viewport. At the bottom of the menu, check **Cavity**:

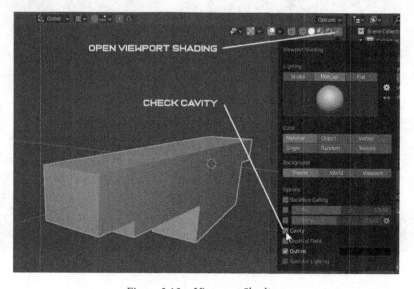

Figure 2.12 – Viewport Shading

This will expand the menu with some more options. We want to open the **Type** box and select **Both**. This will further expand the menu with a few sliders. Now, crank all the sliders to their maximum values:

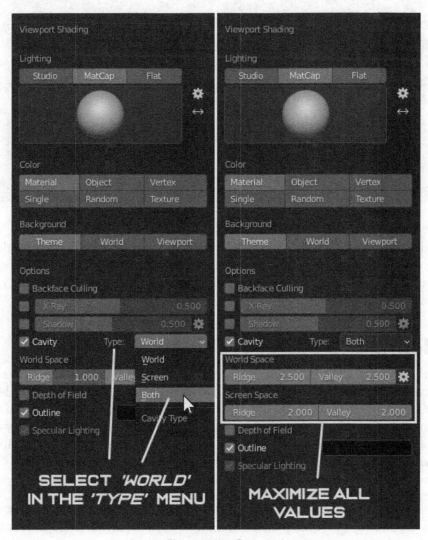

Figure 2.13 – Cavity

With these settings, the mesh has some slightly different shading settings, which make it more aesthetically pleasing and fun to work with:

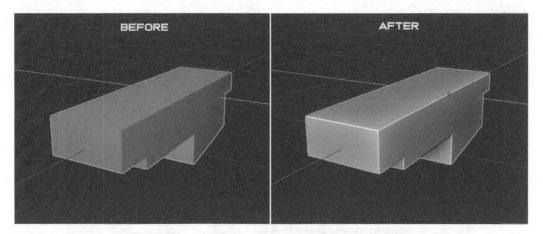

Figure 2.14 – Before and after cavity shading

The shading settings are just a gimmick, but they make the modeling process a little more exciting. There are several other settings in the **Viewport Shading** menu so feel free to explore them. Now, we have created some nicer shading for our model, and we can continue modeling our FN SCAR.

Modeling the upper receiver

Next, let's move on to the upper part of the receiver. We need a cube on top of the mesh we just created, but we need to be pretty precise with where we place the cube, so let's use our 3D Cursor. The **3D Cursor** is a powerful tool used for manipulating objects in 3D space, and we will use it a lot later. Every time we add an object, it is added exactly on the 3D Cursor. We will talk about the 3D Cursor and its abilities more in *Chapter 3, Adding More Details with Polygon Modeling and Modifiers.*. For now, we will place the 3D Cursor exactly where we want to create a cube, and then we will create the cube:

1. Place the 3D Cursor on the face at the back of the lower receiver. To do this, select the face and open the **Snap** menu with *Shift + S*. In the menu, chose **Cursor to Selected**. As the name implies, this will snap the 3D Cursor to the selected polygon:

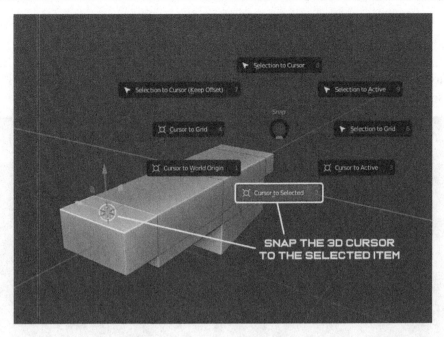

Figure 2.15 – Snapping the cursor

2. Add the cube and move it on top of the surface; we will use this cube to create the upper receiver and the handguard:

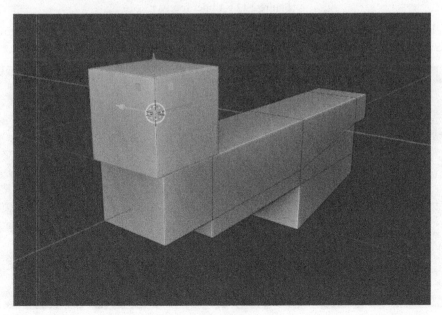

Figure 2.16 – Adding a cube

3. In the side view, align the edges of the cube with the lines in the reference. For now, align the height of the cube with the part of the blueprint shown in *Figure 2.17*. Let's push the side of the cube to the right so it matches the length of the body. The top and bottom of this object will vary in width, so we will model those parts using some different techniques:

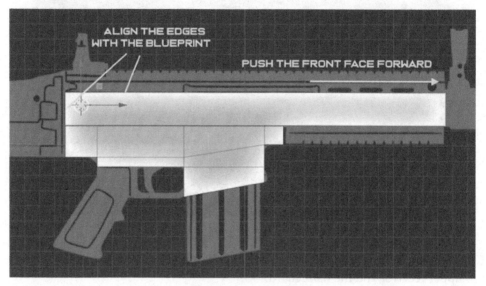

Figure 2.17 – Upper receiver

4. Next, add two loop cuts along the shape and scale them up on the *y* axis by pressing *S* to scale and *Y* to only scale on the *y* axis:

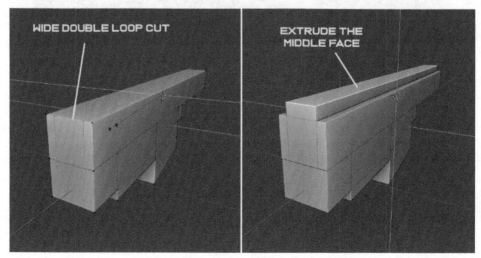

Figure 2.18 – Loop cutting

5. Extrude the face at the top between the two loop cuts. Only extrude that up a little and then repeat the same step once more to create another step. We should now have three steps on each side:

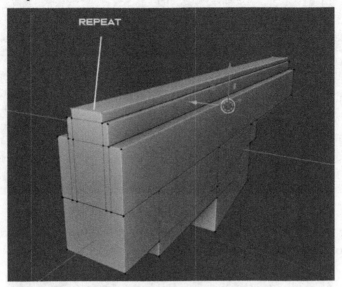

Figure 2.19 – Repeating the step

6. Bevel the bottom steps by selecting their edges and pressing *Ctrl + B* to create a bevel.

There are a few properties that can be changed when adding a bevel. For now, we will just change the width and the number of edges. To change the width, push the mouse cursor away from the bevel or pull it closer to increase or decrease the bevel width, respectively. We will also change the number of edges on the bevel, which will make it look smoother. This can be done by simply scrolling the mouse wheel up or down to increase or decrease the number of edges, respectively.

Set the number of edges to five or six and try to copy the bevel width from *Figure 2.20* (right):

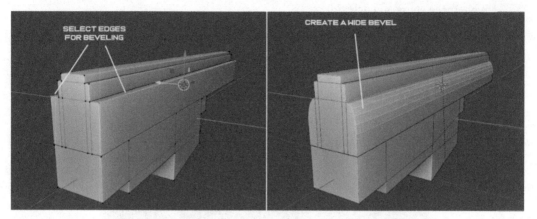

Figure 2.20 – Selecting edges (left) and creating a bevel (right)

7. Bevel the second step. We will repeat the same process from *step 6* with the same number of edges, but narrower bevels:

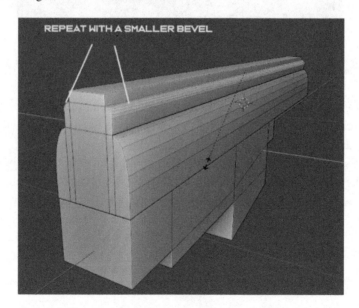

Figure 2.21 – Beveling the upper steps

We are not going to bevel the top step because we need it for creating the railing later. For now, we will just leave it as it is.

8. Now is a good time to clean up the mesh a little by dissolving some unnecessary edges and faces. We can do that by selecting all the faces in the back and the front of the upper receiver, pressing *X*, and selecting **Dissolve Faces**. This will remove the excess edges and turn the faces into **N-gons**.

An **N-gon** is a face with more than four sides. If we have a flat surface with edges cutting through it, we often don't need those edges and we can dissolve them to keep our model tidy:

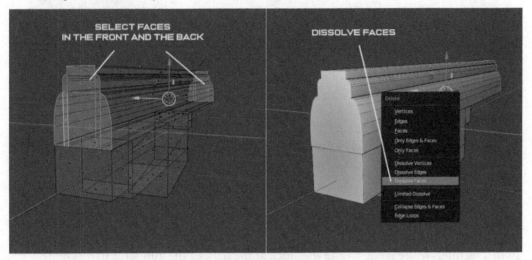

Figure 2.22 – Dissolving faces

We will do the same thing on the side of the lower receiver because it has plenty of unnecessary edges. In this case, the edges are also making it difficult to create bevels:

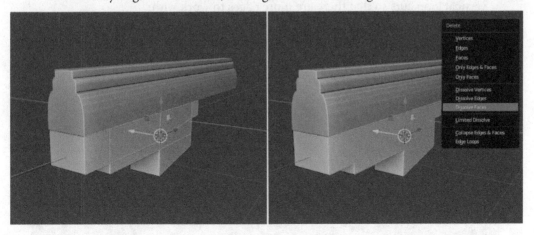

Figure 2.23 – Dissolving side faces

Some bevels on the lower receiver will help us achieve the shape that we want. So, let's add a bevel to the inner edge, then two more bevels to the sides:

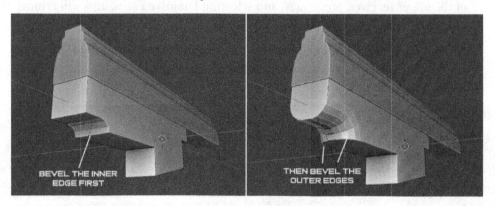

Figure 2.24 – Inner bevel (left) and side bevel (right)

We now have the basic shapes of the main body of the gun, consisting of the upper and lower receiver. From here, we can just keep attaching basic shapes for the other parts of the gun.

Creating the stock

In this section, we are going to add the stock at the back of the gun. This part is quite simple, and we will use similar steps that we used before to shape the receiver:

1.   Add a cube and place it over the top part of the stock in the side view. Also, add four vertical loop cuts so that there are more edges to work with:

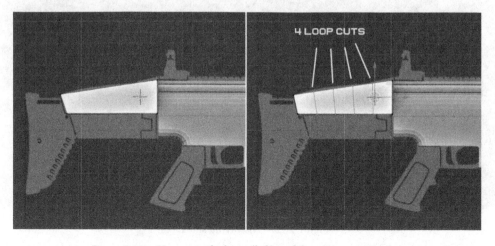

Figure 2.25 – Upper stock shape (left) and four loop cuts (right)

2. Align the edges on the loop cuts with the reference image. Repeat the same step to create the other two shapes of the stock:

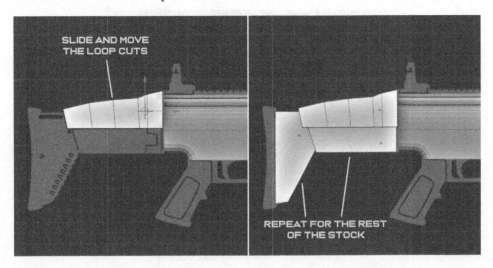

Figure 2.26 – Adjusting loop cuts (left) and other stock shapes (right)

3. Add bevels to the edges. Make sure that the three pieces have different widths so that their surfaces don't overlap; the top part should be the widest and the back part should be the narrowest:

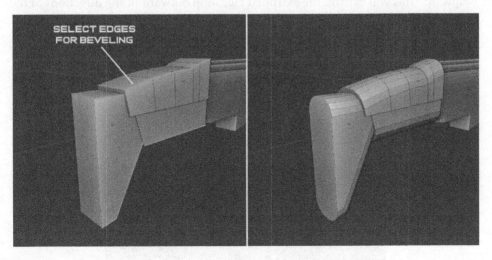

Figure 2.27 – Selecting edges (left) and beveling edges (right)

4. Extrude the face in the far back of the stock. This is the rubber padding that is pushed against the shoulder of the rifleman:

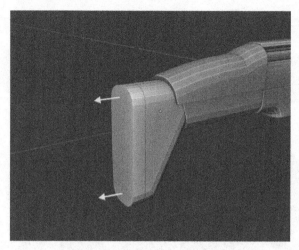

Figure 2.28 – Extruding the back end

5. Select the face loop we just create and extrude it, and immediately press the right mouse button. This will confirm the extrusion and create new faces and edges, but it will not make a visible change because there is no thickness. We will add thickness to the selected loop by using the *Alt + S* shortcut and moving our mouse cursor upward. This will expand the extruded face loop outward in the directions of the individual faces:

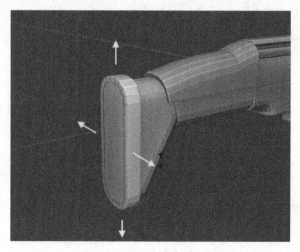

Figure 2.29 – Pad thickness

This is enough to serve us as a basic shape for our stock, and we can move on to the next part.

Adding a handgrip shape

Next, we will create a simple handgrip shape by once again creating a cube, aligning the vertices with the image, and adding a loop cut to adjust the shape. Adding any more detail to the handgrip is a little complicated, so for now, we will just leave it like this:

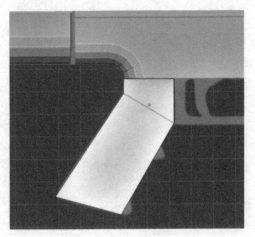

Figure 2.30 – Handgrip shape

Similarly, we going to create the outline of the trigger frame with simple extrusion and loop cuts like before:

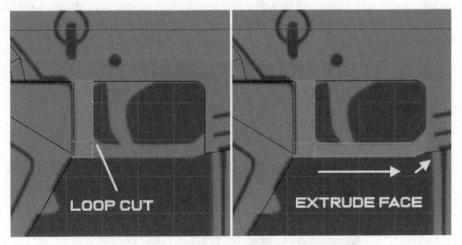

Figure 3.31 – Loop cut (left) and extruding trigger frame (right)

Use the same technique to shape the trigger as well. We now have some basic shapes for our trigger and handgrip.

Creating attachment rails

In the next few steps, we will create the top and bottom attachment rails:

1. Place a plane at the bottom of the rifle with the help of the 3D Cursor:

Figure 2.32 – Handguard plane

2. Align the plane with the handguard so it's overlapping.

    When we do this, there will be some distortion on the surface of the plane. This is because there are multiple faces in the exact same place and Blender doesn't know which one to display, so it displays parts of each face simultaneously:

Figure 2.33 – Clipping distortion

One way to fix this is to just move the plane down a little. Blender will then be able to figure out which face to display first. In this case, we will reshape the surface so the plane will not overlap with the faces above.

3. Next, add a loop cut along the plane and move the new edge downward, creating a near-90-degree angle between the two faces on the plane we created in *step 1*. We will then add a three-edged bevel to that edge and scale it up on the *y* axis to make it a little wider:

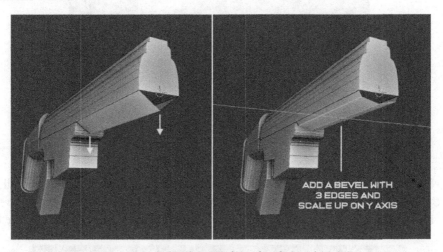

Figure 2.34 – Edge down (left) and wide bevel (right)

4. Fill in the edge loops in the front and the back by selecting their edges and pressing the *F* key:

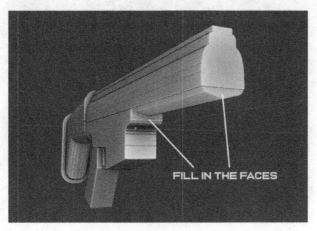

Figure 2.35 – Fill faces

5. We need one more bevel at the bottom to make the surface flat and easier to extrude. This one will be a two-edged bevel made on the edge in the middle at the bottom:

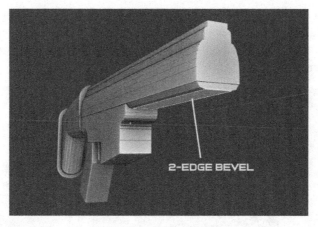

Figure 2.36 – Flat bottom

6. Now, we have a flat face at the top and at the bottom of the rifle body. We will use these two flat faces to extrude a basic shape for the attachment railing. In the side view, we can see on our reference how far up or down we have to extrude the faces:

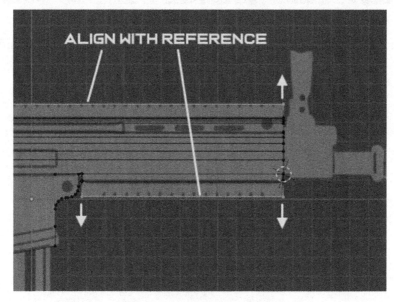

Figure 2.37 – Attachment rails

7. Next, we add two loop cuts around the top and the bottom rails:

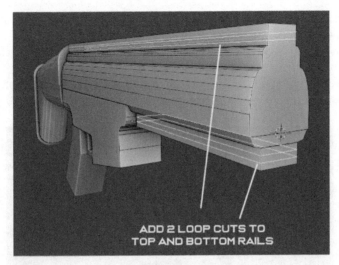

Figure 2.38 – Rail loop cuts

8. Use these loop cuts to shape the rails. Select only the upper edges on the top rail and only the lower edges on the bottom rail, and scale them up on the y axis to make their sides pointy:

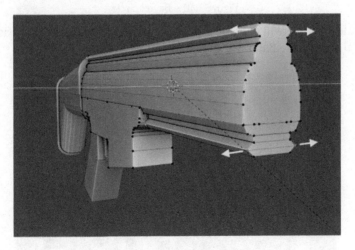

Figure 2.39 – Widening edges

Much like the handguard, finishing the rails is going to be a little trickier than this, but for a basic shape outline, the shapes we just created are perfect.

Shaping the barrel

In the next few steps, we will create the barrel shape, which will later also support the iron sights. The barrel and the sights are arguably the most detailed and sophisticated parts of any gun, so we will only create the simple shape of the barrel without the sights:

1. Using the 3D Cursor, add a circle to the front end of the gun and rotate it by 90 degrees around the y axis. This circle is the base of the barrel:

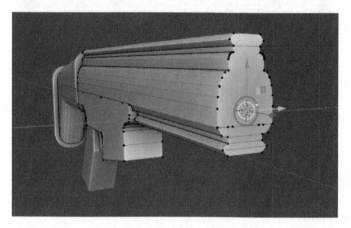

Figure 2.40 – Barrel circle

2. In the side view, we will extrude the circle and move it along the x axis until it reaches the tip of the barrel:

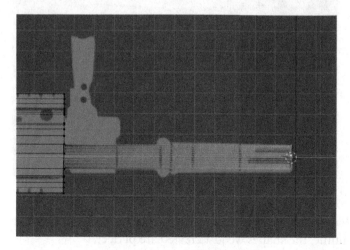

Figure 2.41 – Extruding the barrel

3. Add two loop cuts to create the ring on the middle of the barrel:

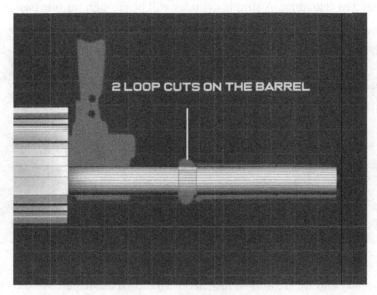

Figure 2.42 – Barrel loop cuts

4. Widen the ring using the same technique as before. First, extrude it with *E* but leave it in place by clicking the right mouse button. Then, expand it by pressing *Alt* + *S* and moving the mouse cursor upward. From now on, we will refer to this technique as **solidification**:

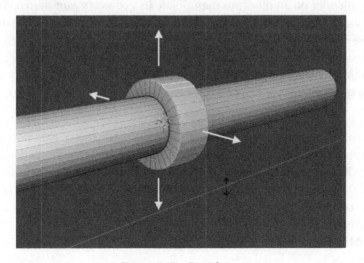

Figure 2.43 – Barrel ring

5. Above the main barrel, the FN SCAR has another smaller barrel that is used for gas-operated reloading. A simple cylinder will be enough for our basic shape here:

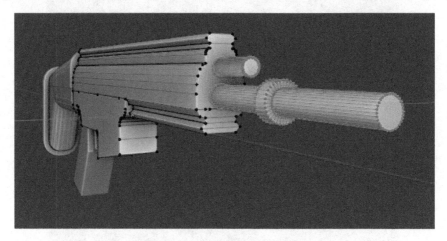

Figure 2.44 – Barrel basic shape

The barrel is ready and we are almost finished with our basic shapes. We only need to create a simple magazine before our FN SCAR is ready for detailing.

Mirroring an object with a Mirror modifier

In this section, we are introducing the **Mirror modifier**. **Modifiers** are operations performed by Blender on an object to manipulate its geometry *non-destructively*. This means that Blender will change the object in a certain way, depending on which modifier(s) we create, without making irreversible changes, therefore, the change can be undone by simply removing the modifier. Modifiers are usually used for actions that would be too time-consuming or difficult to perform manually (https://docs. blender.org/manual/en/latest/modeling/modifiers/introduction. html).

A **Mirror** modifier is a simple modifier that just reflects the mesh over a certain point, making it perfectly symmetrical over that point. The symmetry point can be changed, but by default, it is the object's **origin**. The origin is the point where an object is located in 3D space. Every object has an origin that is set to the object's center of mass by default and can be placed anywhere else using the 3D Cursor, which we will explore further in *Chapter 3, Adding More Details with Polygon Modeling and Modifiers*. Let's look at an example of a **Mirror** modifier operation.

Suppose we created a monkey with a horn, as in *Figure 2.45*, and we want to copy the horn to the other side as well:

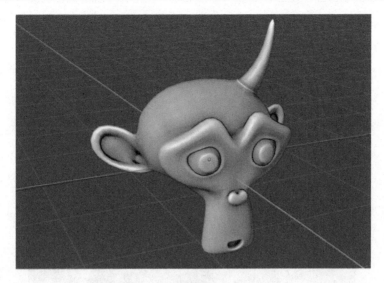

Figure 2.45 – Object for mirroring

Here are a few steps to mirror the object with a **Mirror** modifier:

1. Delete half of the object and keep the half that you want to mirror. It is best to select the half in orthographic projection using the **Box Select** tool, activated with *B*. Make sure to select the half exactly up to the middle:

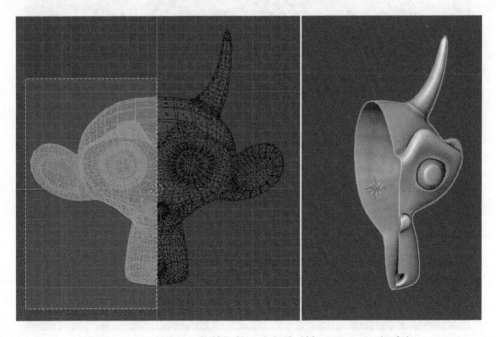

Figure 2.46 – Deleting half (left) and the half for mirroring (right)

2. With the targeted object selected, add a **Mirror** modifier by navigating to the **Modifier** tab and opening the **Add Modifier** menu:

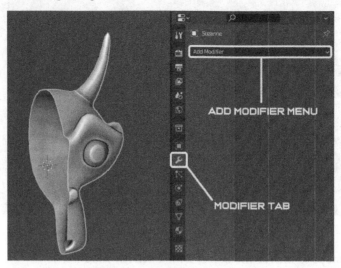

Figure 2.47 – Adding a Mirror modifier

3. In the **Add Modifier** menu, select **Mirror**:

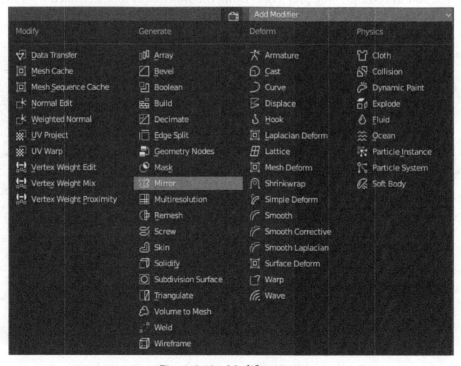

Figure 2.48 – Modifier menu

4. Set the **Axis** settings in the modifier menu to whatever gives the desired result:

Figure 2.49 – Mirror axis

5. Apply the modifier in **Object Mode** (press *Tab* to toggle between **Object Mode** and **Edit Mode**). This will confirm the changes performed by the **Mirror** modifier and create new polygons that we can continue working with:

Figure 2.50 – Applying the modifier

Applying a modifier is **destructive**, meaning that the operation is confirmed and difficult to undo manually. Because of this, it is important to be careful when applying a modifier. We want to be sure that the result is exactly what we want because it cannot be changed afterward.

Now that we have quickly learned how to use the **Mirror** modifier, we will apply it to our modeling process. We will use the **Mirror** modifier quite often, so remember to revisit these five steps when necessary. Next, we will apply the **Mirror** modifier to a part of our FN SCAR.

> **Tip**
> You can slide an edge loop along an edge, after already creating it, by pressing
> *G* twice.

3. Add a two-edged bevel to each loop cut so it matches the width of its ridge:

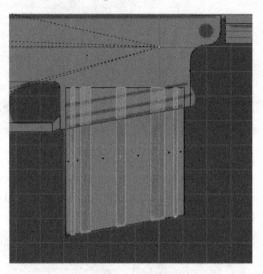

Figure 2.53 – Beveling the loop cuts

4. Add a horizontal loop cut at the top and the bottom of the magazine to create the
    ends of the ridges:

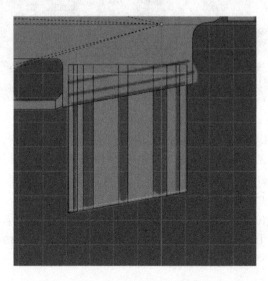

Figure 2.54 – Top and bottom loop cuts

> **Tip**
> You can slide an edge loop along an edge, after already creating it, by pressing *G* twice.

3. Add a two-edged bevel to each loop cut so it matches the width of its ridge:

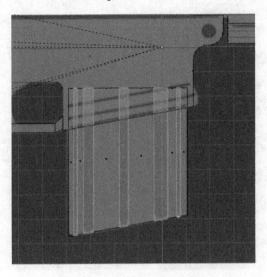

Figure 2.53 – Beveling the loop cuts

4. Add a horizontal loop cut at the top and the bottom of the magazine to create the ends of the ridges:

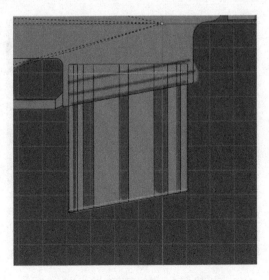

Figure 2.54 – Top and bottom loop cuts

5. Dissolve the edges between the ridges to keep things a little cleaner and to help us with bevels afterward:

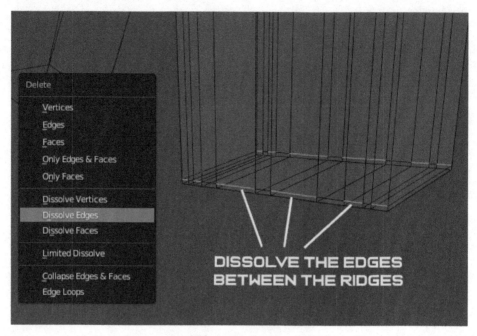

Figure 2.55 – Dissolving edges

6. Add a **Mirror** modifier after deleting one-half of the magazine, but do not apply it yet. This will make shaping the magazine a little easier and quicker:

Figure 2.56 – Mirroring the magazine

7. Extrude the ridges inward a little. Since we are using a **Mirror** modifier, the same extrusion will be repeated on the other side of the magazine:

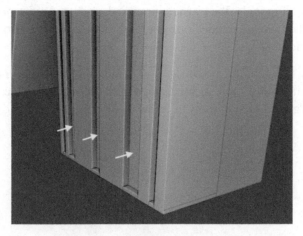

Figure 2.57 – Extruding magazine ridges

This is the last basic shape we need for our FN SCAR outline. When we zoom out and look at what we have until now, it should look something like *Figure 2.58*:

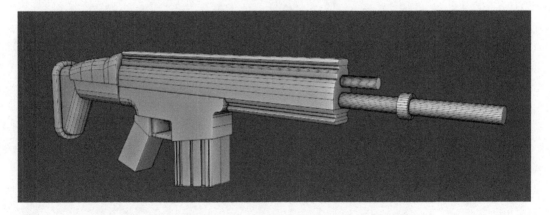

Figure 2.58 – FN SCAR basic shapes

Now, our basic shapes are complete, and we can use this model as a foundation. Keep in mind that a lot will be changed or redone, and the purpose of this model is only to guide us in the right direction. Feel free to add a few more basic shapes for some other parts if you feel it is necessary, such as the iron sights or a scope.

Summary

In this chapter, we developed a low-detail version of the FN SCAR assault rifle by using some essential modeling tools. We learned, prepared, and used references, created objects, and used basic tools such as extrude, loop cut, grab, and so on. We also got a grasp of the **Mirror** modifier and bevels.

In the next chapter, we will increase the level of detail on our current model by reiterating every part and adding more sophisticated shapes and pieces. We will learn to use more modifiers and polygon modeling tools to create a complex and realistic model.

3
Adding More Details with Polygon Modeling and Modifiers

In this chapter, we will continue working on our FN SCAR by increasing the level of detail on the basic shapes we created in *Chapter 2, Creating Basic Shapes for an FN SCAR*.

Previously, we learned how to use basic modeling techniques that were sufficient for creating basic shapes. Now, we will expand our arsenal of tools and modeling techniques and learn how to model almost any detail we come across.

Again, we will work part by part on different sections of the FN SCAR. By the end of this chapter, you will have experience in creating a complex high-poly 3D model and you will also have a finished model ready for texturing and rendering.

This chapter is broken down into the following sections:

- Introducing the 3D Cursor
- Modeling the handgrip
- Detailing the receiver
- Completing the rails with the **Array** modifier

- Finishing the stock
- Modeling iron sights and detailing the barrel

Technical requirements

This chapter requires you to have access to Blender. Internet access for finding reference images is recommended but is not a requirement.

Introducing the 3D Cursor

Before we begin increasing the level of detail on our model, let's talk more about the 3D Cursor. The 3D Cursor is arguably one of the most powerful and versatile tools in Blender. In *Chapter 2*, *Creating Basic Shapes for an FN SCAR*, we mentioned that it is used for manipulating objects in 3D space and that every time we add a new object, it is created exactly at the 3D Cursor.

The 3D Cursor has much more functionality and can be useful in many ways, but the best way to understand its abilities is to try using it. Let's explore what it can do with a few simple steps:

1. Place your 3D Cursor next to the cube by left-clicking, like this:

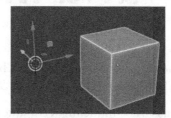

Figure 3.1 – Placing the 3D Cursor

2. Find the **Transform Pivot Point** menu at the top of your screen and select **3D Cursor**.

Figure 3.2 – 3D Cursor as pivot point

3. Now try scaling and rotating the cube and see what happens.

This simple result can be very useful when making precise **transformations**. Transformation is the collective name for the rotate, move, and scale functions. You can be precise with a transformation by typing in the number of units while performing it. Try initiating the rotate function around the *Z* axis by pressing *R* + *Z*, then type 180 and hit *Enter*. The cube should rotate around the 3D Cursor by exactly 180 degrees. You can also use this to scale by a certain factor or move by a certain number of units.

> Tip
>
> You can mirror an object across the 3D Cursor by pressing *S*, typing -1, and hitting *Enter*. Also try setting an axis before typing in the value.

Now we can get back to detailing our FN SCAR. Remember to change the pivot point back to **Median Point** in the **Transform Pivot Point** menu when you want to return to the normal settings.

Modeling the handgrip

We will start increasing the detail by finishing our handgrip because it currently looks quite unimpressive. Let's take a step-by-step approach to make this part look more complete:

1. Add bevels to the vertical edges on each corner of the shape. Try to make it so that every face on the now cylindrical-looking shape is roughly the same width.

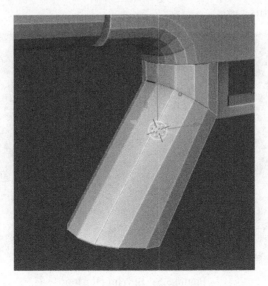

Figure 3.3 – Beveling the edges

2.   Extrude the front-facing faces in the top section of the handgrip and flatten them by scaling them to 0 on the *X* axis. To do this, press the *S* key to scale, then press *X* to scale only on the *X* axis, and then press 0 to multiply the scale by zero (which makes it flat). Press *Enter* to confirm the action.

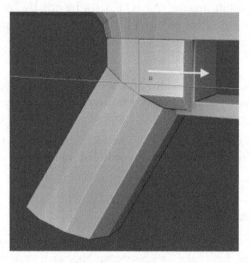

Figure 3.4 – Extruding the front

3.   Select the edges that separate the top and the bottom sections of the handgrip and add another bevel. Do this in wireframe mode to avoid clipping. **Clipping** occurs when edges or vertices pass through each other in an unnatural way, or if the bevel is too wide, in this case.

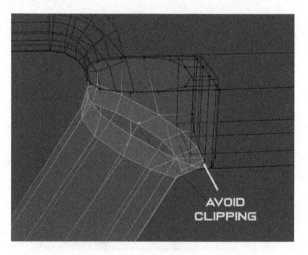

Figure 3.5 – Beveling the loop

4.   Add loop cuts and use them to create the bumps on the handgrip.

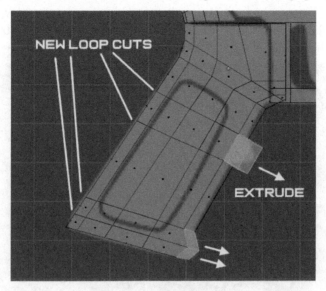

Figure 3.6 – Edge loop bevel

5.   Scale down the extruded part a little to make it pointier.

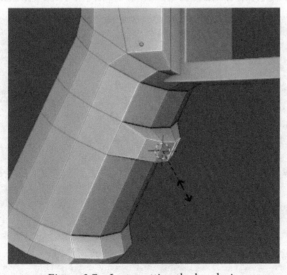

Figure 3.7 – Loop cutting the handgrip

6.   Select the flat surfaces at the top and front of the upper section like in *Figure 3.8* (left), then dissolve the faces. This will create a bent n-gon. Since we need every face to be flat, we will correct that and turn it into two flat n-gons by taking the two corner vertices and joining them together with an edge by pressing *J*.

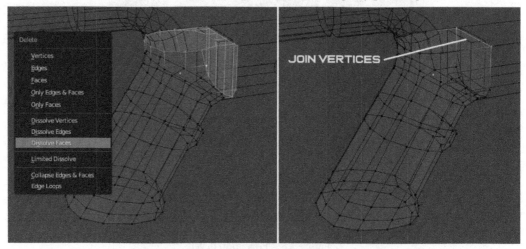

Figure 3. 8 – Dissolving faces (left), joining vertices (right)

7.   Next, add a **Subdivision Surface** modifier from the **Add Modifier** menu.

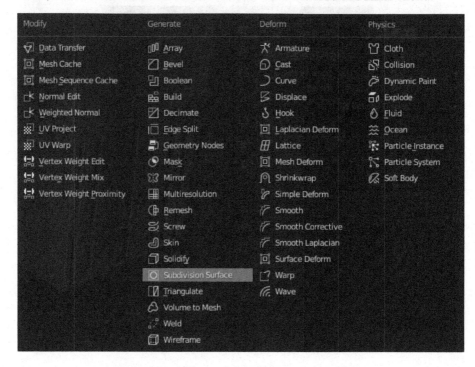

Figure 3.9 – Adding a Subdivision Surface modifier

The **Subdivision Surface** modifier will make the object a lot smoother and rounder, but it doesn't look nice. We have to add a few more things before it's complete.

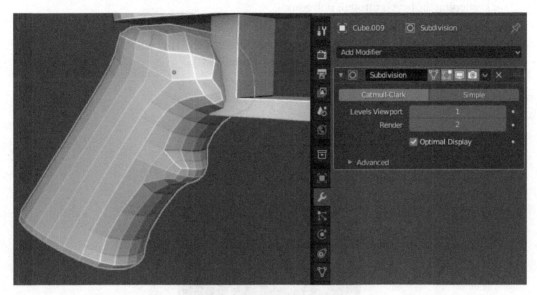

Figure 3.10 – Subdivided handgrip

8.   Add bevels to the flat faces at the bottom, top, and front of the handgrip, as shown in *Figure 3.11*.

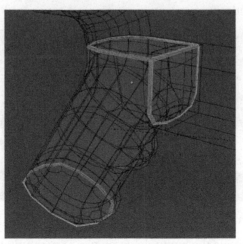

Figure 3.11 – Beveling flat faces

This will make those parts of the handgrip much sharper than you saw in *Figure 3.10*. We can see the improvement in *Figure 3.12*.

> **Tip**
> When creating a bevel, press *C* to toggle **Clamping**. This will allow or prevent
> clipping the bevels through polygons.

9. Add loop cuts close to the ones we created previously. This will tighten the mesh
   and give us a sharper look around those loops.

Figure 3.12 – Tightening with loop cuts

10. Optionally, add a few more adjustments such as thinning the bumps or narrowing
    the top of the handgrip.

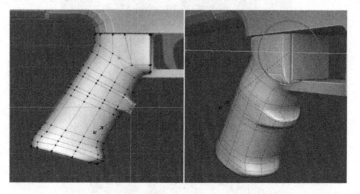

Figure 3.13 – Dual-axis scaling (left), proportional editing (right)

In *Figure 3.13* (left), we scale the bump down on two axes simultaneously by pressing *S*
to scale, then *Shift + Y* to scale on all axes except the *Y* axis. In *Figure 3.13* (right), we also
narrow down the top part of the handgrip using **Proportional Editing**, which is toggled
with the *O* key. When scaling, scroll the mouse wheel up or down to increase or decrease
the influence area, respectively.

Now the handgrip is finished, we can move on to a different part of the rifle. Before we move on to the next part of our FN SCAR, let's take a moment to talk about the 3D Cursor and what it can do.

Detailing the receiver

Let's continue working on this part by adding bevels to each edge of the large bevels we created in *Chapter 2, Creating Basic Shapes for an FN SCAR*:

1. Create a three-edge bevel on each of the edges. Don't bevel the sharp edges at the top, bottom, or middle. Remember to do this on both sides of the gun.

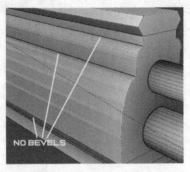

Figure 3.14 – Beveling the bevels

2. Make the spaces between the edges a little more constant. We can use a set of tools called **LoopTools** to help us with this, but we have to activate it in **Blender Preferences**, which we can find in the **Edit** menu in the top-left corner of the screen. In the **Add-ons** tab in the **Blender Preferences** window, search for LoopTools and enable the add-on.

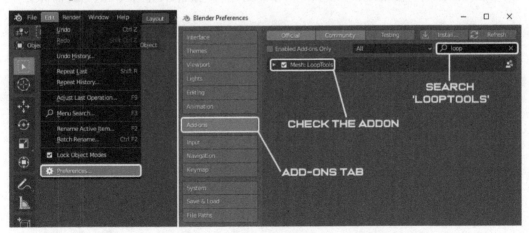

Figure 3.15 – Blender Preferences (left), enabling LoopTools (right)

3. Select the edges in the bottom curve but not the top one. You can do this quickly by selecting the bottom edge and then holding *Ctrl* while selecting the top edge. With the edges selected, press *W* to open the **Edge** menu. In the **LoopTools** section, select **Space** to evenly space the edges.

Afterward, do the same but this time, click the **Relax** button to *relax* the edges. This will make the edges flow more smoothly. Remember to do both of these steps on the same edge loop on the back of the gun, and on the other side.

Figure 3.16 – Space (left), Relax (right)

4. Repeat the same process of spacing and relaxing on the upper bevel, but this time we will only select the round edges and not the straight edge at the bottom, like in *Figure 3.17*. Again, remember to do this on the back and on the other side as well.

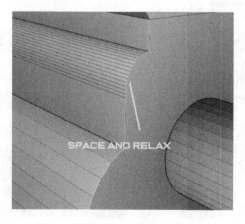

Figure 3.17 – Spacing and relaxing

5. Add a cube with beveled edges that clips through the receiver just a little, like in *Figure 3.18*. Use the reference image we created at the beginning of *Chapter 2, Creating Basic Shapes for an FN SCAR*, to locate exactly where this should be placed.

    Then, press *F2* to rename the object, and name it something recognizable. The letter *A* is a good name because it will appear at the top of a list we will visit in a few moments.

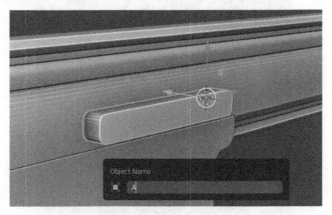

Figure 3.18 – Object Name

6. Select the rifle and add a **Boolean** modifier. We will use this modifier to cut a hole in the object, in the shape of the other object that we just created and renamed.

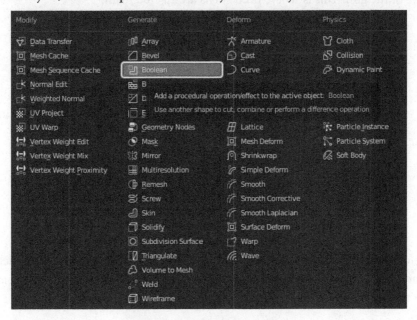

Figure 3.19 – Boolean modifier

7. Find the object named *a* in the **Object** list. Make sure that **Boolean** is set to **Difference**.

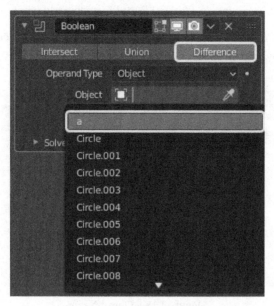

Figure 3.20 – Boolean objects

Once we apply the modifier and delete the object, we have a rectangular hole in the side of the gun. This is where fired shells are ejected from.

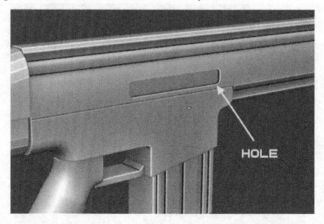

Figure 3.21 – Boolean hole

Before we move on, have you noticed that the surface of the gun looks much smoother in *Figure 3.21*? This is because we enabled **Shade Smooth**. You can do this in the **Object** menu in the top-left corner of the screen.

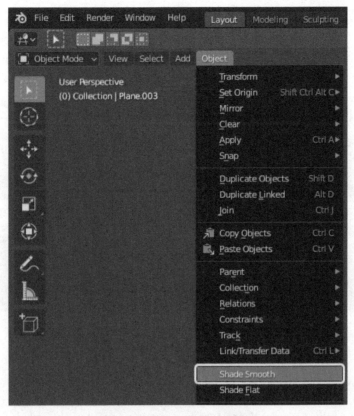

Figure 3.22 – Smooth shading

8. By default, smooth shading on a complex object will give us a messy result, so we have to enable **Auto-Smooth** in the **Object Data Properties** tab. This will tell Blender to keep the shading sharp on edges below a certain angle. Most of the time, 45 degrees is the best angle, but feel free to play around with the number to find the best result.

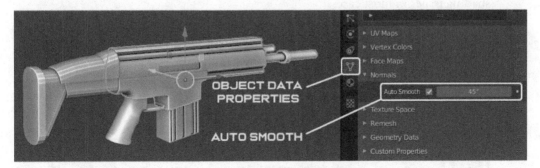

Figure 3.23 – Auto Smooth

When applying the **Boolean** modifier, you will sometimes notice that no hole is created. This can be because of the *normals* of the object used for cutting the hole. Always make sure to correct the normals by selecting an entire object in **Edit Mode** and pressing *Ctrl + N* (*Shift + N* in older versions of Blender).

Let's use the **Boolean** modifier to add more holes to the rifle. Use the reference image to see the shape, size, and placement of the holes.

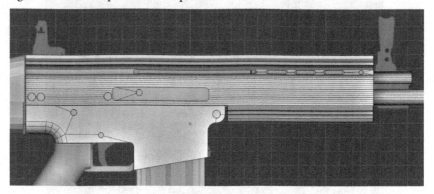

Figure 3.24 – Adding more holes

Tip

When you add a circle, an **Add Circle** menu appears at the bottom left of your screen. In the menu, you'll find a **Vertices** bar for controlling the number of vertices in the circle. Set this to 12 when creating circles for cutting holes.

Sometimes, cutting holes on flat surfaces will cause some weird shading issues, especially when smooth shading is enabled. This can be fixed by selecting all edges surrounding the flat surface except one. With the edges selected, press *V* and then right-click to rip the edges. This will register the edge as a sharp edge and fix shading issues in most cases.

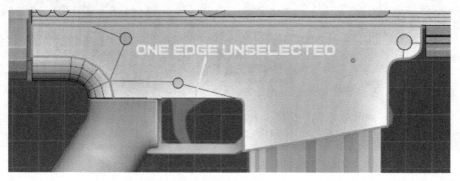

Figure 3.25 – Ripping edges

> **Tip**
> You can stitch back ripped edges by selecting a mesh and pressing *Shift + W*
> to merge vertices by distance. This will turn vertices that are in the same place
> into one vertex and close the invisible gap between them.

We added some rough details to the receiver, but we still need to create some fine detail. Let's use some examples to simplify the fine detail creation process into a four-step workflow that can be used to create other details at the same level.

Simplifying detail creation

Taking the time to create small details is what separates decent models from exceptional ones, but it's very fun and easy to do. Here are two separate four-step workflows for two small and simple but advanced-looking details.

As our first example, let's take a look at a small object on the side of the receiver and break down the creation process:

1. Create a cube and shape it so it's wide and thin. The front face should be a little smaller than the back one. As always, add some bevels to the edges.

2. Use a cube with loop cuts and bevels to create this weird-looking shape. This will be used with a **Boolean** modifier to cut a hole in the object.

3. Add and apply a **Difference** Boolean and add small bevels to some of the edges.

4. Add a few more circles to cut some more holes or create some random objects. Be creative here and do whatever you like, and feel free to look at some other gun photos for reference. The smaller the pieces you create, the better the model will look afterward. Finally, enable smooth shading and auto-smoothing to make the object more realistic.

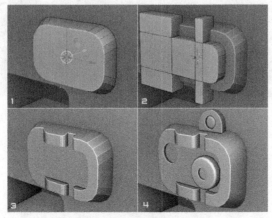

Figure 3.26 – Four-step detail workflow

As the second example, let's create a fire mode switch lever in another four simple steps:

1. Create a short cylinder with a loop cut around the middle and extrude a few faces on the top.

2. Scale the extruded faces to zero using dual-axis scaling and dissolve the unwanted edges. Make sure to dissolve the same edges on the back part of the switch lever.

3. Add a bevel to the point of the lever and the top of the cylinder.

4. Stretch a cube and add some bevels to every edge to complete the object. Remember to enable smooth shading and auto-smoothing on every object.

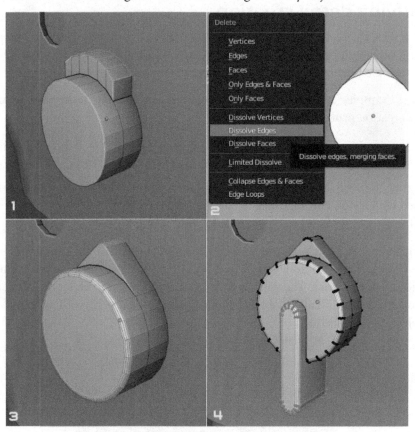

Figure 3.27 – Four-step switch lever workflow

There are plenty of similar details all over the FN SCAR, such as the cocking handle. Check some images of the FN SCAR online and keep creating as many of these details as you can. The more details you create, the better the model will look. Next, let's look at how to create some screw heads to further increase the level of detail.

Modeling screws

Screws are very versatile details because they can be placed on almost any hard-surface model, so let's look at a few steps to create a simple screw head:

1. Start by creating two circles on the hole that we previously made with a **Boolean** modifier. One circle will have 12 vertices (like the hole) and it will be about twice as large as the inner circle, which only has six vertices. Select both circles, press *W* to open the **Edge** menu, and then click **Bridge Edge Loops**.

Figure 3.28 – Bridging edge loops

> **Tip**
> If you created the circles as separate objects, you can join them into one by selecting them both and pressing *Shift + J*.

2. After bridging the edge loops, extrude the circles to create some thickness for the screw. Obviously, the middle circle is used to create the hole in the screw. If you're in the mood to split some hairs, you can add some thin bevels to the edges of the circles.

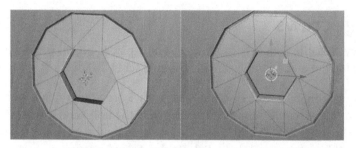

Figure 3.29 – Extruding the screw (left), beveling the edges (right)

3. Using the *Shift + S* shortcut, snap the 3D Cursor to the bottom of the hole that we made for the screw earlier. It may be easier to do that in wireframe mode. When the 3D Cursor is in place, go back to the **Object** menu and set the origin to the 3D Cursor. This origin placement will help us duplicate and precisely move the screw to other places on the gun.

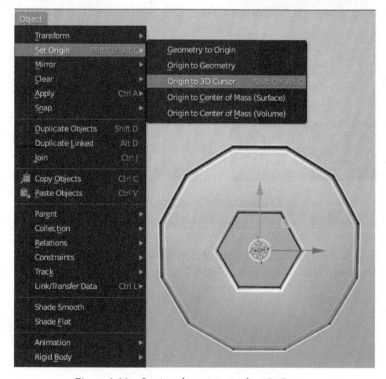

Figure 3.30 – Setting the origin to the 3D Cursor

4.   Snap the 3D Cursor to the bottom circle of another hole. Duplicate the screw using *Shift + D* and move the new screw to the 3D Cursor using the **Selection to Cursor** button in the snap menu.

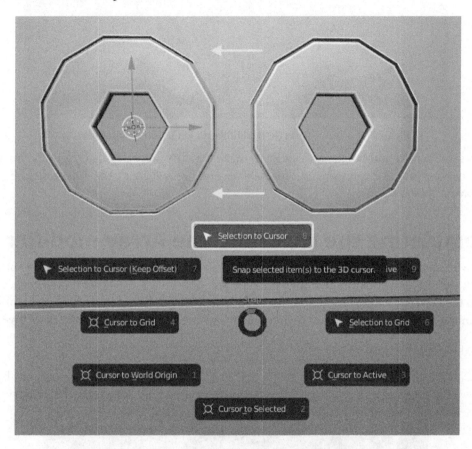

Figure 3.31 – Snapping the screw to the 3D Cursor

The screw origin is located exactly at the bottom and middle of each hole. Whenever we snap a selection to the 3D Cursor, the object is moved so that its origin is placed exactly on the 3D Cursor. Now, we can easily duplicate the screw and perfectly place it in any of the holes on our gun.

Let's finish working on the receiver by introducing the **Insert Faces** tool.

5.   Make a shape like the one on the left in *Figure 3.32*. Select the face on the side and press *I* to insert a new face. Rather than simply creating a smaller face, this tool will create a face with edges equally distant to the edges on the face we are inserting it into at every point.

6. Then press *G* twice, slide the outer edges until they merge with the inner edges, and use *Shift + W* to merge vertices.

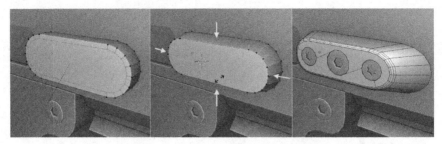

Figure 3.32 – Insert Faces (left), Sliding (middle), Adding screw (right)

Add some screws and bevels to this part to make it a little more detailed. Now, the main part of our FN SCAR is finished. In the next section, we will create the rails using the **Array** modifier.

Completing the rails with the Array modifier

We will now turn the simple shape of our rails into a detailed and finished attachment rail. First, we will create one single step of the rail, and then we will duplicate it many times with the help of an **Array** modifier. The **Array** modifier duplicates an object any number of times we want it to and places them in an array according to the parameters we give.

Let's get started:

1. Start by separating the basic shape of the rail into a new object. We can do this by selecting it in edit mode, pressing *P*, and separating it by **Selection**. If necessary, join the two vertices at the bottom of the shape with *J*.

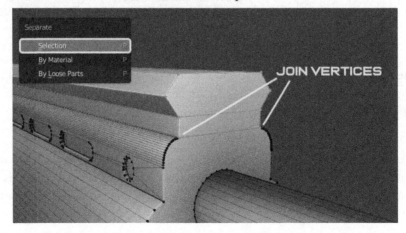

Figure 3.33 – Separating by Selection

2.   Push the front faces of the rail shape all the way to the back to get a thin *slice*. The top of the rail looks a little nicer when thinner, so let's scale it down on the *Z* axis and add some bevels. We will use this shape to create one part of the rail, which we will then duplicate

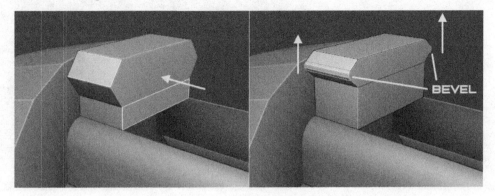

Figure 3.34 – Shortening the rail (left), thinning and beveling (right)

3.   To make the gap between the rails, add a shape and use the **Boolean** modifier to cut a hole.

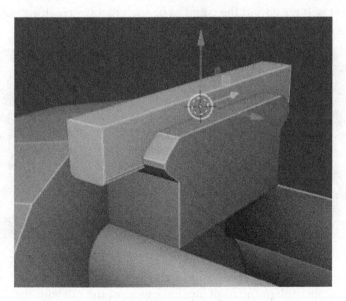

Figure 3.35 – Boolean shape

4.   Now, this is one part of the rail that we can duplicate, so let's add an **Array** modifier.

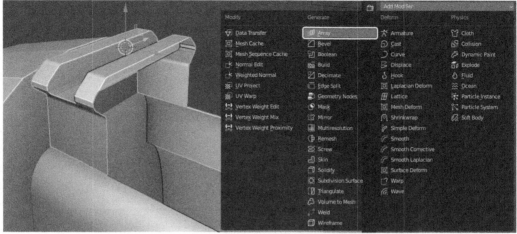

Figure 3.36 – Adding an Array modifier

In the **Array** modifier menu, there is a **Count** slider that lets us choose how many times we want to duplicate the object. The number will vary depending on how long your object is, but we want the count to be such that the resulting object is a little shorter than the length of the gun body.

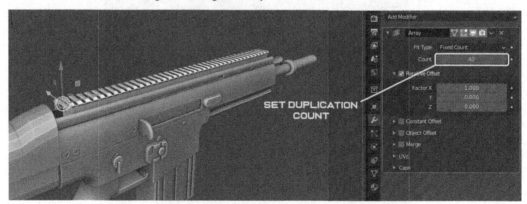

Figure 3.37 – Setting Array Count

5.   When you have the right count and length, apply the modifier. Then use the 3D Cursor to scale to align the front and back faces of the rail with the rest of the gun, by scaling to zero on the X axis.

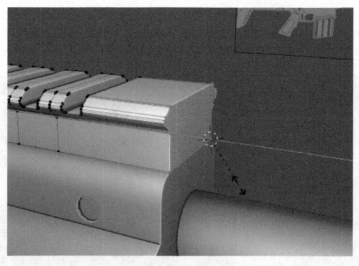

Figure 3.38 – Aligning the rail

6. Duplicate one part of it and separate it into a new object. This part will be used to create the side rails, so we want it to be short. Try to duplicate approximately the same length as in *Figure 3.39*. Place the 3D Cursor between the two vertices at the end and set the origin to that point.

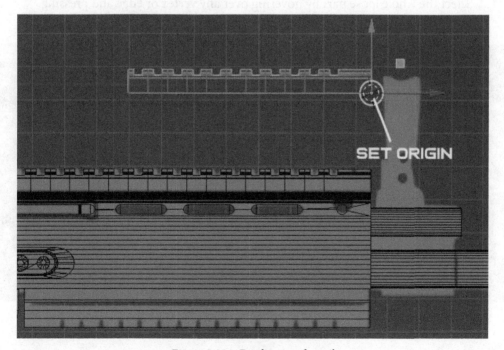

Figure 3.39 – Duplicating the rail

7. Snap this part of the rail to the side of the handguard and rotate it by 90 degrees. Remember to do this on the other side as well. The base of the top rail is quite thick while the side rail has a much thinner base, so bring it a little closer to the gun.

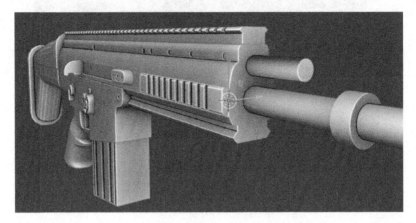

Figure 3.40 – Side rail

The basic shape we created before doesn't really match our current rail shape, so we will delete it and redo it.

8. Select the whole loose part by hovering over any vertex or edge and pressing the *L* key.

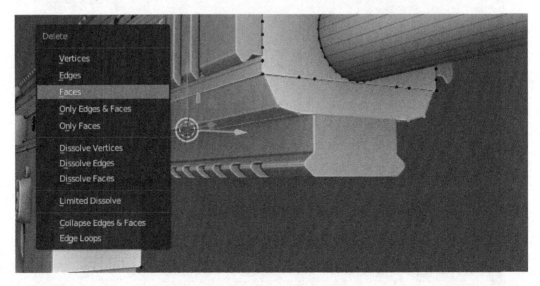

Figure 3.41 – Deleting the loose part

9. Extend the base of the lower rail so it reaches the bottom of the handguard. You can do this precisely by scaling it to zero with the 3D Cursor as the pivot point. We will also add a few loop cuts around the base, like in *Figure 3.42*.

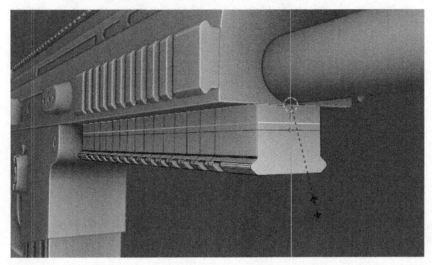

Figure 3.42 – Bottom rail

10. Scale this face loop on the *Y* axis until it's just a little narrower than the handguard and dissolve the edge marked in *Figure 3.43*. Dissolving this edge will allow us to create cleaner bevels.

Figure 3.43 – Bottom rail base

11. Finish the bottom rail by adding bevels to those edges. We also add a thin two-edge bevel to the bottom of the upper receiver.

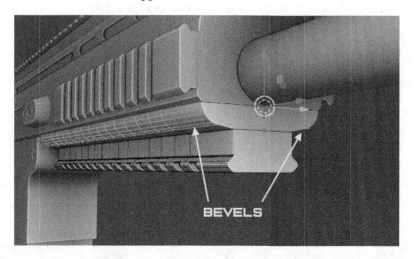

Figure 3.44 – Beveling the bottom rail

12. To finalize the rails, we can add some more screws to the ends and add a thin cover to the end of the gun body, right behind the barrel. This can be done by duplicating the faces at the ends, extruding them a little to add some thickness, and slightly beveling their edges.

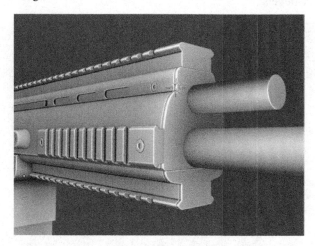

Figure 3.45 – Finishing the rails

We now finished detailing the body of our FN SCAR. We still have to complete the stock at the back and the barrels and sights at the front. In the next section, we will work on the stock before finally moving on to the latter.

Finishing the stock

We are now going to turn the simple shapes we created for the stock in *Chapter 2, Creating Basic Shapes for an FN SCAR*, into more detailed and sophisticated ones:

1. Add lots of loop cuts and bevels to the shape to increase the complexity of the surface. We are doing this because having more edges lets us create cleaner cuts with the **Boolean** modifier. Try playing around with the spacing and relaxing loop tools to get a better result. Also delete the faces from the front, back, and bottom of the object.

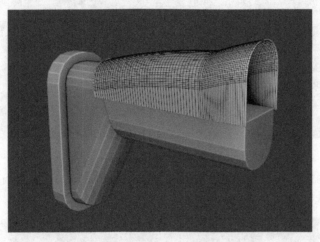

Figure 3.46 – Increasing polygon density

2. Add a few loop cuts to the bottom shape and extrude it up so that it is just below the surface of the upper object.

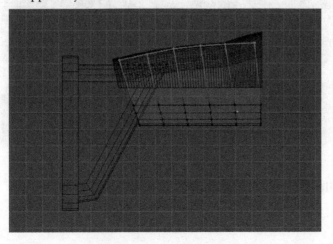

Figure 3.47 – Lower stock

3. Add bevels to the edges we just extruded. Make sure that every part of the lower stock piece is below the upper part, so that nothing is clipping through the cover.

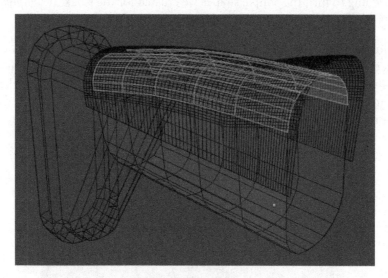

Figure 3.48 – Beveling the lower stock

4. Using the 3D Cursor, scale the upper stock down on the *X* axis so that there is a little gap between the stock and the body of the gun.

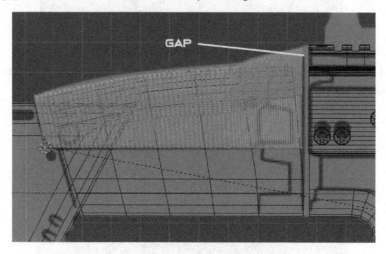

Figure 3.49 – Gap

5. Add a **Solidify** modifier to the upper stock piece.

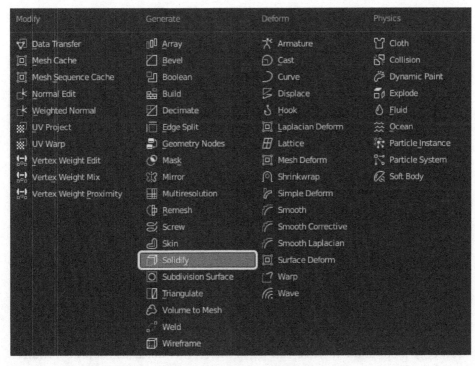

Figure 3.50 – Solidify modifier

The **Solidify** modifier adds thickness to a surface, like in *Figure 3.51*. The thickness is not always constant across the entire object, so make sure to check **Even Thickness**.

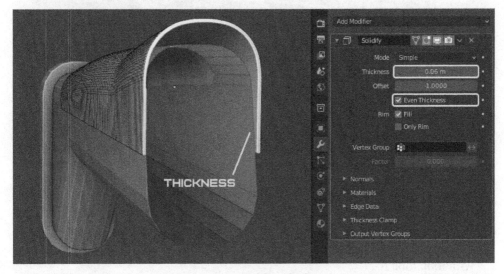

Figure 3.51 – Adding thickness

6. Add some more cuts with the **Boolean** modifier. We will trim the corner in the front and cut a circle in the back.

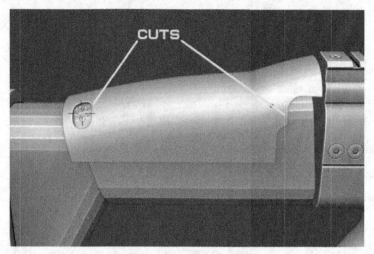

Figure 3.52 – Upper stock cuts

7. Repeat the same process for the lower stock piece. This time, we will delete a few edge loops at the top to create a gap there. Afterward, also apply a **Solidify** modifier here.

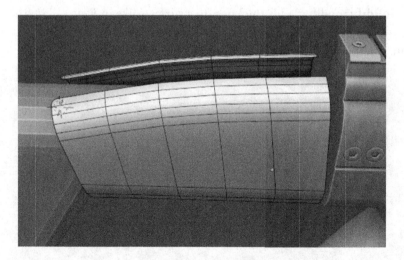

Figure 3.53 – Lower stock

8. At the back of the stock, we will increase the polygon density using the same technique we used on the body by adding bevels, then spacing and relaxing them with loop tools.

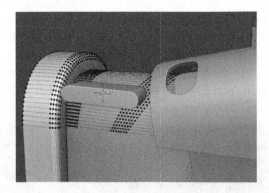

Figure 3.54 – Rear stock detail

Notice how the polygon density varies on the surface. Some parts have lots of vertices, while others don't have many. This is because we need to have approximately the same vertex density on the object we're cutting and the object we're using to make the cut.

The rounded parts of our cutting object obviously have more polygons than the straight parts, so the parts where the cut will be round on the target object need to have a higher vertex density.

9. Create some grips on the bottom part of the stock using a thin cylinder with an **Array** modifier. This time, we set the **Relative Offset** factor for both the X and the Z axes. This is because we want the array to duplicate upward and slightly forward as well. Your factor might need to be a little different, depending on the angle you need.

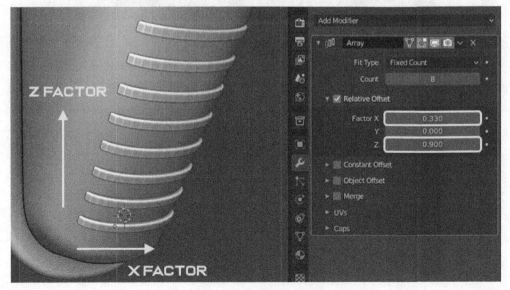

Figure 3.55 – Grip Array

10. Let's move the stock backward a little so that we can work on the part that connects the stock and the body or the receiver. We need a vertical cylindrical cut along the back edge, but this time we won't do it with a **Boolean** modifier. Instead, we can create a bevel and use the **Shape** slider in the **Bevel** menu that appears at the bottom left of your modeling screen when you create a bevel. Set the value to something between 0.040 and 0.050 to get a circular shape.

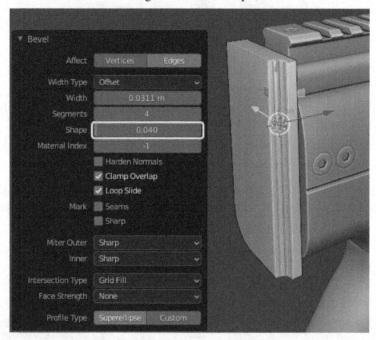

Figure 3.56 – Bevel shape

11. Create a circle at the bottom of the bevel and change its shape with proportional editing. Extrude the shape upward to add some thickness to it, like in *Figure 3.57*.

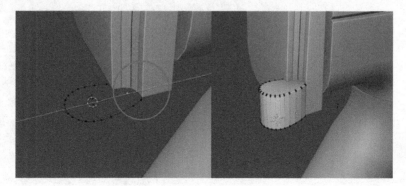

Figure 3.57 – Proportional editing circle (left), stock connector shape (right)

12. Duplicate the shape twice and arrange it as in *Figure 3.58*. This will act as a hinge, which can be used to fold the stock.

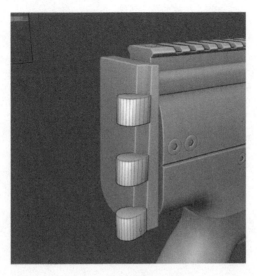

Figure 3.58 – Stock connector

13. When we bring the stock back, we have to shorten it a little to prevent the hinges from clipping the upper stock piece. We will scale that part down a bit with **Proportional Editing**.

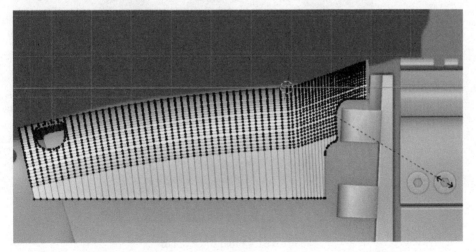

Figure 3.59 – Shortening the upper stock with proportional editing

14. Duplicate the hinges a few more times and rotate them so they connect the stock to the body.

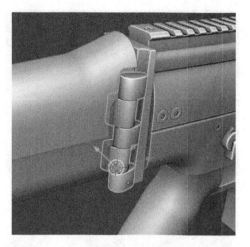

Figure 3.60 – Finishing the stock connector

15. Finish this part by inserting a thin shape between the stock connector and the gun body. In real life, the shape looks something like in *Figure 3.61*, but you can get creative and shape it however you like.

Figure 3.61 – Final stock detail

The stock is now finished on our FN SCAR. Essentially, we used the simple shapes we created in *Chapter 2, Creating Basic Shapes for an FN SCAR*, and we turned them into more detailed ones. We also added a few more items to make the model more complete.

Modeling iron sights and detailing the barrel

Next, we are going to add more details to the barrel, and we will create an iron sight. In this section, it is not very important to follow the steps too closely because many of the details are improvised and not necessarily realistic:

1. Connect the two barrels with a smooth shape. Do this by filling some of the edges with *F* and making them smoother with some loop cuts, bevels, or **LoopTools**.

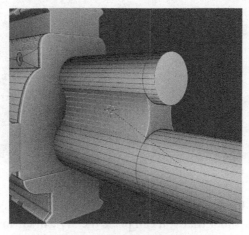

Figure 3.62 – Connecting the barrels

2. Push the shape forward to create a small gap between the receiver and the barrels. In that gap, we extrude two circles to connect the shapes.

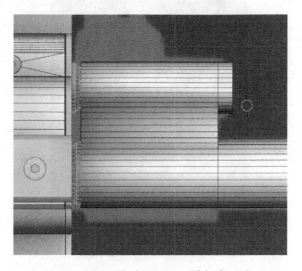

Figure 3.63 – The beginning of the barrels

3. Add some shapes to create the iron sight mount. This is the part that holds the iron sight in place, and it looks different on the many variations of the FN SCAR, so feel free to get creative here as well.

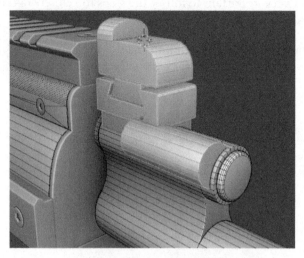

Figure 3.64 – Sight mount

4. Create an outline for the iron sight by extruding some edges out of a circle and mirroring it. Remember that you can place the 3D Cursor in the middle of the shape, then duplicate and scale the selection to -1 on the *Y* axis. When you do this, make sure to correct the normals with *Ctrl + N*.

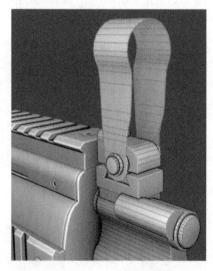

Figure 3.65 – Sight outline

5. Solidify the outline and fill in the middle part. When we do this, the hole will not be circular. To make it circular, select all the edges there and use the **Circle** option in **LoopTools**. Sometimes, this option is a little messy, but a **Boolean** modifier will also do the trick here.

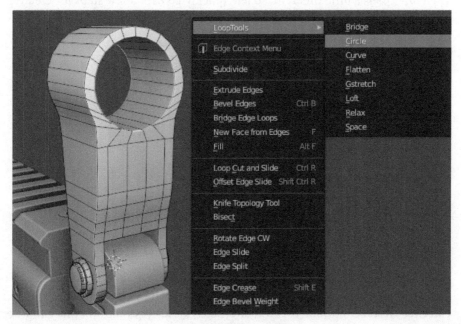

Figure 3.66 – Iron sight

6. Finally, cut some shapes into the end of the barrel with a **Boolean** modifier. Again, we have to increase the vertex density at the rounded parts of the cut.

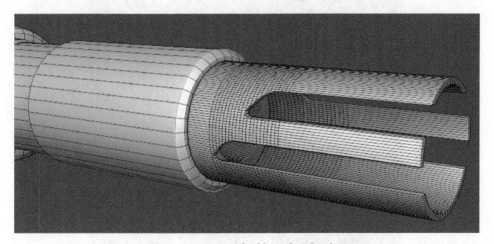

Figure 3.67 – Finished barrel and sights

The iron sight consists of two parts – one at the barrel and one at the back of the railing on top of the gun. The back part is also quite straightforward and can be created using the modeling techniques we already covered. The adjustment wheel in *Figure 3.68* is a little different, so let's quickly go over a few steps for creating a shape like this.

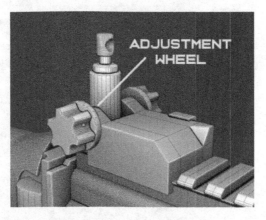

Figure 3.68 – Adjustment wheel

7.   Add a cylinder with 12 sides and select the faces on the sides. In edit mode, you will find the **Select** menu at the top left of the modeling screen, which contains a **Checker Deselect** option. This will alternately deselect every other face that we selected. In our case, only 6 of the 12 faces will remain selected.

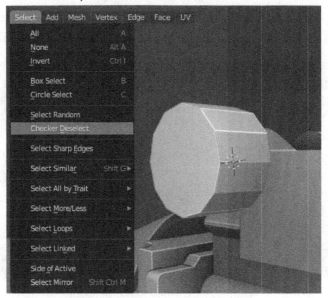

Figure 3.69 – Checker Deselect

8. Set the pivot point to **Individual Origins**. This will let us transform each selection individually, based on its individual origin or center of mass.

Figure 3.70 – Individual Origins

9. Use dual-axis scaling to scale up the selected faces. Each face is being scaled individually without moving, which will narrow the faces in between. **Individual Origins** can also be helpful when rotating multiple objects.

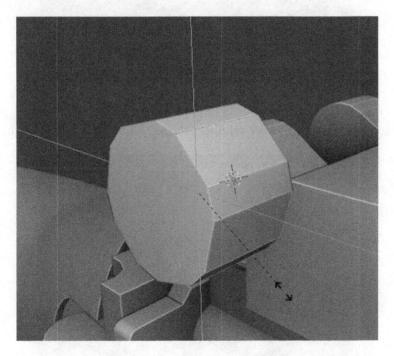

Figure 3.71 – Scaling individual faces

10. Press *E* to extrude. Because we set the pivot point to **Individual Origins**, each face will be extruded individually in its own direction. After extruding, scale the faces down just a little.

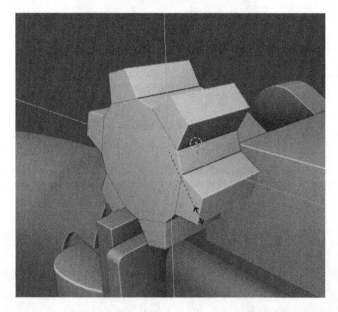

Figure 3.72 – Extruding individual faces

11. Add some bevels and another cylinder as a base to attach this to the sight base.

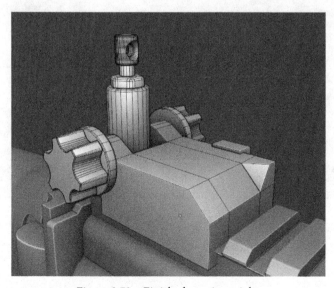

Figure 3.73 – Finished rear iron sight

> **Tip**
> Pretend you're aiming down the sight to make sure your sights are
> aligned correctly.

Finally, we can revisit the magazine. This is probably the easiest part to detail
because we only need to add some bevels. If you'd like to, add some more detail
to the bottom or to the sides with a **Boolean** modifier.

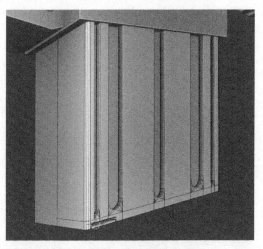

Figure 3.74 – Finished magazine

With all these details complete, the FN SCAR should look something like this:

Figure 3.75 – Finished FN SCAR model

In this section, we applied the techniques we learned throughout this chapter to create an
iron sight and detail our barrel and magazine. Now our FN SCAR model is finished. If you
want to keep working on this model, try using the techniques we covered in this chapter
to add some attachments, such as a front grip or a scope.

Summary

In this chapter, we finished modeling our FN SCAR assault rifle. We learned how to use new modeling tools and techniques and multiple new modifiers. Now, we can create almost any detail we come across without needing to introduce new techniques. Of course, though, there are many more tools and techniques to explore in Blender.

In the next chapter, we will introduce materials, PBR texturing, and basic lighting and rendering techniques to turn our flat-colored model into a beautiful and realistic rendered image.

4

Texturing and Rendering the FN SCAR

In *Chapter 3*, *Adding More Details with Polygon Modeling and Modifiers*, we finished modeling the FN SCAR assault rifle and learned many new tools and techniques. Now, we will learn the basics of Blender's rendering and texturing abilities, as well as some essential texturing techniques.

In this chapter, we will wrap up our FN SCAR project by creating materials and textures for the model and rendering it into a portfolio image.

First, we will create some simple color materials for the model. Then, we will apply some Blender-generated textures to make the materials look more realistic. When the materials and textures are ready, we will set up the lighting and the scene before finally rendering the project.

This chapter is broken into the following sections:

- Creating materials
- Generating an Edge Mask
- Creating Edge Wear
- Rendering the Scene

Creating materials

In this section, we will learn how to create materials to give color to our currently colorless model. Before we start creating materials, we must understand how Blender creates materials using **Material Nodes**.

Understanding Material Nodes

When creating materials in Blender, we usually use Material Nodes. Material Nodes are operations created in Blender to control the appearance of a material. There is an incredible variety of things that can be created with the wide array of nodes available to us in Blender, but we will not go into too much detail regarding the functions of each node. Instead, we will learn how to use some simple nodes to create basic materials.

Let's go over a few steps to set up our Workspace for material creation and create a simple material:

1. Enter the **Shading** Workspace by clicking on the **Shading** button at the top of the screen.

Figure 4.1 – Shading Workspace

2. Expand the Shader Editor window by hovering the mouse over the top of the window and dragging it up.

Figure 4.2 – Shader Editor

3. In the Shader Editor, click on **New** to create a new material for our object.

Figure 4.3 – Creating a new material

The new material consists of two nodes: the **Principled BSDF** node and the **Material Output** node. These are the two most fundamental nodes that are present in almost every material. In short, **Principled BSDF** is like a junction point where we put all our material settings together, and the **Material Output** node is just where we plug everything to display it on our object. By default, every material is a plain white color, as is shown on the model and in the **Base Color** part of the **Principled BSDF** node.

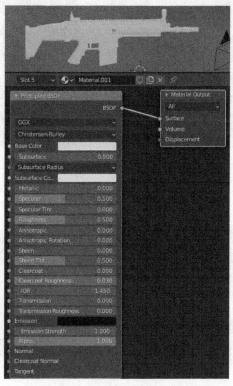

Figure 4.4 – Nodes

4. In the **Principled BSDF** node, click on **Base Color**.

    In this **Base Color** menu, there are multiple ways to control colors. My preferred way is to use the **HSV** (**hue, saturation, value**) control. In the **HSV** control, it is easier to manipulate the saturation and value (brightness) directly. For now, we need a beige base color. To get this color, drag the color wheel pointer to approximately the same place as shown in *Figure 4.5*, and turn down the value using the black and white bar on the right:

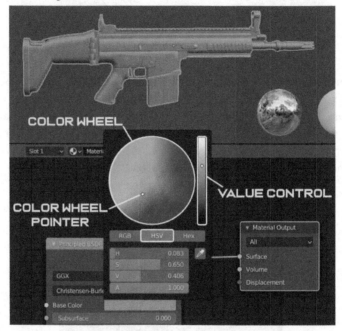

Figure 4.5 – Color wheel

5. Set the **Metallic** value in the **Principled BSDF** node to 1.000 by dragging the slider to the right.

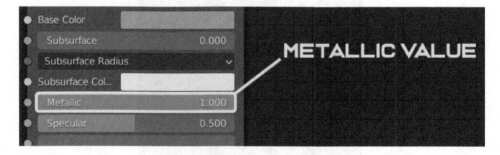

Figure 4.6 – Metallic value

The **Metallic** value is an example of another property we can control in the **Principled BSDF** node. **Roughness** is also commonly changed, and it determines how shiny a material is. These properties can be controlled not only using the sliders in **Principled BSDF** but also with other nodes.

Let's explore that a little further.

Combining nodes

Figure 4.7 is a simple example of how we can use a node to assign an image or texture to the surface of an object. An **Image Texture** node is used to load an image or texture from a file, and the color output of that node is plugged into the **Base Color** plug on the **Principled BSDF** node. This way, we can apply any image to the surface of our model instead of just having a base color. In *Figure 4.7*, an **Image Texture** node with an image of a smiley is plugged into the **Base Color** plug of the **Principled BSDF** node and cast on the surface of a plane:

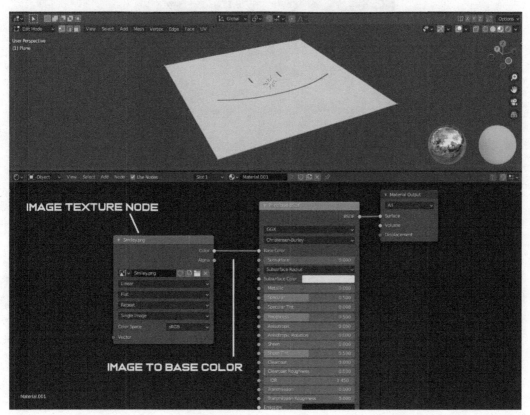

Figure 4.7 – Material Node example

As you can imagine, any of the properties in the **Principled BSDF** node can be controlled using an **Image Texture** node, or any other node for that matter. There are also nodes that allow us to generate textures such as clouds or a checker pattern, which can be used in the same way. We will use more nodes later in this chapter, but for now, we need a few more basic materials for our FN SCAR.

Adding multiple materials

We will now create a few more materials to assign to our FN SCAR:

1. In the **Material Properties** tab, create a new material slot using the plus (+) button.

Figure 4.8 – New material 2

2. In **Edit Mode**, select the upper receiver by hovering over it and pressing *L*, then create a new material in the slot and click on **Assign**.

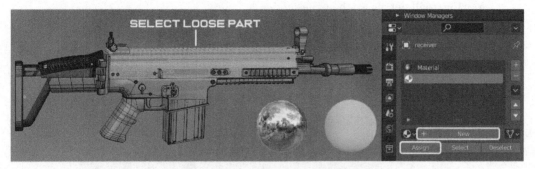

Figure 4.9 – Assigning a new material

3. Set **Base Color** for the new material to a slightly more golden-looking color. Remember to set the **Metallic** value to 1.000 once again.

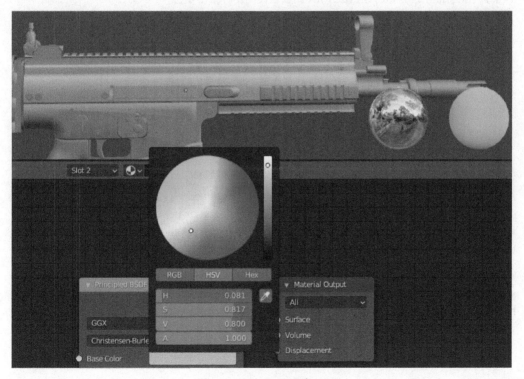

Figure 4.10 – Base Color 2

4. Repeat steps *1*, *2*, and *3* to create and assign two more materials for the details. Use a *metallic black* for the larger details, such as iron sights and railings, and a *metallic gray* for small details, such as the screws.

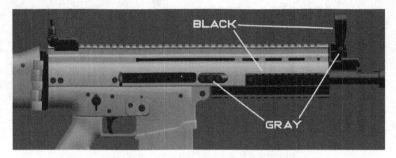

Figure 4.11 – Black and gray details

Before we move on to the next section and continue texturing the FN SCAR, let's take a look at the shading issues on the lower receiver in *Figure 4.12*:

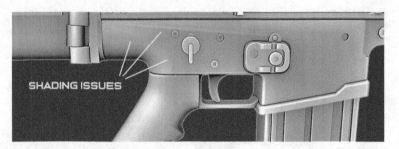

Figure 4.12 – Shading issues

As we mentioned in *Chapter 3, Adding More Details with Polygon Modeling and Modifiers*, shading issues can appear when cutting holes in a shape or beveling its edges. Although we fixed this problem before, it can reappear if we make small changes to the model like the ones shown in *Figure 4.12*.

As we did before, we will fix the problem by selecting the edges surrounding the surface (marked with a checkered line in *Figure 4.13*) and pressing *V* to rip the edges, then clicking the right mouse button. Try to do this in any other place where you find noticeable shading issues.

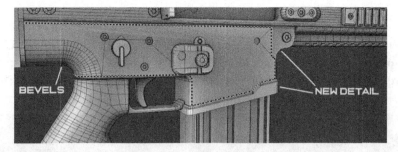

Figure 4.13 – Ripping edges

After ripping the edges, the model should look much cleaner, as shown in *Figure 4.14*. With the help of this technique, we can cut holes in our models much more easily without undesired side effects:

Figure 4.14 – Clean surface

We created some basic materials and assigned them to different parts of the model. Next, we will create an edge wear effect to make our FN SCAR look more natural and realistic.

Generating an Edge Mask

In this section, we are going to use Blender's Cycles render engine to generate an Edge Mask. In other words, we will tell Blender to detect sharp edges and create an edge wear effect around those areas. This technique will significantly improve the appearance of our model, and we will apply it to the other models we create in this book.

Detecting edges

We begin by creating an edge detection node setup, which we will refer to as an Edge Mask. Essentially, this is a combination of nodes that will create white areas around the edges of our FN SCAR. We will later turn these white edges into edge wear on our basic materials from the *Creating materials* section.

Here are the steps to creating the Edge Mask:

1. Select all faces of the FN SCAR, and in **Edit Mode**, press *U* to open the **UV Mapping** menu. In the menu, select **Smart UV Project**. This will unwrap the entire model onto a 2D surface. Before unwrapping, correct the normals by pressing *Shift + N* to make sure the entire gun is a single object.

Figure 4.15 – Smart UV Project

2. In **Object Mode**, duplicate the entire FN SCAR and move it upward, away from the original.

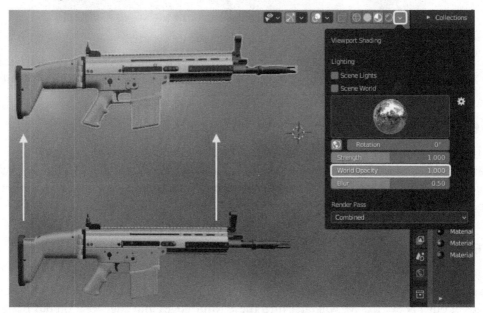

Figure 4.16 – Duplicating

> **Tip**
>
> You can remove the background image in the viewport settings. Click on
> the arrow shown on the top right of *Figure 4.16* and drag the **World Opacity**
> slider down.

3. Create a new material and assign it to the duplicated model. In the new material,
    delete the **Principled BSDF** node. The result should be a completely black object.

Figure 4.17 – New material

4. In the **Render Properties** tab, set **Render Engine** to **Cycles**. An Edge Mask will not work in **Eevee**.

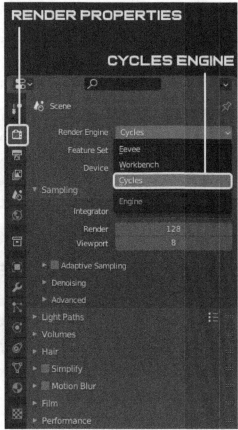

Figure 4.18 – Cycles render

5. In the Shader Editor, open the **Add** menu by pressing *Shift + A* and click on the **Search** bar. Search for `bevel` and add a **Bevel** node.

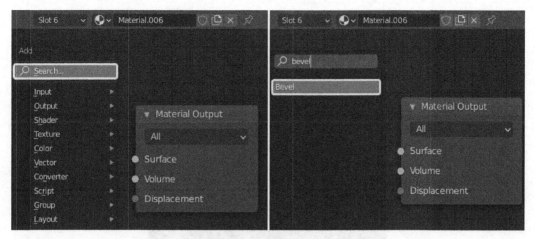

Figure 4.19 – Add node (left), Bevel node (right)

6. In the **Bevel** node, set **Samples** to 10 and **Radius** to 0.07. Below the **Bevel** node, also add a **Geometry** node.

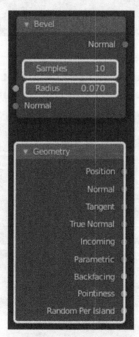

Figure 4.20 – Bevel and Geometry nodes

7. In the **Add** menu, search for and add the **Vector Math** node and place it as shown in *Figure 4.21*. When added, the node will appear as **Add** by default.

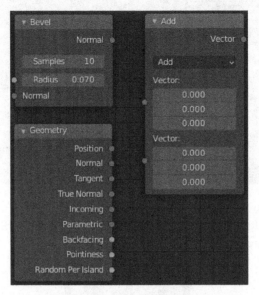

Figure 4.21 – Vector Math node

8. In the **Vector Math/Add** node, change **Add** to **Dot Product**, and plug the **Normal** output from the previous two nodes into the **Vector Math** node.

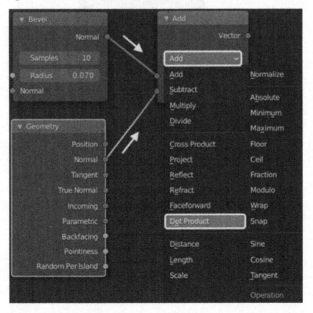

Figure 4.22 – Dot product

9.   Lastly, add an **Invert** node after the **Vector Math** node.

10. Plug **Value** from the **Vector Math** node into the **Color** input of the **Invert** node. Plug the **Color** output of the **Invert** node into the **Surface** input of the **Material Output** node.

When you switch to **Rendered View**, in the top-right corner of the 3D viewport, the edges on the model should appear white on an otherwise black model.

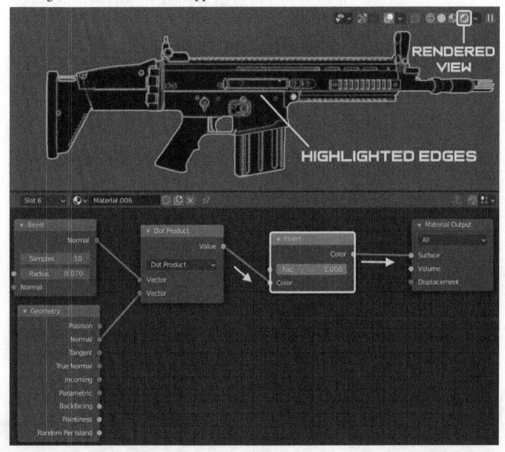

Figure 4.23 – Invert node

Our edge detection process is now complete. The next step is to turn this result into an edge map that we can use to create an edge wear effect on our materials.

Baking an edge map

In the following few steps, we'll turn the Edge Mask into an edge map. This means that we will turn the material we just created for highlighting edges into an image texture. We will then be able to use that image texture to control the base colors on the basic materials we created in the previous section. So, to get started, execute the following steps:

1. Find the Image Editor in the bottom left of the **Shading** Workspace. In the Image Editor, we can create a new image using the **New** button at the top of the window.

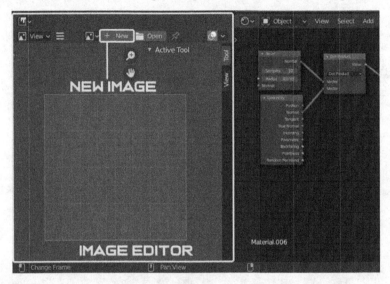

Figure 4.24 – Image Editor

2. Set the name to Edge Map and resolution to 2048 px. Check **32-bit Float** and click **OK**. This will create a plain black image. We will use the following image to bake our edge map:

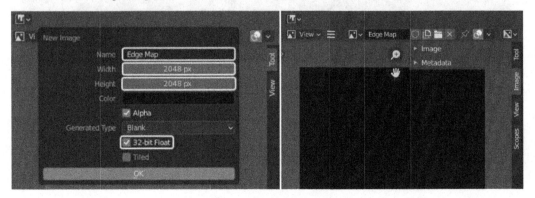

Figure 4.25 – Edge map

3. Next to the nodes we created for our Edge Mask in the Shader Editor, search for and add an **Image Texture** node. Open the image browser in the node and load the edge map that we generated in *step 2*.

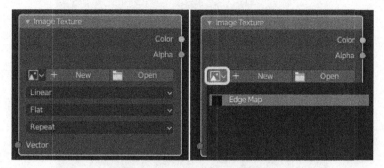

Figure 4.26 – Image Texture node

4. Break the model up by moving apart some overlapping parts. This will help create a better result. For example, the top part of the stock is normally covering the rest of the stock, which can lead to some issues on our edge map.

Since we are using the duplicated model to bake the edge map, only break apart that model.

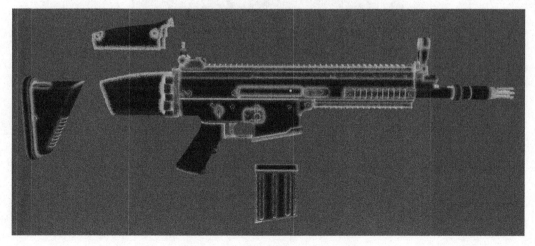

Figure 4.27 – Breaking up the model

5. With the duplicated FN SCAR selected, go to the **Render Properties** tab and open the **Bake** menu. Here, set **Bake Type** to **Emit** and click **Bake**.

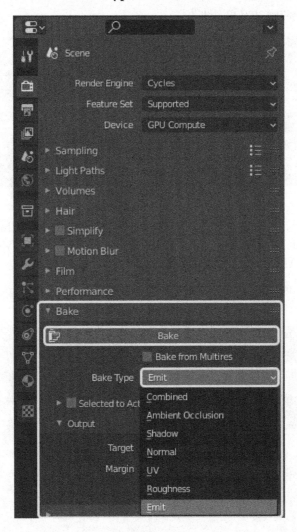

Figure 4.28 – Baking

After a few minutes, the black image we generated will turn into a baked edge map, which should look something like in *Figure 4.29*:

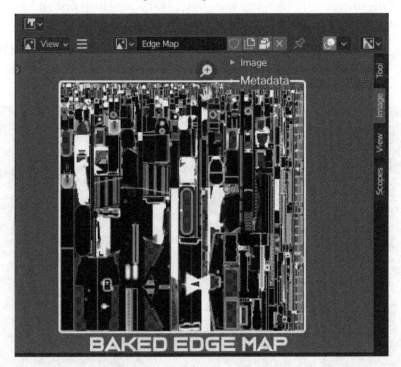

Figure 4.29 – Baked edge map

We can now use this image to change the appearance of the materials we created in the first section.

Creating edge wear

In this section, we are going to process the edge map to create edge wear on our model. The edge map will be combined with various nodes to produce a highly customizable result, which will help create more realistic models.

Let's begin by applying the edge map to our first material:

1. Select the material to which you want to apply the edge map first and add an **Image Texture** node. In the **Image Texture** node, load the edge map.

    Plugging the **Image Texture** node into **Base Color** of the **Principled BSDF** node will replace that material with the edge map texture we baked in the previous section.

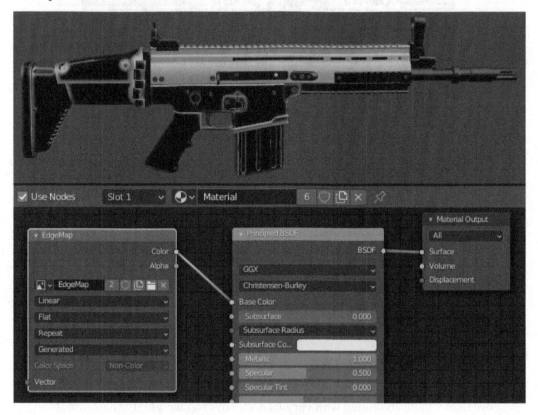

Figure 4.30 – Loading the edge map

2. Search for and add a **Mix RGB** node. Place it between the **Image Texture** node and the **Principled BSDF** node.

    This node mixes colors and we will use it together with the **Image Texture** node to control where we want to display which color.

Figure 4.31 – Mix RGB node

3. Set **Color1** to beige, the main color of the object. Set **Color2** to black, which is the color of the edges. The effect is not noticeable yet, but we will add a few more nodes to improve it.

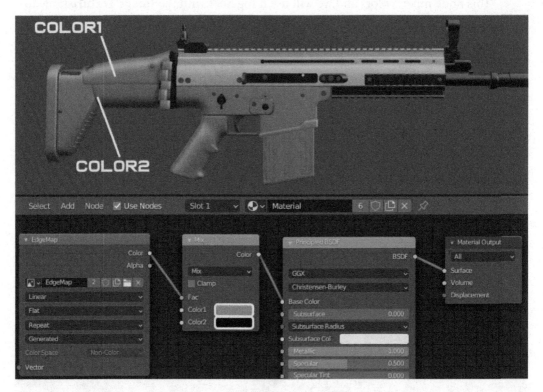

Figure 4.32 – Color1 and Color2

4. Add a **Math** node between the **Image Texture** node and the **Mix RGB** node. By default, it is named **Add** when created. Set the operation for this node to **Power**. This node will amplify the effect of our edge map.

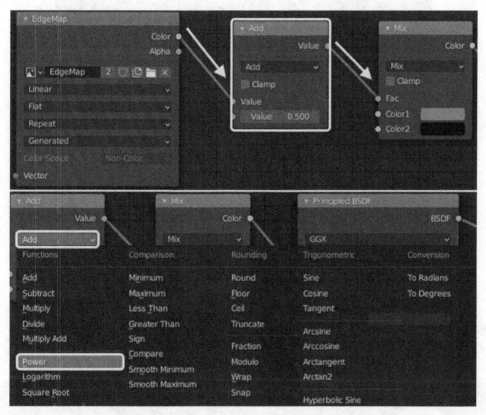

Figure 4.33 – Math node (up), Power node (down)

5. Reduce the **Exponent** value to 0.200 to make the edge shading darker.

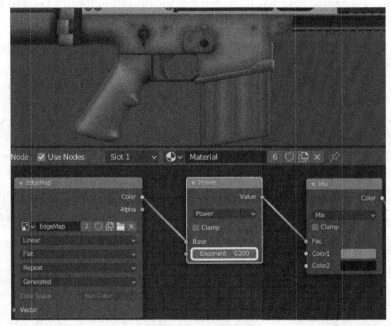

Figure 4.34 – Exponent

6. Duplicate the **Image Texture** node with the edge map and plug **Color** from the **Image Texture** node into **Color2** on the **Mix RGB** node. This will create white edges on top of the shading we generated so far.

Figure 4.35 – Color2 node

7. Add a **ColorRamp** node between the duplicated **Image Texture** node and the **Mix RGB** node. The sliders on **ColorRamp** will let us control the presence of the colors on the edge map, which will in turn change the look of the white edges we created in *step 6*.

Figure 4.36 – ColorRamp

8. Set the sliders to get a desirable effect. Pushing the black slider to the right will make the white edges thinner. Pushing the white slider to the right will make them sharper.

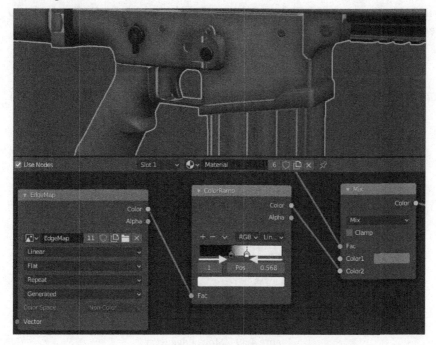

Figure 4.37 – Sliders

9. Click on the white slider and adjust the color in the color wheel.

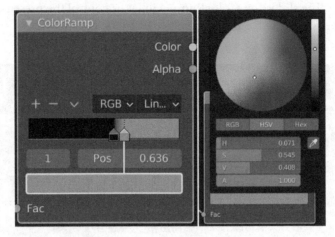

Figure 4.38 – ColorRamp color

We have now created edge wear from the Edge Mask. Next, we will correct inconsistencies in edge wear that appear on some parts of the model.

Separating materials

We applied the same material to the stock, but the edge wear and shading look too thick here:

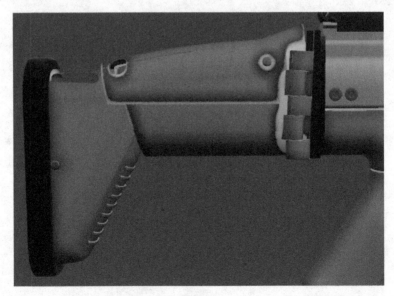

Figure 4.39 – Stock edge wear

We can fix these issues by tweaking the material on this part of the model, but not on the other parts. To do so, lets separate the material in just a few quick steps:

1. Create a new material slot and load the same material from the Material Browser.

Figure 4.40 – New material slot

2. Duplicate the material using the **New Material** button, marked in *Figure 4.41*:

Figure 4.41 – Duplicating a material

3. Assign the duplicated material to the parts where you want to change the edge settings.

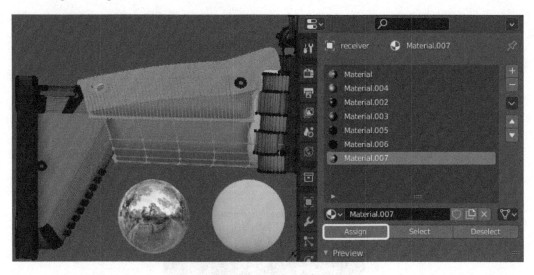

Figure 4.42 – Assigning a material

4. In the duplicated material, change the colors of **ColorRamp** to black. In the **Power** node, increase the exponent to around 0.700.

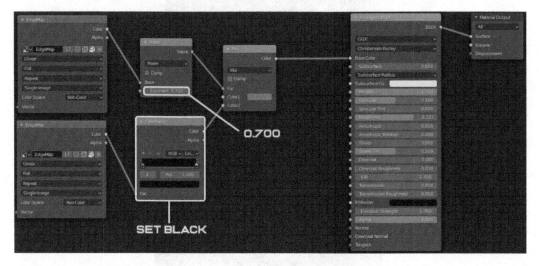

Figure 4.43 – Duplicated material

This should reduce the thickness of the edges on the stock. At this point, the model should look something like in *Figure 4.44*, in the material view:

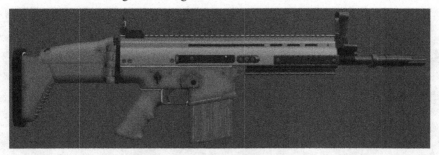

Figure 4.44 – Stock material

Now, the edge shading no longer looks excessive, and it can be controlled separately. You can do this any number of times, on any part of the model.

Copying nodes to other materials

Our first material is ready, but we need the same effect on the other materials as well. Luckily, we don't need to manually create the same nodes each time, but we can just copy and paste them from the first material:

1. Select all the nodes from the finished material, except **Principled BSDF** and **Material Output** since they are already in every material. Once selected, copy them by pressing *Ctrl + C*.

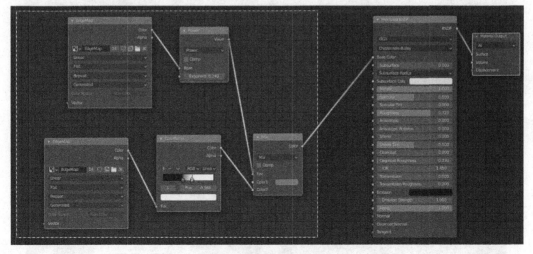

Figure 4.45 – Copying nodes

2. Paste the nodes in the Shader Editor of the second material, using *Ctrl + V*. Plug **Color** from the **Mix RGB** node into **Base Color** of the **Principled BSDF** node.

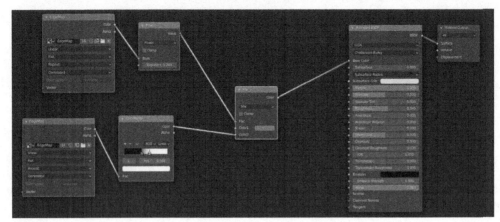

Figure 4.46 – Pasting nodes

3. Set the correct color in the **Mix RGB** node. We pasted the nodes from the previous material, so it will carry the color from that material. Also, decrease the roughness a little on this material.

    You will most likely need to adjust some of the properties on different materials to get a better result since not all parts of the model have the same edge wear.

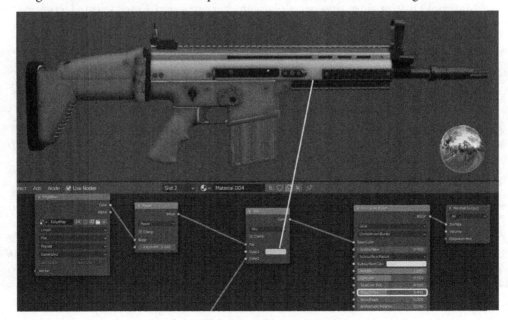

Figure 4.47 – Adjusting copied nodes

For example, adding a **Power (Math)** node between **Image Texture** and **ColorRamp** for **Color2** on the black metal material will improve the look of the edges. You may also need to adjust the markers and the color in the **ColorRamp** node.

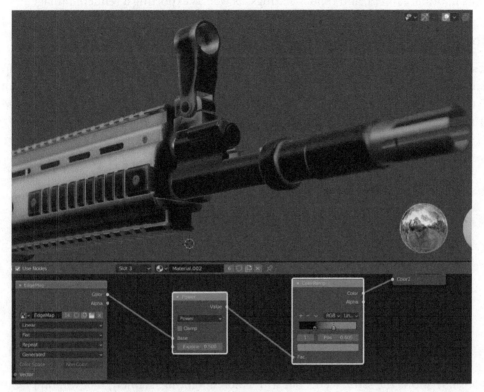

Figure 4.48 – Adding nodes

4. Continue adjusting all the materials until the FN SCAR is ready. When you finish, it should look something like in *Figure 4.49*:

Figure 4.49 – Finished materials

Lighting and rendering

In this section, we are preparing a scene to render our FN SCAR. This consists of setting up the lighting, camera, and render settings, as well as exporting a rendered image.

Lighting the scene

Let's take a moment to discuss how we will create the lighting. *Figure 4.50* shows a simple scene consisting of an object in the center and four plain white point lights placed around the object. The scene is well lit and the object is clearly presented, but it does not look very natural or aesthetically pleasing:

Figure 4.50 – Lighting example 1

Figure 4.51 shows the same scene, but with colored lighting. Namely, the twopoint lights on the right side project a light-orange color, and the ones on the left project a light-blue color. As a result, the scene looks much better:

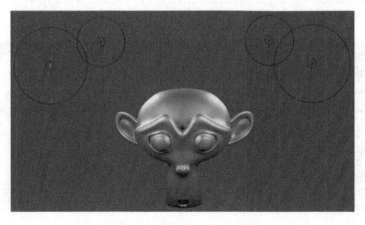

Figure 4.51 – Lighting example 2

The key here is that one side of the object is lit with a warm color, while the other side is lit with a cold color. This is the principle we will follow when lighting our FN SCAR.

In the following steps, place lights into our scene:

1. Add an **Area** light from the **Light** section of the **Add** menu.

Figure 4.52 – Area light

2. Place the light on the right side of the model and rotate it so that it is facing the model.

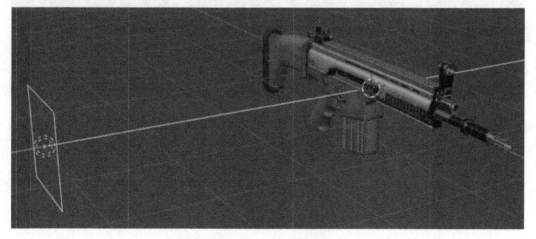

Figure 4.53 – Light placement

3. Duplicate the light multiple times and rotate it around the *Z* axis so that there are four or five lights on the right side of the model, all facing the center. When done, select all the lights but select the middle light last, and use *Ctrl + L* to apply **Link Object Data**.

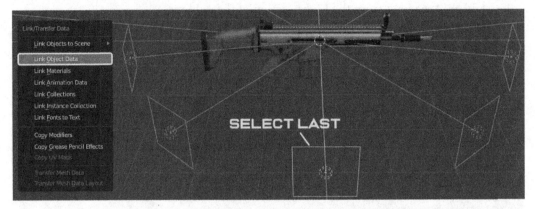

Figure 4.54 – Link Object Data

4. Select the middle light and open the **Light** properties menu. In the menu, set **Color** to a light orange and **Power** to 50 W.

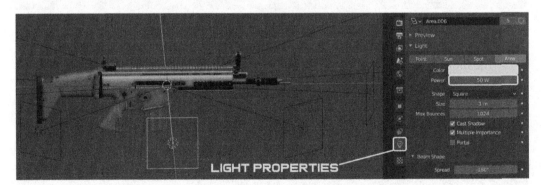

Figure 4.55 – Light properties

5. In the front view, rotate the lights so that they lie at an angle of approximately 20° from the *Z* axis.

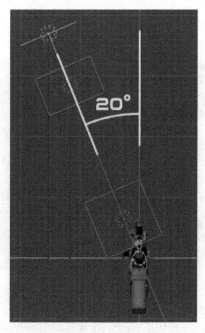

Figure 4.56 – Light angle

6. Repeat *steps 1-4* on the other side of the FN SCAR. Set the color for these lights to a light blue and the power to 600 W.

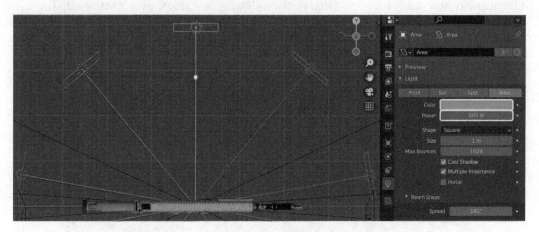

Figure 4.57 – Blue lights

7. Add one last area light under the model, facing upward. Also, set the color to light blue and set the power to 30 W.

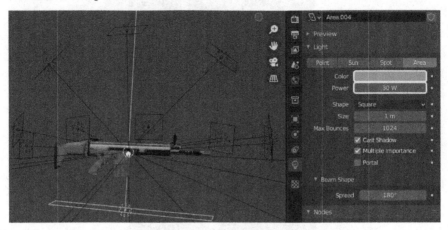

Figure 4.58 – Floor light

We created some lights to make our object visible in the scene, and we aligned and colored them to create a more aesthetic result. Next, we will turn our scene into a savable image.

Rendering the scene

Our scene is now ready for rendering. In the following few steps, we are setting up the camera and render settings to produce a rendered image:

1. Place the 3D view at an angle from which you want to render the scene. In this scene, the lighting is set up best for an angle similar to that of *Figure 4.59*:

Figure 4.59 – Aligning the view

2. Add **Camera** from the **Add** menu and press *Ctrl + Alt + Num 0* to align it with the view.

Figure 4.60 – Adding a camera (left), aligning the camera with the view (right)

3. In the Camera properties tab, you can adjust the focal length to 40 mm.

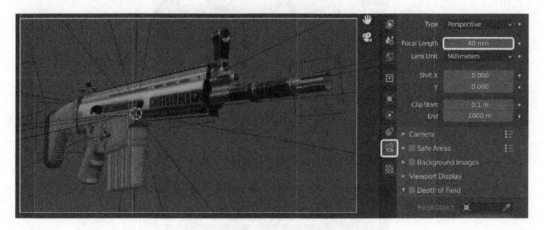

Figure 4.61 – Focal Length

4. To improve the render, try switching the Shader Editor to **World Mode** and replicating this node setup for a background gradient.

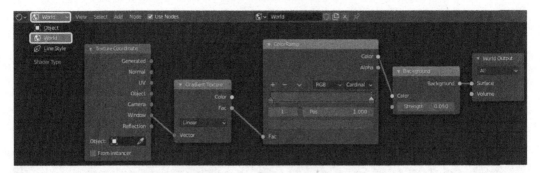

Figure 4.62 – Background color

5. In the **Render Properties** tab, find the **Sampling** menu and set the **Render** number to 512. You may also want to check the **Render** box in the **Denoising** menu to prevent noise in the render.

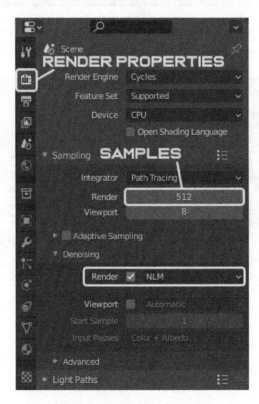

Figure 4.63 – Render Properties

6. In the Output properties tab, adjust the **Resolution** settings of the render.

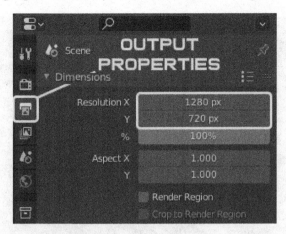

Figure 4.64 – Output Properties

7. Render the image by opening the **Render** menu in the top left and selecting **Render Image**. Alternatively, use the shortcut *F12*.

Figure 4.65 – Render Image

The following screenshot, in *Figure 4.66*, shows the final render:

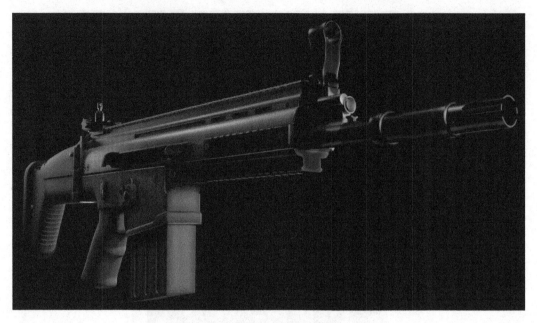

Figure 4.66 – Render result

After a few minutes, Blender turns the scene into a rendered image after calculating the colors, lights, shadows, and reflections.

Summary

In this chapter, we learned how to create materials and apply them to a model. We also learned how to use material nodes to create an Edge Mask, which was used to shade the edges and simulate edge wear. Finally, we set up the lighting for the scene and rendered the image. These skills are necessary to turn any 3D model into a presentable result and will likely be used in nearly every project you work on in the future.

In the next chapter, we will continue learning about modeling techniques and getting some practice with the ones that we already learned about by creating a futuristic sci-fi race ship. We will also learn about some new texturing techniques.

Part 3: Modeling a Sci-Fi Race Ship

This section consists of creating a concept race ship model in medium-poly and introducing some ways to make a model appear more detailed than it really is, by implementing texturing techniques and normal decals.

We will cover the following chapters in this section:

- Chapter 5, *Modeling a Sci-Fi Race Ship*
- Chapter 6, *Texture Painting the Sci-Fi Race Ship*

5
Modeling a Sci-Fi Race Ship

In this chapter, we are going to model a medium-poly sci-fi race ship. We will learn how to create a model with a lower level of detail than the FN SCAR, but with enough detail to still make it impressive. The model will be used in *Chapter 6, Texture Painting the Sci-Fi Race Ship*, to demonstrate techniques that can simulate higher levels of detail.

By the end of this chapter, we will produce a model with a medium level of detail, which makes it suitable for use in games and animation. This is important because highly detailed models will often not work well for such purposes, and they must be replaced with less sophisticated ones.

We will cover the following topics in this chapter:

- Modeling basic shapes
- Adding details
- Modeling armor panels
- Adding more parts
- Finishing the model

Modeling basic shapes

In this section, we are going to create the basic shapes for our race ship. We will begin by creating the cockpit, since that is the central part of the ship. Everything else, including the wings, engine, and armor, will be attached to the cockpit.

In the following steps, we will create the basic shapes of the race ship using techniques that we have already covered:

1. Add a cube and shape it into the nose of the ship by simply moving the edges.

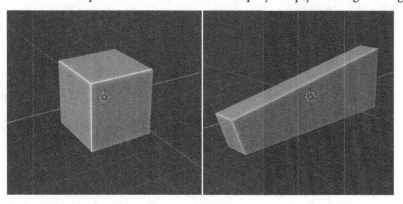

Figure 5.1 – Cockpit nose

2. Extrude the back of the nose a few times using *E* to extrude and *S* to scale the individual segments.

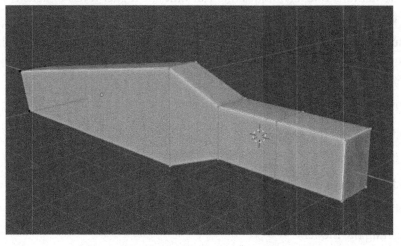

Figure 5.2 – Extruding the cockpit

3. Add another cube to the side and reshape it, as shown in *Figure 5.3*. We are using a **Mirror** modifier on this shape to copy it to the other side.

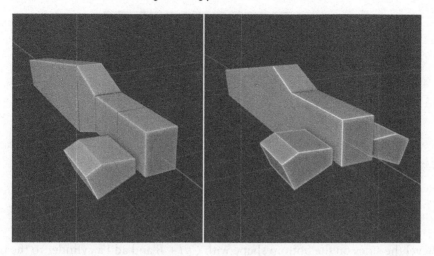

Figure 5.3 – Side shape

4. Extrude the side a little further and create two loop cuts, as shown in *Figure 5.4*. Using the *P* shortcut, separate the face loop between the loop cuts and narrow it using *Alt + S*. This will scale the shape down while ensuring every edge is equally distant from its starting point.

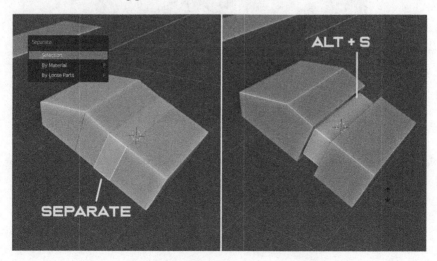

Figure 5.4 – Separating and narrowing

5. Rejoin the part we separated in *step 4* with the original shape using *Ctrl + J* after selecting both objects. Also, fill the faces with *F*, as shown in *Figure 5.5*.

Figure 5.5 – Filling

6. Bevel the sides on the bottom shape with *Ctrl + B* and add a cylinder to the back. With the help of more bevels and extrusion, smooth the shape and create a hole in the back. This shape will be the propulsion system.

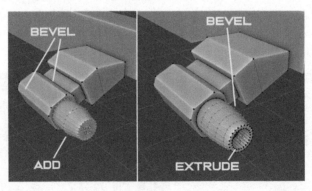

Figure 5.6 – Propulsion

Next, let's attach some more basic shapes to our ship.

7. Add a cube at the back of the fuselage to hold the engine.

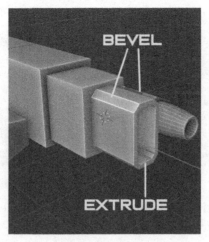

Figure 5.7 – Engine

8. Add another cube and extend it toward the front of the cockpit to create a basic shape for the wing. Rotate the shape so that it aligns with the shape that is already in place.

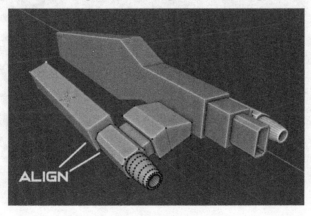

Figure 5.8 – Wing shape

9. Duplicate the face at the front of the shape with *Shift + D* and move it a little further to the front. Extrude the face to create another shape.

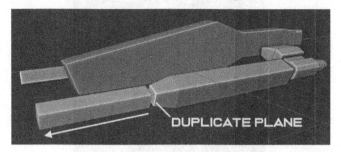

Figure 5.9 – Duplicating the wing shape

10. Repeat to create another shape that's approximately twice the length of the previous one. Use *Ctrl + R* to create a loop cut in the middle of it.

    Using the *Alt + S* shortcut, the face will be pushed in the direction it is facing. Push it towards the middle of the ship, as shown in *Figure 5.10*.

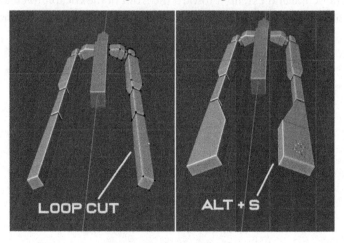

Figure 5.10 – Front wing

11. To get some more space between the wings, push the entire wing outward.

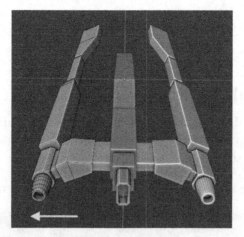

Figure 5.11 – Wider wing

12. Extrude the face at the back of the cockpit shape upward with *E* and pull the front edge up higher than the back edge.

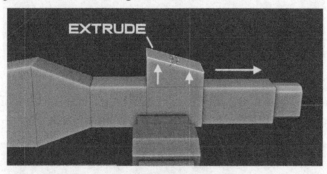

Figure 5.12 – Back of the cockpit

13. Add a cube and use it to make the basic shape of the windshield.

Figure 5.13 – Windshield

We have now finished creating the basic shapes for our race ship and we have enough shapes to form our ship. Next, we will add more details to the basic shape and replace some of them with more sophisticated objects.

Adding details

We made enough basic shapes to form the ship. Now, we will continue by increasing the level of detail on the ship and adding more objects to the existing shapes. Here, we will improve the look of the ship without making it too sophisticated:

1. Duplicate the face at the top of the nose with *Shift + D* and move it upward.

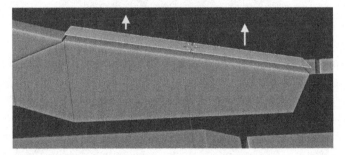

Figure 5.14 – Nose cover

2. Extrude the face downward with *E* and add a loop cut at the back of the shape. Remember to correct the normal with *Shift + N* after extruding.

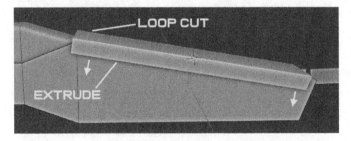

Figure 5.15 – Extruding the nose cover

3. Extrude the face at the bottom of the loop we just created and use it to create a frame for the windshield. *Figure 5.16* shows how to create the frame in four steps using extrusion.

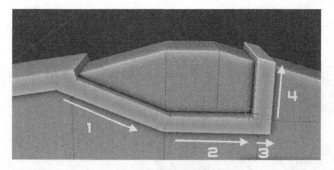

Figure 5.16 – Windshield frame

4. You may need to make the windshield wider or larger so it fits the frame better.

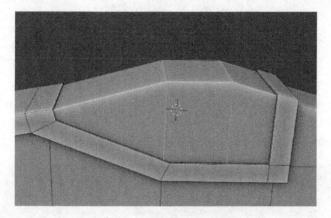

Figure 5.17 – Adjusting the windshield

5. Next, use *Ctrl + B* to bevel some of the edges of the nose cover, windshield, and the back of the windshield frame. This will make the shape flow better.

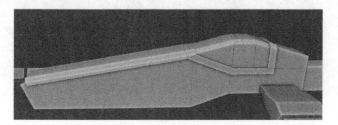

Figure 5.18 – Beveling the cockpit

6. Duplicate the faces at the front of the shape we created next to the cockpit and extrude them to get a similar shape.

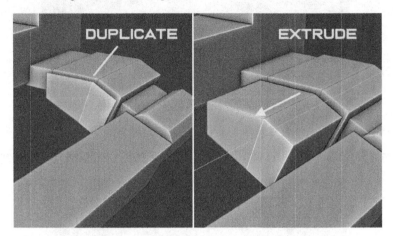

Figure 5.19 – Extruding a new shape

7. Move the edge back toward the wing to create an angle on the shape. Press *I* with the faces selected to insert new faces, then press *E* to extrude, moving the face inward to the desired depth, creating the air intake.

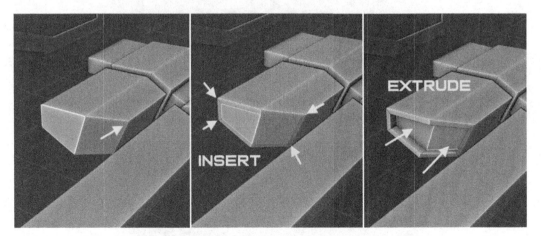

Figure 5.20 – Air intake

8. Duplicate the two faces at the bottom of the air intake and move them down. You can use *Alt* + *S* to move them in the direction they are facing. Extrude them downward to create a similar shape.

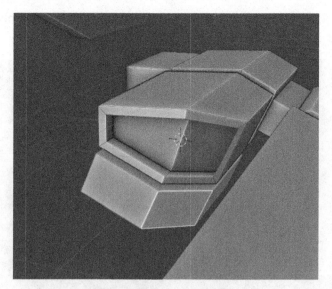

Figure 5.21 – Lower intake

9. Once again, insert faces to create another air intake.

Figure 5.22 – Inserting faces

10. Bevel the edges at the top and bottom of the cockpit. At the top, only bevel the front edges, and slide the vertices up by double-pressing *G*.

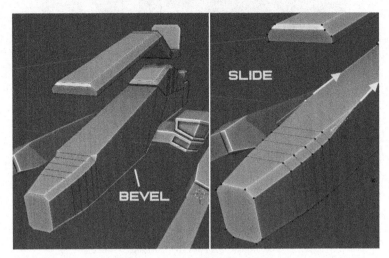

Figure 5.23 – Nose bevels

11. Select the faces at the top of the nose and extrude them, then press the right mouse button to snap them back into their original place.

12. Place the 3D Cursor at the front edge, as shown in *Figure 5.24,* and scale the faces to *0* on the *Z* axis to flatten them.

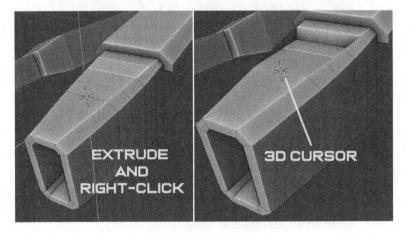

Figure 5.24 – Nose dent

13. Scale the edges down individually so that the dent becomes narrower at the back.

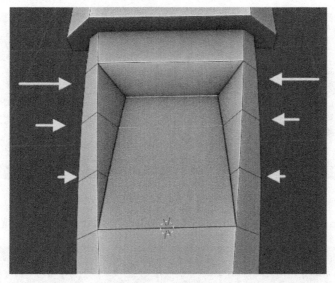

Figure 5.25 – Scaling edges

14. Add a small cube into the hole we just created on the nose and bevel the edges at the top. Insert a face at the front by pressing *I* and extrude it to create another air intake.

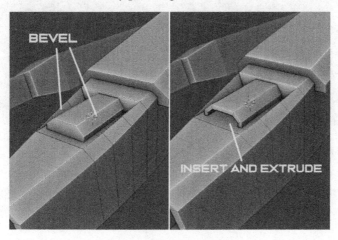

Figure 5.26 – Nose intake

15. Using the same technique, add a similar object to the side of the cockpit.

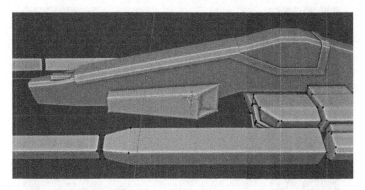

Figure 5.27 – Cockpit attachment

16. Add two more shapes to the front of the object to make it look like a gun.

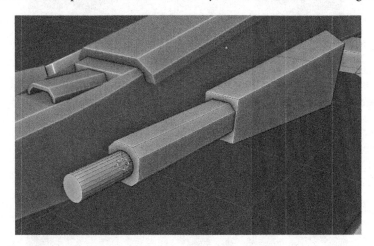

Figure 5.28 – Gun shape

17. Select the circle at the end of the gun and activate the **Shear** tool on the left of your screen. Drag the top slider backward to shear the surface. After dragging the slider, you can manually adjust the offset value in the **Shear** menu.

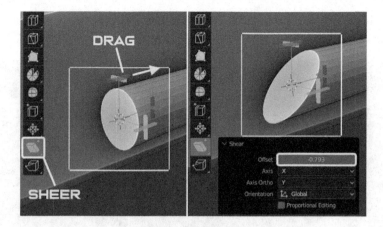

Figure 5.29 – Shear

We increased the level of detail by adding a few more objects to the model. Let's stop adding details for a minute and learn how to make armor panels to protect the ship and improve its aesthetic.

Modeling armor panels

We will now learn how to create armor panels to cover the exterior of the ship. We will use a new object and apply modifiers to it so that we can shape the armor panels. This will allow us to improve the appearance of the ship:

1. Duplicate the top face at the back of the cockpit and separate it so that it's a new object. We are going to use a **Mirror** modifier here, so delete one half of the face.

Figure 5.30 – Duplicating a plane

2. Add a **Solidify** modifier and a **Mirror** modifier. In the **Solidify** modifier, set the thickness to **0.1m** and check the **Even Thickness** checkbox.

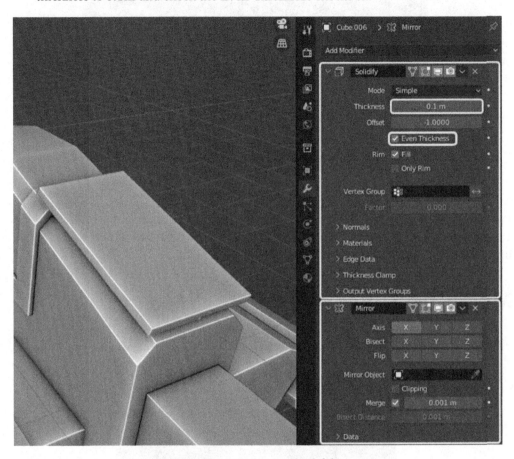

Figure 5.31 – Mirroring and solidifying

3. Extrude an edge from the side and pull it down to form an armor panel. Remember that you can slide a vertex by double-pressing *G*.

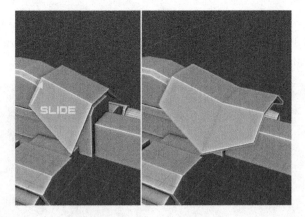

Figure 5.32 – Armor panel

4. Add a few loop cuts to this shape and push the rear edge inward, as shown in *Figure 5.33*.

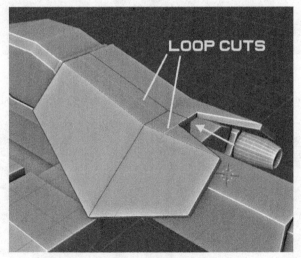

Figure 5.33 – Loop cutting the armor panel

5. Place a cube on top of the engine and shape it so it fits the shape we cut out of the armor panel. Bevel the edges with *Ctrl + B*, then insert and extrude a face at the back. This will become the exhaust pipe.

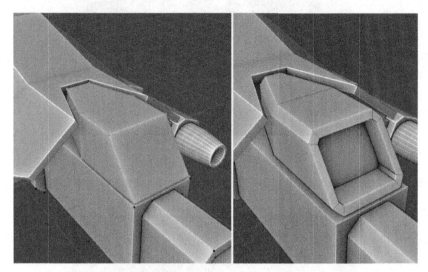

Figure 5.34 – Rear exhaust

6. Repeat this process to create two more pipes coming out of this shape.

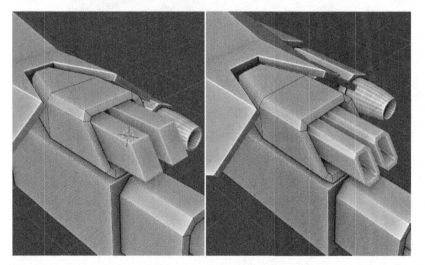

Figure 5.35 – Exhaust pipes

7. Add another armor panel at the beginning of the wing.

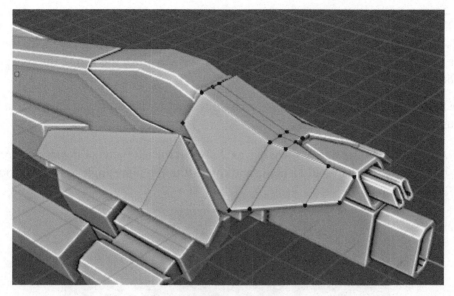

Figure 5.36 – Wing armor

8. When extruding new parts of the armor panel, you can ensure they have the same angle as another face by extruding the edge first and then scaling it outward using the 3D Cursor, as shown in the middle panel of *Figure 5.37*.

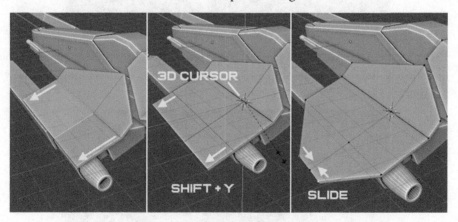

Figure 5.37 – Shaping the wing armor

We have now learned how to create armor panels using simple modeling in combination with the **Solidify** modifier. We will use this technique more as we continue modeling the race ship. Next, we will create more details on the model.

Adding more parts

In this section, we will continue adding more parts details to the ship and replace the rest of our basic shapes with more sophisticated ones. We will finish the wings, the cockpit, and the back of the ship, and add other details.

In the following few steps, we will apply techniques that we have already learned to add various details to our model:

1. Add a shape to the side of the wing, as shown in the left panel of *Figure 5.38*. At the front of the shape, add a plane and rotate it to the same angle as the previously created shape.

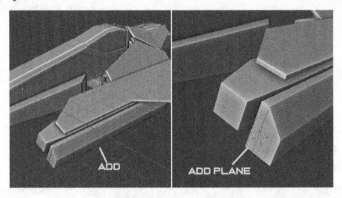

Figure 5.38 – Wing side

2. Using loop cuts, separate the plane into two smaller ones. Extrude planes in the direction of the front of the ship and add two loop cuts on each shape, as shown in *Figure 5.39*.

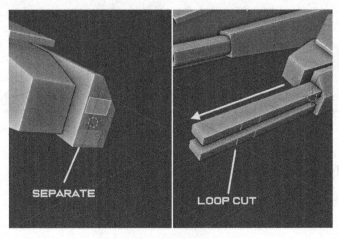

Figure 5.39 – Extruding planes

3. Push the outer faces outward using the *Alt + S* shortcut to ensure they move in the right direction. Do the same to the faces on the other side of the shape.

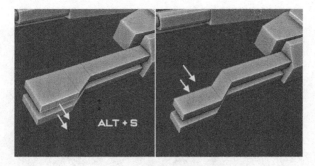

Figure 5.40 – Moving faces

4. Add a cube and make it long and thin by using *S* to scale.

5. Add two loop cuts to the cube and push the back edges forward.

6. Add another loop cut so that another shape can be extruded and push the edges forward again.

7. Extrude the thin and long faces further and push the edges forward again.

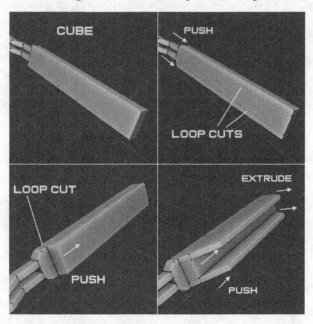

Figure 5.41 – Middle wing shape

8. Create another cube in front of this shape and push an edge from the back forward. Then, add loop cuts so that another shape can be extruded and push the edges together, as shown in *Figure 5.42*.

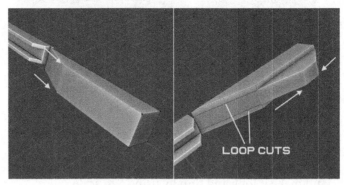

Figure 5.42 – End wing shape

9. On the outside of the wing, add a cube and scale it up on the *Y* axis so that its length matches the length of the wing. Bevel the outer edges.

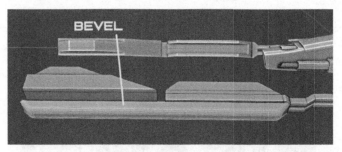

Figure 5.43 – Side wing shape

10. Add a smaller cube to the side of this shape and bevel it in the same way. Separate this to a new object by pressing *P*.

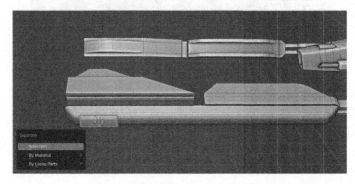

Figure 5.44 – Separating by selection

11. In the modifier properties tab, add an **Array** modifier to copy this shape multiple times and place it along the wing.

Figure 5.45 – Array modifier

12. Add a small cube to connect the two parts of the wing. Move the top face to the side so that the shape is angled.

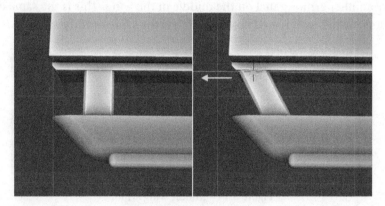

Figure 5.46 – Connector

13. Add an **Array** modifier to this shape.

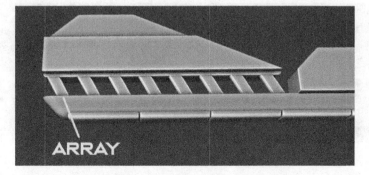

Figure 5.47 – Connecting the wing shapes

14. Duplicate this array and move it below the first one to make the shape look more intricate.

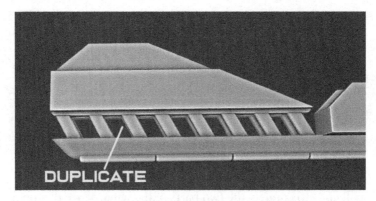

Figure 5.48 – Duplicating the array

15. Create another armor panel on the middle of the wing. This is the same object as the armor panels we created before, so it has the same modifiers.

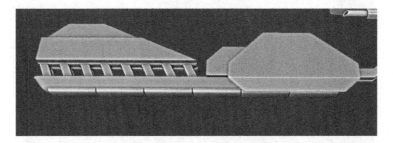

Figure 5.49 – Middle wing armor

16. Duplicate the new armor panel and move it to the front end of the wing, where it acts as the wing's protection. Then, simply reshape it so it better fits this part of the wing.

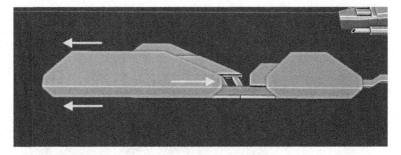

Figure 5.50 – Front wing armor

17. Reshape the armor panel by moving vertices individually. Snap the 3D Cursor to a vertex with *Shift + S* and scale up another vertex with the 3D Cursor set as the pivot point.

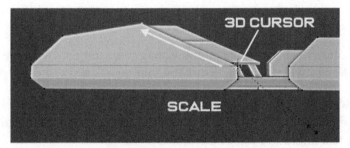

Figure 5.51 – Moving the vertex

18. Use dual-axis scaling (*S* followed by *Shift + Y*) with the 3D Cursor and scale the vertex to 0 to ensure it is aligned correctly.

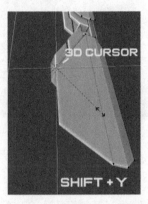

Figure 5.52 – Dual-axis scaling

19. Add more air intakes underneath the front armor panel that we have just created.

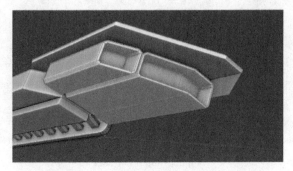

Figure 5.53 – Front intakes

We have added some more items and details to the wings of the ship, making it appear much more complete. Next, we will add some more objects to various parts of the ship to make it look even more complete.

Creating smaller details

We will now create a final layer of details by adding some more items to the model. We need to fill in the empty space at the rear of the ship, so let's add some more objects there:

1. Use the technique we used to create air intakes in the *Adding details* section to create a similar shape at the back of the ship. Adding grilles by applying an **Array** modifier to a thin shape can be a nice detail.

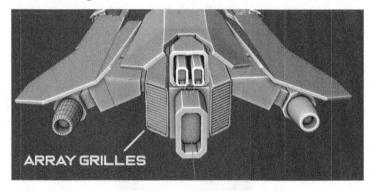

Figure 5.54 – Rear exhaust

2. Use a plane and extrude its edges to form a diffuser in the back. Then, add a **Subdivision Surface** and a **Solidify** modifier to the shape.

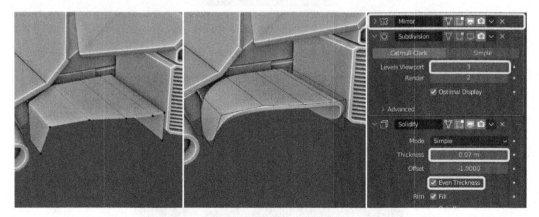

Figure 5.55 – Diffuser

3. Create a few more similar shapes to add more detail to the diffuser.

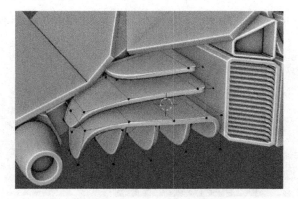

Figure 5.56 – Diffuser detail

4. Add an object to the side of the wing to make this part of the ship appear bulkier. Feel free to get creative and make the shape different from what you see in *Figure 5.55*.

    You can also remodel the armor panels to whatever shape you like so that it better fits the ship.

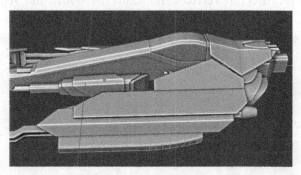

Figure 5.57 – Side object

5. Add a pipe connecting the back and the front part of the wing. Do this by extruding a circle.

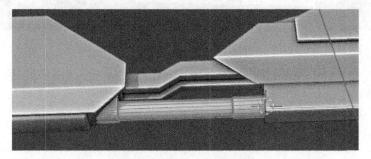

Figure 5.58 – Wing pipe

6.   Add more armor panels to cover the gun on the side of the cockpit.

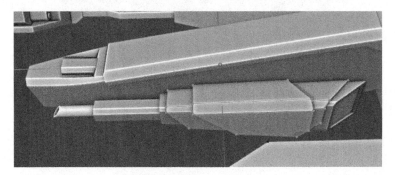

Figure 5.59 – Gun armor

7.   Bevels can also be added to individual vertices. Select a vertex and use the *Shift + B* shortcut to initiate beveling, then click the left mouse button to apply it. A **Bevel** menu will appear in the bottom-left corner of the screen.

In the menu, set **Affect** to **Vertices** and adjust the **Width** and **Segments** values of the bevel.

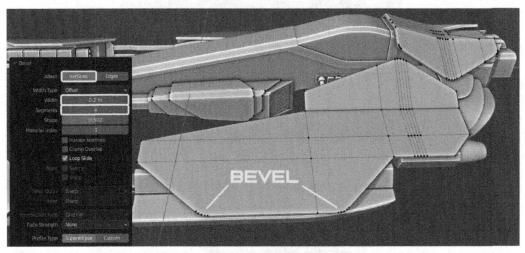

Figure 5.60 – Vertex bevel

It is now time to add finer details to the ship. Use the techniques that we have learned so far and try to come up with new things to add to the model.

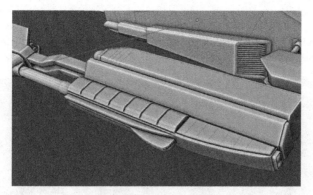

Figure 5.61 – Side details

> **Tip**
>
> Searching online for images of airplanes, race cars, industrial vehicles, or any other machines can help with inspiration for new details.

We have further increased the level of detail on the ship by adding more complex parts to it. Next, we will quickly go over a few more detailing ideas to finalize the model.

Finishing the model

We will now finish the model by adding some more final details all over the race ship. Here are a few more random things that I have added to the ship by using the tools and techniques that we have learned so far. Feel free to change them or create more details.

Figure 5.62 is the inner part of the wing, created by applying an **Array** modifier to a cube with beveled edges and a few round shapes at the back.

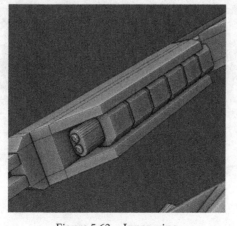

Figure 5.62 – Inner wing

I also added another layer to the windshield, some pipes to connect the cockpit to the wings, and some more intakes on the nose of the ship. The intakes are created the same way as the intake at the tip of the nose. *Figure 5.63* shows a few more details added to the cockpit.

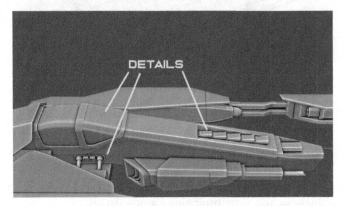

Figure 5.63 – Cockpit details

We can check whether the normals are oriented correctly by checking **Face Orientation** in the **Viewport Overlays** menu. Correct normals will appear blue, while incorrect normals will appear red.

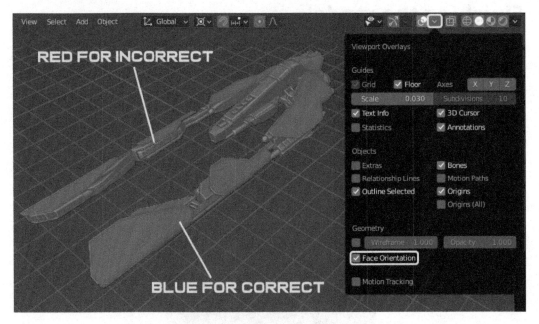

Figure 5.64 – Face orientation

Figure 5.65 is a top-view screenshot of the finished ship. It is okay if your model looks different from this, as the purpose of this chapter is to exercise creativity and bring your own ideas into Blender.

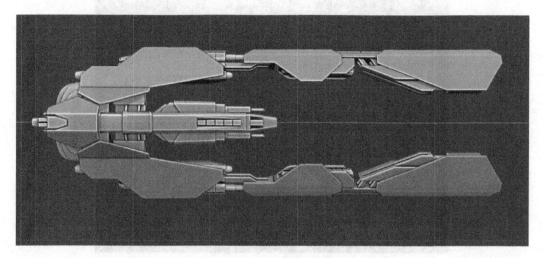

Figure 5.65 – Top preview

Our model is now finished. Before we proceed, let's apply a MatCap to give us a better idea of what the model will look like when we create materials and put it in a scene.

Applying a MatCap

We will now apply a **Material Capture (MatCap)** shader to get a better preview of the model. This will simulate some shading and lighting to show us what our model would look like in a scene, without requiring us to manually create a material.

To apply a MatCap, open the **Viewport Shading** menu and set **Lighting** to **MatCap**. Clicking on the sphere will allow you to choose between many different MatCaps.

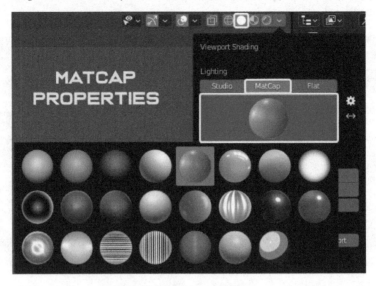

Figure 5.66 – MatCap

After choosing a MatCap, set **Color** to **Single** and pick a color for the object. A dark gray MatCap suits this model well, but you can set it to whatever you like. We can use this as a reference in *Chapter 6, Texture Painting the Sci-Fi Race Ship*, when we create materials.

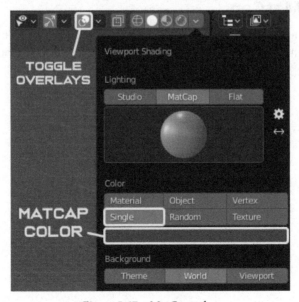

Figure 5.67 – MatCap color

> **Tip**
>
> You can remove the grid floor and axes by disabling the overlays with the
> **Toggle Overlays** button.

Figure 5.68 consists of snapshots of the finished model.

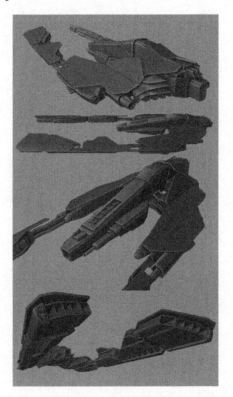

Figure 5.68 – Final preview

We now have a MatCap on our model, which makes it look nicer in the viewport. We are now ready to start texturing the model.

Summary

In this chapter, we modeled a game-suitable race ship from scratch without using any references. We exercised the skills that we acquired in the previous chapters and learned how to create shapes and objects that we can apply to other vehicles or models.

In the next chapter, we will learn how to create custom textures by texture painting our race ship. We will also learn how to create decals and bake normal maps.

6

Texture Painting the Sci-Fi Race Ship

In this chapter, we will texture the sci-fi race ship using texture painting techniques. We will learn how to paint a custom livery for the ship and increase the apparent level of detail on the model using normal maps and normal decals.

We will cover the following topics in this chapter:

- Baking a normal map
- UV unwrapping
- Baking a bevel map
- Texture painting the armor panels
- Painting decals
- Painting normal decals

Baking a normal map

In this section, we will learn how to create a normal map texture from a high-poly object. This will allow us to simulate a bumpy surface by placing a texture on it. In the following steps, we will create a carbon fiber surface and bake it as a normal map so that we can easily place it on any object as a texture:

1. Create two planes and place them as shown in *Figure 6.1*. Add a loop cut in the middle of each plane by pressing *Ctrl + R* and lifting it up:

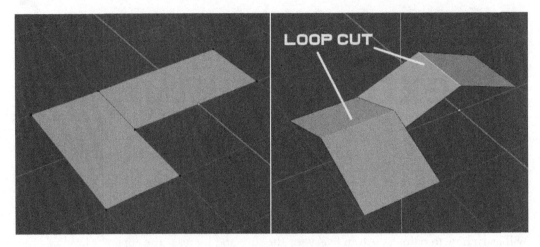

Figure 6.1 – Two planes

2. Bevel the edge created by the loop cut by pressing *Ctrl + B* and turn on smooth shading.

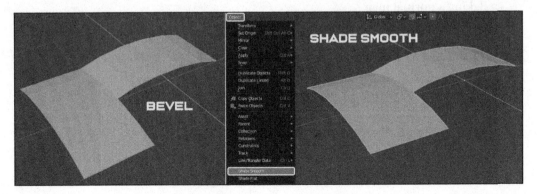

Figure 6.2 – Bevels and smooth shading

3. In the top view, add an **Array** modifier and check **Constant Offset** instead of **Relative Offset**. Set the **X** and **Y** distances so that the shape is tiled perfectly, as shown in *Figure 6.3*:

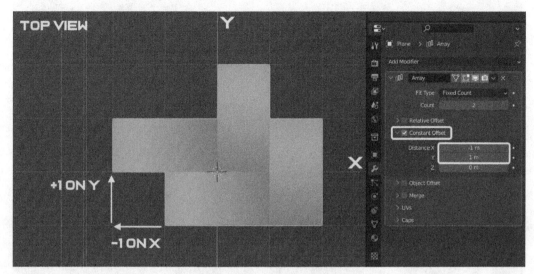

Figure 6.3 – Constant Offset

4. Increase the **Count** value to create a longer tiled pattern.

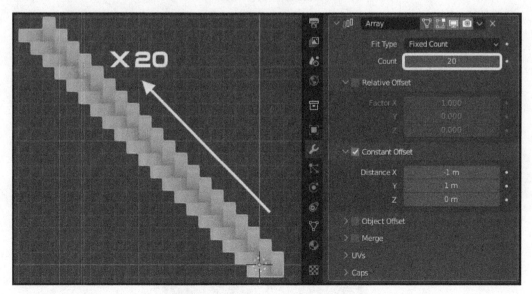

Figure 6.4 – First array

5. Add another **Array** modifier and, once again, adjust the offset values to tile the previous array perfectly.

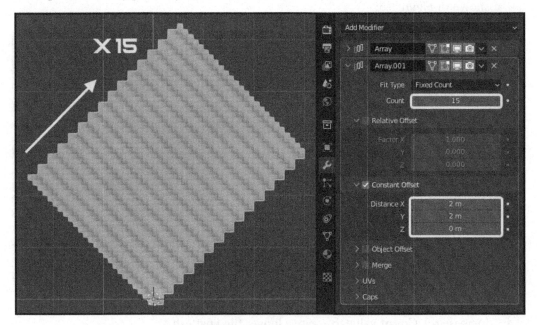

Figure 6.5 – Second array

6. Add a plane in the middle of the pattern and scale it up by any multiple of *2*.

The plane must not stick outside of the pattern. It must be scaled by a multiple of 2 to ensure that the normal map will be seamless. Remember to hold *Ctrl* while moving the plane so that it snaps to the grid. The plane must be just above the surface of the pattern.

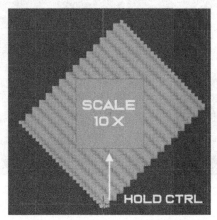

Figure 6.6 – Plane

7. Create a new image named `Carbon_Fiber` in the Image Editor (found in the **Shading** Workspace) and set its resolution to `512 px` x `512 px`.

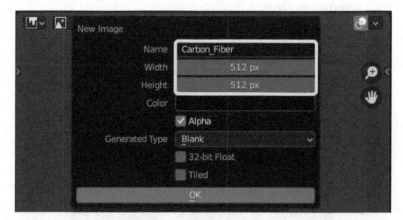

Figure 6.7 – Carbon fiber image

8. Create a new material for the plane. In the material, add an **Image Texture** node and load the image created in *step 7*.

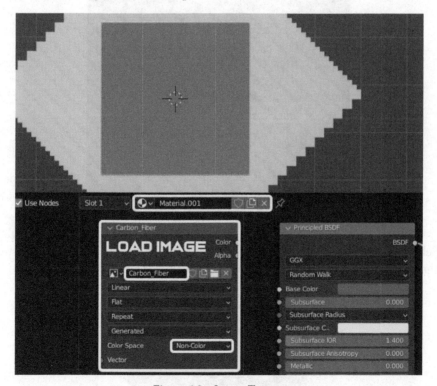

Figure 6.8 – Image Texture

9. Open the **Bake** menu in the **Render Properties** tab. The menu will only appear in **Cycles** render mode. Set **Bake Type** to **Normal** and check the **Selected to Active** checkbox, as shown in *Figure 6.9*:

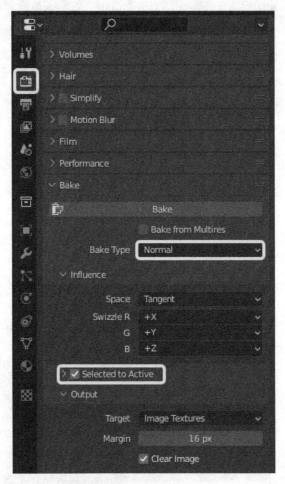

Figure 6.9 – Bake settings

10. Select the pattern first and the plane second. This will allow us to bake the surface of the pattern onto the plane in the form of a normal map.

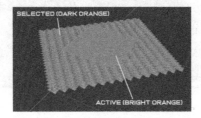

Figure 6.10 – Selected and active

11. Click the **Bake** button in the **Bake** menu to create the normal map.

Figure 6.11 – Bake

12. After a few minutes, the blank image will turn into a normal map, which should look something like in *Figure 6.12*. Save this normal map image on your computer.

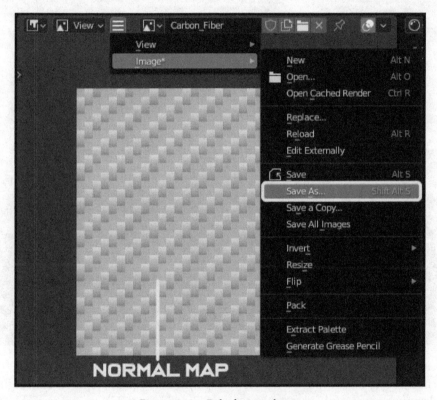

Figure 6.12 – Baked normal map

13. Plug an **Image Texture** node with the normal map loaded into a **Normal Map** node.

Plug the **Normal Map** node into the **Normal** plug of the **Principled BSDF** node. In rendered view, you will notice a bumpy pattern on the plane. To highlight the effect of the normal map, reduce the **Roughness** value on the **Principled BSDF** node.

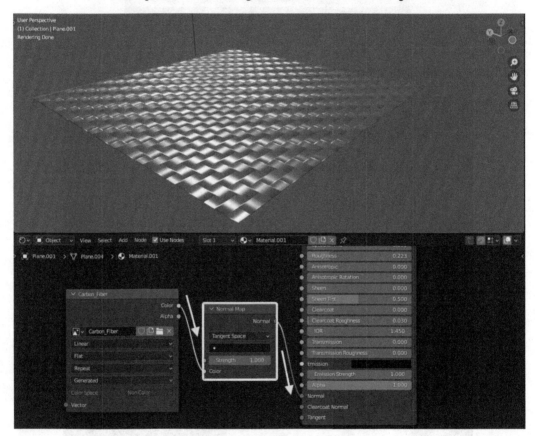

Figure 6.13 – Rendered normal map

We learned how to bake a normal map and display it on a surface to simulate a highly detailed surface on a simple object. Next, we will learn how to UV unwrap an object so that we can use the same technique on a more complex object.

UV unwrapping

In this section, we will learn how to **UV unwrap** an object for texturing. This technique can be used to seamlessly texture any object.

We must first understand what UV unwrapping is and how it works. When we UV unwrap an object, we turn it into a 2D surface. You can think of it as reverse papercraft. We then place the 2D version of the object on an image texture to tell Blender how we want the texture to appear on the surface of the object. If we try to unwrap a simple cube, the result will look like in *Figure 6.14*:

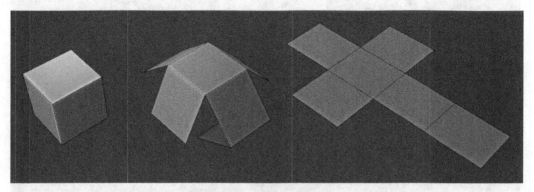

Figure 6.14 – Unwrapped cube

An object can be UV unwrapped in two simple steps:

1. Select the edges that need to be cut to unwrap the object. In **Edit Mode**, press *U* to open the **UV Mapping** menu and select **Mark Seam**. After marking the seams, select **Unwrap** in the same menu.

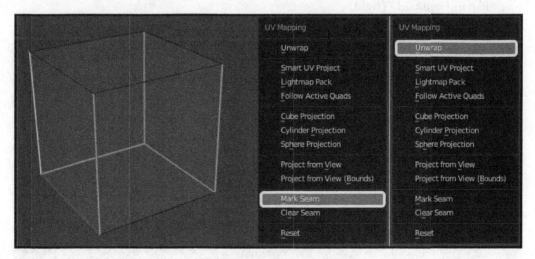

Figure 6.15 – UV Mapping

2. In the **Shading Editor**, switch from **Image Editor** to **UV Editor**. When you select the cube, it will now appear as the unwrapped version in UV Editor.

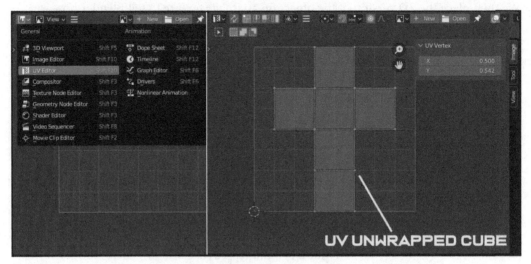

Figure 6.16 – UV unwrapping

We will now apply this method to the diffuser we created at the back of our ship:

1. Mark the seams on the diffuser in the back of our ship, as shown in *Figure 6.17* (left). After unwrapping, the UV map should look something like in *Figure 6.17* (right):

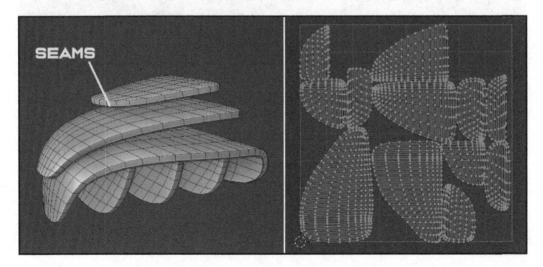

Figure 6.17 – Marked seams (left), UV-unwrapped diffuser (right)

2. Create a new material for the diffuser and load the carbon fiber texture with an **Image Texture** node.

3. Set **Color Space** to **Non-Color** and run the image through a normal map. You should then see the carbon fiber pattern on the surface of the object.

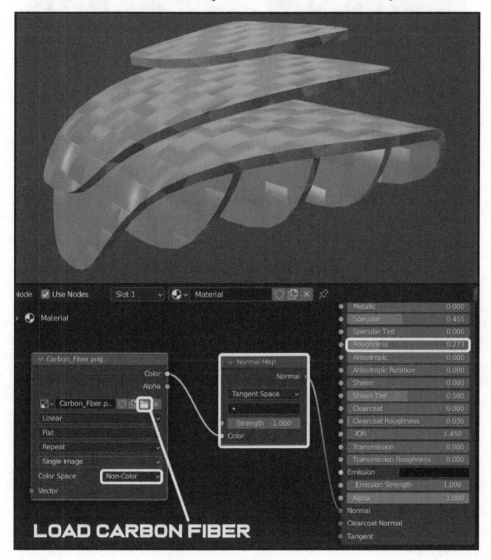

Figure 6.18 – Carbon fiber diffuser

4. Add **Texture Coordinate** and **Mapping** nodes to the material, as shown in
    Figure 6.19, to allow better control over the texture. For example, we can increase
    the scale of the texture by changing the **Scale** figures in the **Mapping** node:

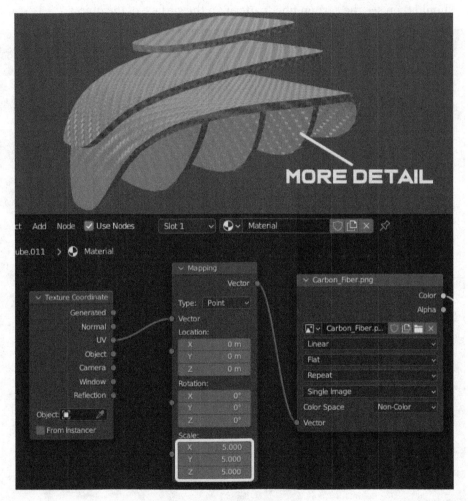

Figure 6.19 – Mapping node

We now have a carbon fiber texture on the surface of our diffuser as a result of UV
unwrapping. Next, we will learn another trick to increase the level of detail and realism
with normal maps.

Baking a bevel map

We will now learn how to simulate smooth bevels using a normal map.

At this point, the object has a bumpy surface, but its edges look too sharp and unrealistic. We can make the edges look nicer by adding bevels, but that will increase the polygon count too much. We can simulate smooth beveled edges using the same normal map techniques we already learned:

1. First, duplicate the object and bevel the sharp edges on the copy with *Ctrl + B*.

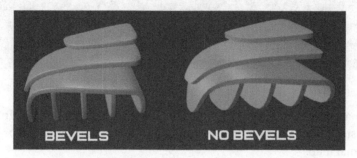

Figure 6.20 – Bevels versus no bevels

2. Move the objects so that they are in exactly the same place.

    Select the original object and in **Edit Mode**, solidify everything slightly using *Alt + S*. This will ensure that the copied object is completely contained by the original object. In the same way we moved the plane above the carbon fiber mesh when baking the previous normal map, we need the surface to be slightly *above* the high-poly mesh.

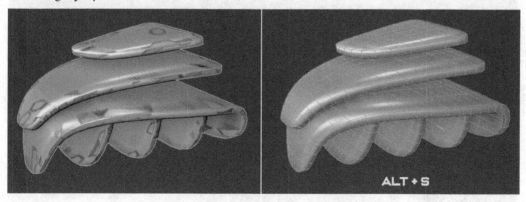

Figure 6.21 – Baking preparation

3. Create a new image onto which we can bake the normal map for the bevels.

Figure 6.22 – New image

4. In the material that we already created, load the new image into the **Image Texture** node instead of the carbon fiber texture. Then, simply repeat the steps for baking the normal map.

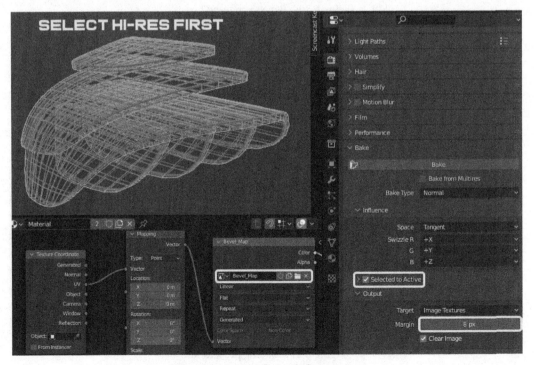

Figure 6.23 – Bevel map bake settings

After baking, you should get a normal map that looks something like in *Figure 6.24*:

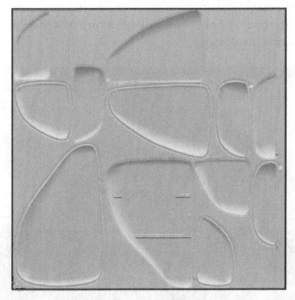

Figure 6.24 – Bevel normal map

Applying the normal map to the unbevelled object using nodes should create a result like in *Figure 6.25*:

Figure 6.25 – Smooth edges

We can easily combine the carbon fiber normal map with the bevel normal map. To do this, create a separate **Image Texture** node for each normal map (accompanied by the mapping and geometry nodes) and connect them using a **MixRGB** node before running them through the normal map node.

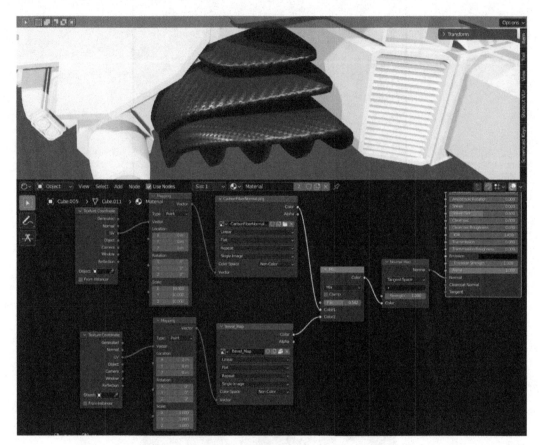

Figure 6.26 – Mixing normal maps

We can now bake multiple different normal maps for an object and render them together on a surface using nodes. Next, we will texture the armor panels on our race ship.

Texture painting the armor panels

In this section, we will learn how to create a custom texture for our race ship using texture painting. This will allow us to create original textures completely independently for any model:

1. Add a new material and assign it to the armor panels. Name this material `Armor`.

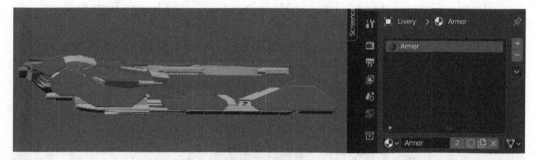

Figure 6.27 – Armor material

2. In **Edit Mode**, press *C* to brush-select the faces at the top of the armor panels. After making the selection, press *I* to insert faces and create an edge around the armor panels.

3. Create and assign a black material named `Carbon Fiber` to the edges. Also assign the black material to the faces on the bottom side.

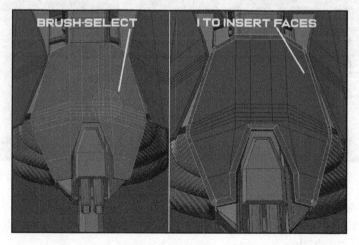

Figure 6.28 – Brush-selecting (left), inserting faces (right)

> **Tip**
>
> Press *C* to activate brush selection, then click and drag the left mouse button to select. Scroll the mouse wheel to adjust the brush size.

You can easily apply the carbon fiber texture to any object without UV unwrapping.

In the **Carbon Fiber** material, plug the **Object** output (instead of UV) from the **Texture Coordinate** node into the **Mapping** node. In the **Image Texture** node, set **Mapping** to **Box**. This will project the texture onto any object based on its shape. Although this makes texturing much easier, it is not always as perfect as manual UV unwrapping.

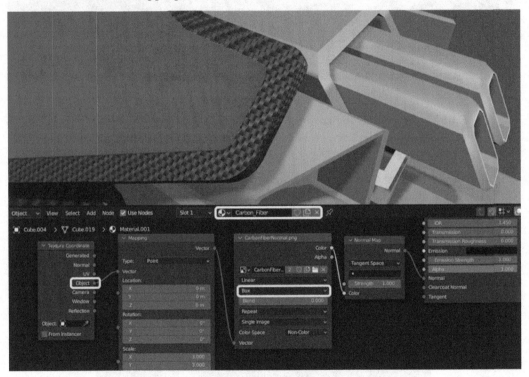

Figure 6.29 – Box mapping

4. Next, select all the colored faces of the armor panels. To do this, select just one and press *Shift + G*. In the **Select Similar** menu, click **Material** to select all the faces with the same material.

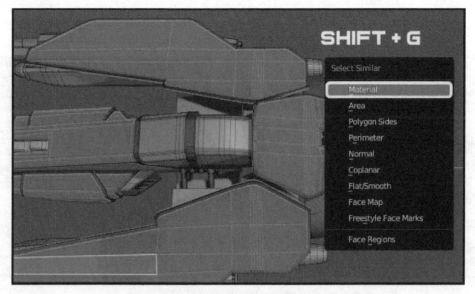

Figure 6.30 – Select Similar | Material

5. Separate the faces into a new object with *P* and UV unwrap the armor panels.

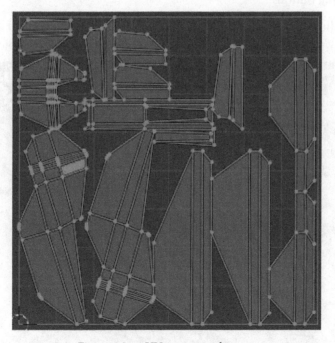

Figure 6.31 – UV-unwrapped armor

6. Create a new image named `Texture_M  ask` for texture painting. Using an **Image Texture** node, plug the image into **Base Color** of the **Armor** material.

Figure 6.32 – Texture Mask

7. Access the **Texture Paint** Workspace by clicking the **Texture Paint** button next to the **Shading** button.

After loading the last image, you can immediately start painting on it with a simple brush. Try playing around with some of the settings, such as the color or brush size.

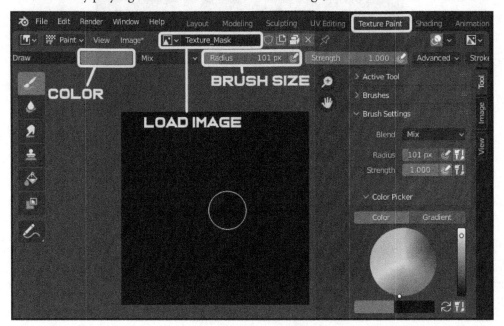

Figure 6.33 – Texture painting

You can also use the brush to paint on the object in the 3D view on the right side of the **Texture Paint** Workspace.

Figure 6.34 – 3D texture painting

8. When texture painting, make sure that only the object you are painting is selected in **Object Mode** to ensure no other objects are affected. Use the menu in the top left of the 3D Workspace to change between **Object Mode** and **Texture Paint** mode.

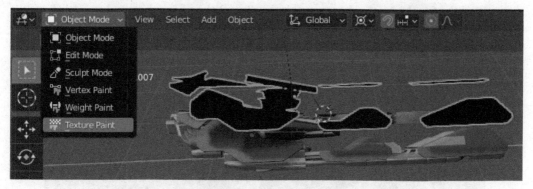

Figure 6.35 – Texture Paint mode

Now that we have finished setting up, we can begin our texture painting:

1. Ensure that the image is completely black by painting over it with a large black brush.

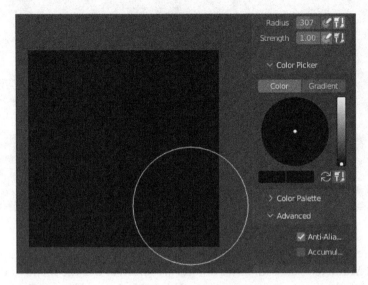

Figure 6.36 – Black

2. Find the **Stroke Method** menu in the toolbar at the top of the window and change it from **Space** to **Line**. This will allow us to paint straight lines.

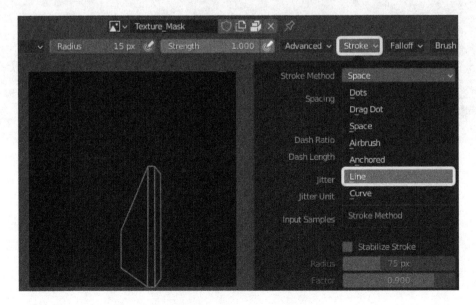

Figure 6.37 – Stroke method

3. Using a white brush, click and drag the left mouse button to create straight lines at the edges of the armor panels.

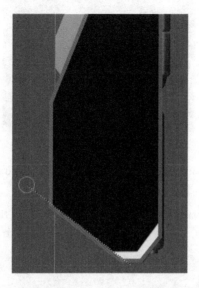

Figure 6.38 – Line painting

4. Paint some outlines and shapes on all the armor panels using this tool. *Figure 6.39* might give you some ideas:

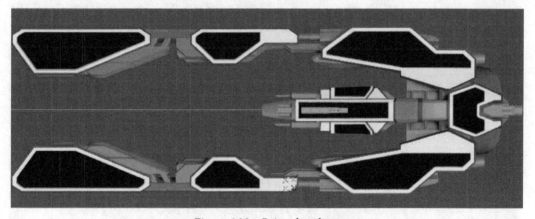

Figure 6.39 – Painted outlines

> **Tip**
>
> Align the view with a selected face with *Shift + 7* and enter Orthographic View by pressing *Num 5*. This will give you a better angle when texture painting.

Figure 6.40 is a view of the back of the ship after some texture painting:

Figure 6.40 – Painted armor

5. Add a **MixRGB** node between the **Image Texture** node and the **Principled BSDF** node.

Plugging the texture color output into the **Fac** input of the **MixRGB** node will allow us to replace the black and white colors we painted with any other color.

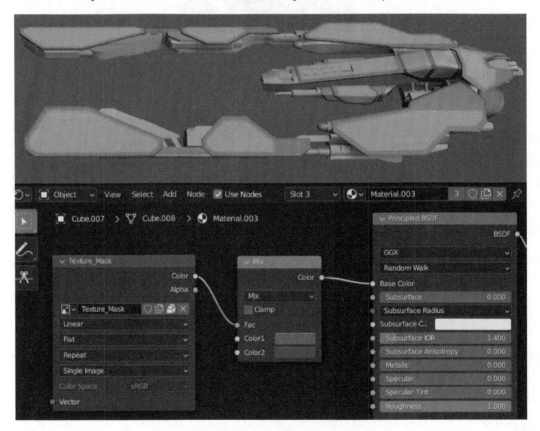

Figure 6.41 – Mixing colors

We can also replace the colors with a texture. For example, we can generate a **Checker Texture** node, as shown in *Figure 6.42*, and plug it into one of the inputs of the **MixRGB** node. Try copying the nodes from *Figure 6.42* to get a pattern on the armor:

Figure 6.42 – Checker Texture

6. Add another **Image Texture** node to the material and leave it disconnected.

7. Create a new image and change the bake settings, as shown in *Figure 6.43*. This will allow us to save our material as an image and paint over it freely:

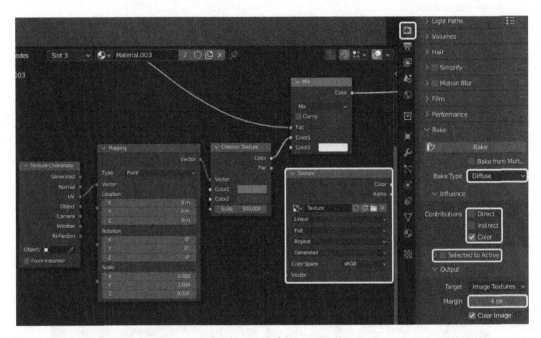

Figure 6.43 – Baking a texture

8. After baking, replace all the other nodes with just the baked texture loaded in an **Image Texture** node.

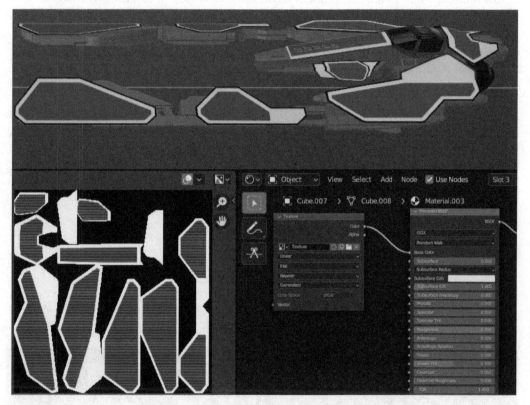

Figure 6.44 – Baked texture

We now have a basic texture for the race ship as a saved image displayed on the surface of the armor. We can use this image as a texture painting canvas and paint decals on it, which is what we will learn about in the next section.

Painting decals

In this section, we will paint custom decals on the race ship. You can use any image from your computer and put it onto the surface of the model. In this case, we need stickers with transparent backgrounds. You can easily find such stickers by searching decal png in your internet browser and downloading images with checker (transparent) backgrounds, as shown in *Figure 6.45*:

Figure 6.45 – Decal PNG

1. In the **Texture Properties** tab, click the **New** button to create a new texture. You can then open any decals or stickers you downloaded.

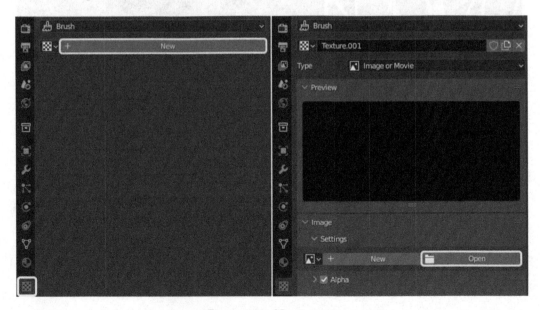

Figure 6.46 – New texture

2. On the right-side toolbar of the **Image Editor** window in the **Texture Paint** Workspace, you will find a **Texture** menu and a **Texture Mask** menu.

In the **Texture** menu, select the decal that we just loaded. Set the mapping to **Stencil** and correct any stretching by clicking on **Image Aspect**.

In the **Texture Mask** menu, simply set **Mask Mapping** to **View Plane**.

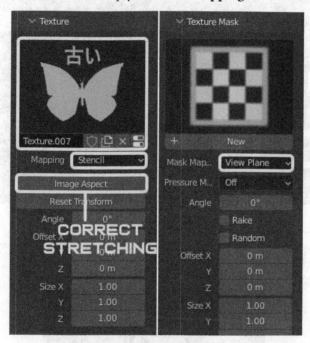

Figure 6.47 – Texture (left), Texture Mask (right)

3.   Change **Stroke Method** back to **Space**.

Figure 6.48 – Space stroke

4.   You will now see the sticker in your 3D view, and you can paint over it to place the sticker anywhere on the model.

Figure 6.49 – Painting a decal

5.   Download as many stickers or decals as you like and get creative with placing them on the model. *Figure 6.50* shows some more stickers that I placed on the ship:

Figure 6.50 – Painted decals

> **Tip**
> Search online for images of race cars to get some inspiration for painting the model.

We learned how to paint decals onto a surface using texture painting. Next, we will use the same technique to create normal map decals and simulate a bumpy surface.

Painting normal decals

In this section, we will combine normal map baking with texture painting to create custom normal decals. This technique is useful for creating additional small details on a surface without adding any new geometry.

Baking a normal decal

In the following few steps, we will create a shape and bake it as a normal decal:

1. Create a new file in Blender and model a simple metal hatch.

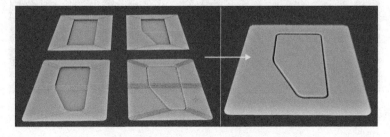

Figure 6.51 – Decal modeling

2.　Add a plane above the hatch. We will use this plane to bake a normal map, as we did with the carbon fiber pattern.

3.　Create a material with a new image sized 512　px x 512　px so that we can bake a new normal map.

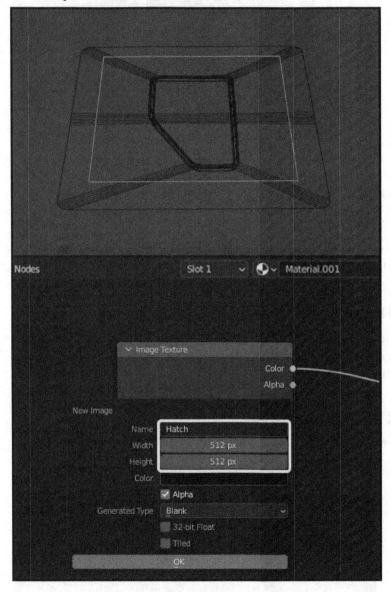

Figure 6.52 – Creating the decal image

Baking a normal map will sometimes produce an odd result, as shown in *Figure 6.53*. This means that the normals of the mesh are not oriented correctly:

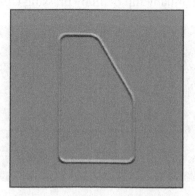

Figure 6.53 – Incorrect normal decal

4. Check the normals by opening the **Viewport Overlays** menu in **Edit Mode** and enabling **Face Orientation**.

When this is enabled, correctly oriented normals will be colored blue while incorrectly oriented normals will be colored red.

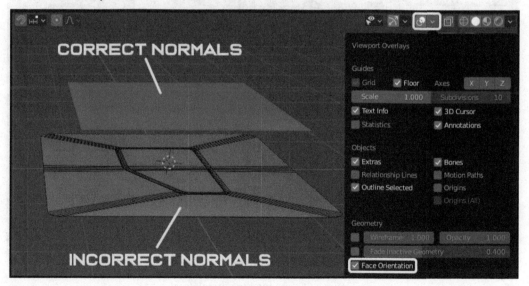

Figure 6.54 – Face Orientation

5. To correct normals, select the entire mesh in **Edit Mode** and press *Shift + N* to automatically calculate the normals. If the normals are still not corrected, select all the red surfaces and manually flip them by pressing *Ctrl + W*.

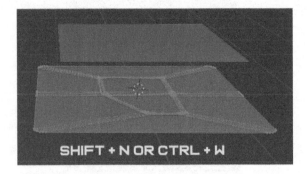

Figure 6.55 – Correcting normals

6. After correcting the normals, repeat the steps from the *Baking a normal map* section to bake a normal map, as shown in *Figure 6.56*. Save this image to your computer:

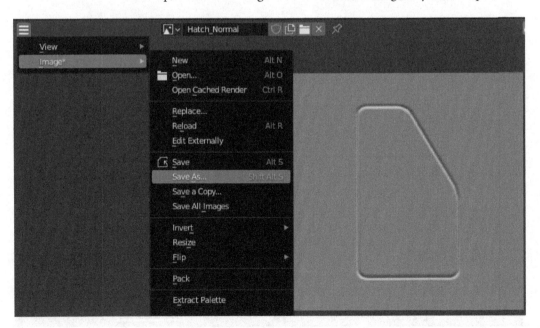

Figure 6.56 – Saving the normal decal

Now we have a normal decal ready. Next, we will prepare the decal for texture painting and place it on our ship.

Painting the decal

In the next few steps, we will create a base for texture painting the normal decal and place it on the ship:

1. Load the .blend file with the race ship model again and create a new image in the **Armor** material.

    This time, instead of keeping the image black, we will set its **Hex** code to 8080FF. This will give us the base on which we can paint the normal map bumps.

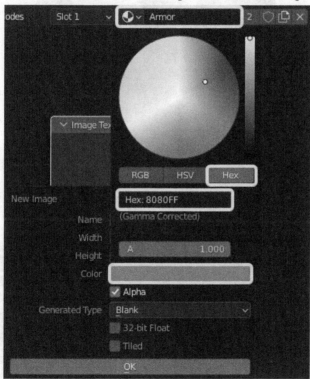

Figure 6.57 – Normal map base

2. In the **Texture Properties** tab, load the newly baked normal map.

Figure 6.58 – Loading a new image

3. Load the image in the **Texture** menu. You may need to correct the image aspect. Here, you can also rotate the stencil by changing the angle.

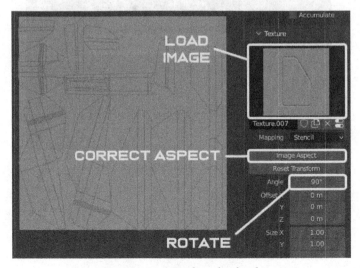

Figure 6.59 – Loading the decal

4. Place the stencil anywhere on the ship and paint over it to create the normal decal. You can move the stencil by clicking and dragging it with the right mouse button.

Figure 6.60 – Texture painting the normal decal

After painting the normal decal, it appears as if we modeled the hatch into the armor. This is a good way to create a lot of detail without adding any new objects or increasing the poly-count of the model.

Figure 6.61 – Painted normal decal

5. Invert the image by scaling it to -1.00 on the *Y* axis to paint it on the other side of the ship, the same way we would invert an object when modeling.

Figure 6.62 – Inverting the stencil

6. Use the techniques covered in this chapter to add as much detail to the model as you can. *Figure 6.63* shows the final result:

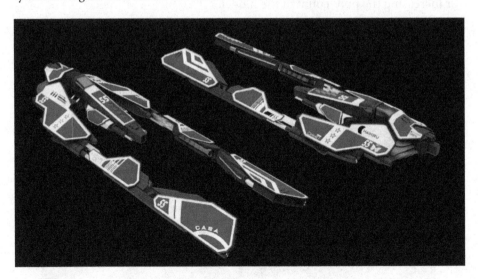

Figure 6.63 – Finished sci-fi race ship

We now have a finished sci-fi race ship with a custom-painted livery.

Summary

In this chapter, we learned how to increase the apparent level of detail of a model using normal maps and texture painting. We learned how to bake normal maps for three purposes: simulating bumpy surfaces, placing details such as bevels on low-poly objects, and painting decals onto surfaces to create more details.

In the next chapter, we will begin the third, final, and most advanced project of this book, where we will model, rig, texture, and render a high-poly T-72 tank using all the techniques we have learned so far.

Part 4: Modeling a T-72 Tank

The final project is a highly detailed T-72 tank. Here, all the tools and techniques learned so far, as well as others, will be used to achieve the highest level of detail. This section also introduces basic constraint rigging techniques, which will make the tank tracks functional.

We will cover the following chapters in this section:

- *Chapter 7, Modeling the T-72 Tank: Basic Shapes*
- *Chapter 8, Modeling the T-72 Tank Hull*
- *Chapter 9, Modeling the T-72 Tank Turret*
- *Chapter 10, Modeling Tank Tracks*
- *Chapter 11, Rigging Tank Tracks*
- *Chapter 12, Texturing the Tank*

7
Modeling the T-72 Tank: Basic Shapes

In this chapter, we will create the basic shapes for a T-72 tank. We will use mostly the same techniques we learned in the previous chapters to create a simple version of the tank. We will first model the most important parts of the hull, then we will create a simple shape for the turret, and finally, we will add some wheels.

By the end of this chapter, we will have an outline that we can use as a foundation to create more detailed shapes and objects.

We will cover the following topics in this chapter:

- Modeling a hull
- Creating a skirt
- Adding a simple turret
- Adding wheels

Modeling a hull

In this section, we will create the hull. We will use this part as a base to which we will add all the other basic shapes. In the following steps, we will transform the default cube into a tank hull using tools and techniques that we learned previously:

1.   Check **Edge Length** in the **Measurement** section of the **Viewport Overlays** menu. This will display the length of selected edges in **Edit Mode**.

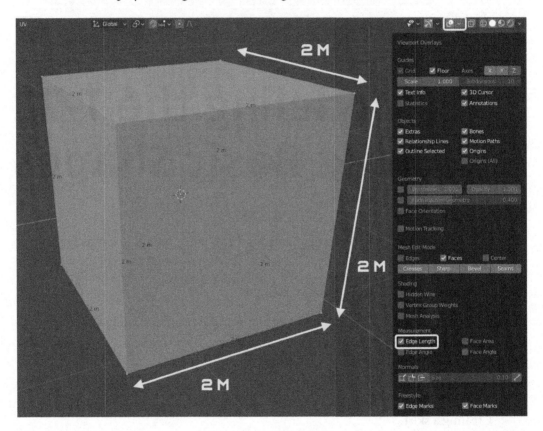

Figure 7.1 – Edge Length

2. Scale the default cube to match the dimensions in *Figure 7.2*:

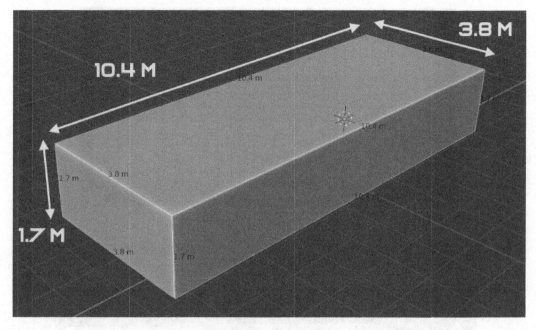

Figure 7.2 – Hull dimensions

3. Add two loop cuts by pressing *Ctrl + R* to get the shape shown in *Figure 7.3*:

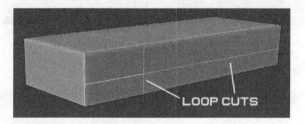

Figure 7.3 – Loop cuts

4. Inside view, move the edges to create a pointy front.

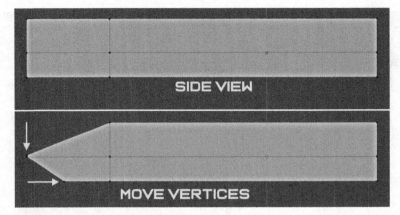

Figure 7.4 – Moving vertices

5. Add two loop cuts to the middle of the object. After loop cutting, we can slightly lower the face in the back, as shown in *Figure 7.5*:

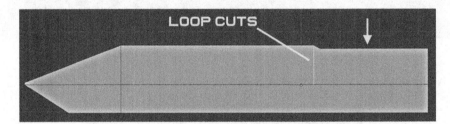

Figure 7.5 – More loop cuts

6. Move the edges at the back to shape the rear of the hull.

Figure 7.6 – The hull rear

7. Add three more loop cuts to the object, as shown in *Figure 7.7*:

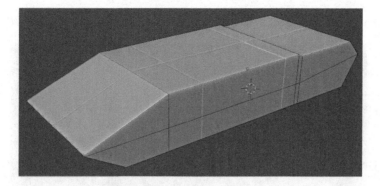

Figure 7.7 – Even more loop cuts

8. Delete all the faces on the left side of the hull.

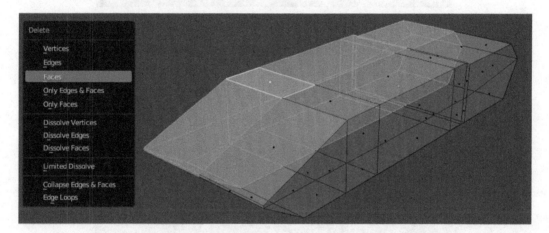

Figure 7.8 – Deleting the faces on the left side

9. Add a **Mirror** modifier to the object.

Figure 7.9 – A Mirror modifier

10. Press *E* to extrude a face on the side of the hull, as shown in *Figure 7.10*:

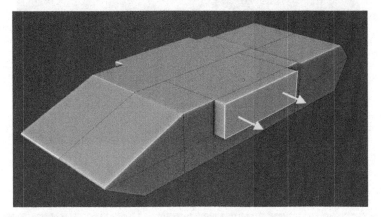

Figure 7.10 – Extruding the side

11. Move the edges to make the extruded face smaller than its base.

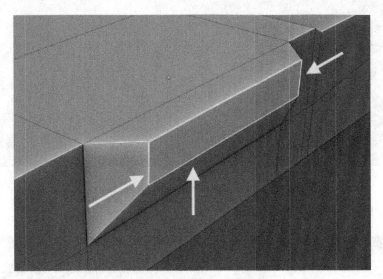

Figure 7.11 – Shaping the side

12. Add multiple loop cuts around the extruded face, as shown in *Figure 7.12*:

Figure 7.12 – Side loop cuts

13. Select the edges like in *Figure 7.13*. Press *W* and select **Relax** in the **LoopTools** menu:

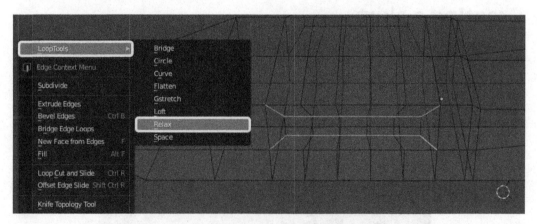

Figure 7.13 – Relaxing the edges

14. Repeat *Step 13* multiple times to make the edges more relaxed. Do this until your result looks like *Figure 7.14*:

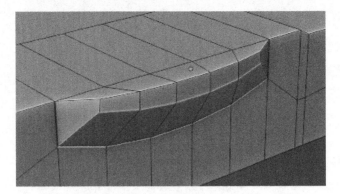

Figure 7.14 – A side shape

Now, we have the basic shape of the hull ready. Next, we will add some shapes and objects to the sides of the hull to create the skirts, or the side armor.

Creating a skirt

In this section, we are using simple shapes to create an outline of the side armor and the track covers. In the next few steps, we will once again add shapes and modify them with basic tools and techniques to create this part of the tank:

1. Add a new plane to the hull in **Edit Mode** and separate it by **Selection**. The plane will have the same origin and modifiers as the hull because it was created as part of the same object.

Figure 7.15 – A new plane

Figure 7.16 is a reference for correctly placing the plane from the top view and side view:

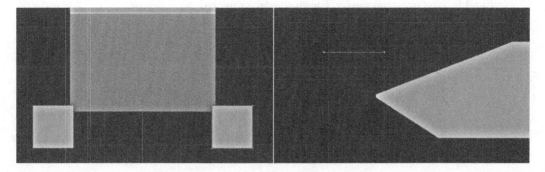

Figure 7.16 – A placement reference

2. Extrude the edge at the front of the plane and lower it to the same height as the hull point.

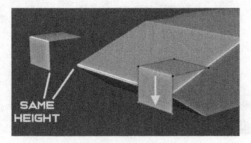

Figure 7.17 – Edge extrusion

3. Press *Ctrl* + *B* to turn the sharp edge into a round one with a bevel.

Figure 7.18 – Bevel

4. Duplicate a single vertex from the corner of the shape, as shown in *Figure 7.19* (left), and lower it down. Once lowered, fill the side by pressing *F*, and triangulate the filled face by pressing *Ctrl + T* with the face selected.

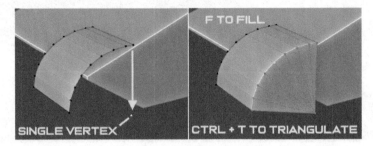

Figure 7.19 – A single vertex (left) and triangulation (right)

5. Bevel the edge with *Ctrl + B* and extend the shape outward slightly.

Figure 7.20 – Beveling and extending

6. Create another small two-edge bevel on the inner edge and slide the inner edge of the bevel downward. Here, the edges created by the triangulation help guide the edges.

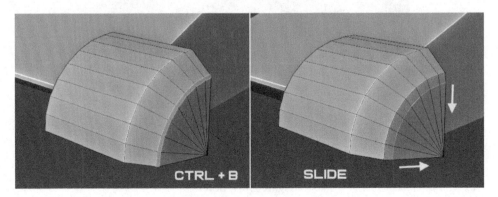

Figure 7.21 – Beveling and sliding

7.   Delete the triangulated faces and repeat *Step 4* and *Step 5* on the inside of the shape.

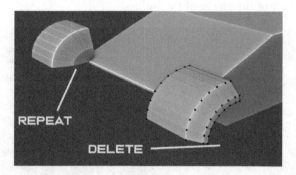

Figure 7.22 – Delete and repeat

8.   Duplicate the edges at the back of the shape by pressing *Shift + D* and extrude them backward. Then, add a loop cut and extrude another shape at the back.

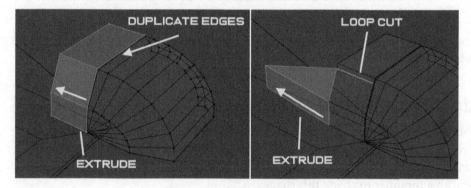

Figure 7.23 – Duplicating edges

9.   Add a cube and use it to create a thin shape, as shown in *Figure 7.24*. Ensure that the edges follow a slope:

Figure 7.24 – A slope

10. Use cubes to create more boxes at the sides of the tank. Make sure to shape them so that they go around the shape of the hull.

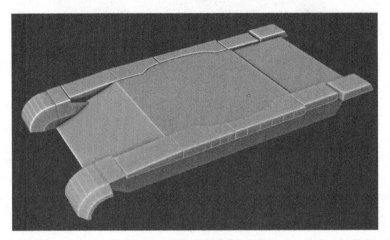

Figure 7.25 – Side shapes

We now have enough objects on the sides of the hull to give a rough idea of what this part should look like. Next, we will add a turret and a turret ring.

Adding a simple turret

In this section, we will create a simple turret shape. The turret is arguably the most difficult part of the tank to model, so for now, we will only create one object, which we will later modify to add more detail to. In the next few steps, we will add a simple cube with a modifier to create this shape:

1. Add a circle at the top of the hull. This will serve as the turret ring.

Figure 7.26 – The turret ring

2. Add a cube with a deleted bottom face on top of the turret ring. Add a **Subdivision Surface** modifier to the cube to make it round, but do not apply the modifier.

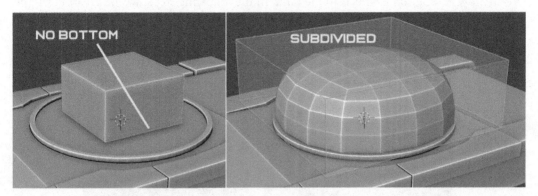

Figure 7.27 – A subdivided turret

3. Scale the object so that the mesh is slightly larger than the turret ring, and adjust the shape so that the front is lower than the back.

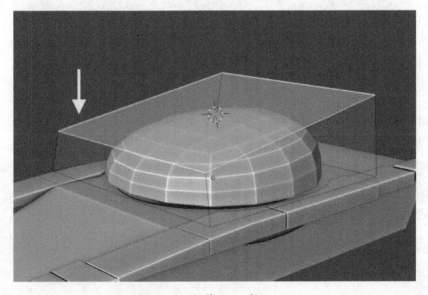

Figure 7.28 – Shaping the turret

We now have a basic shape for the turret. This is the only thing we can create for the turret that will qualify as a basic shape, so we are going to leave it here for now. Next, let's add some wheels to the tank.

Adding wheels

We are now adding some wheels to the tank. In the following steps, we are creating simple cylinders and arranging them so that we know where the wheels will sit:

1. Add a cylinder to the side of the tank.

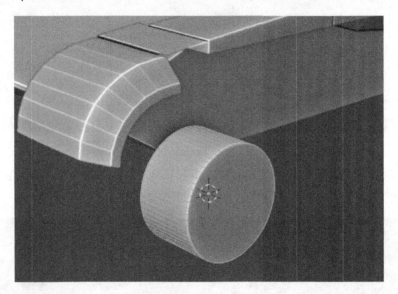

Figure 7.29 – A wheel

2. Add an **Array** modifier to the cylinder to copy the wheel. Set the **Count** value to **6** and the **Constant Offset Y** factor to **1.41 m**.

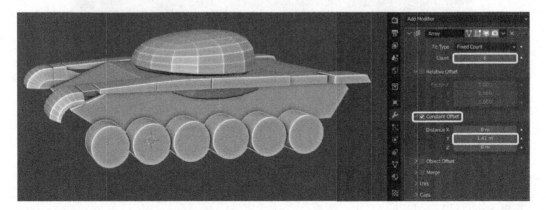

Figure 7.30 – The wheel array

3. Add two smaller cylinders at the front and the back. These will be the sprockets that drive the tracks.

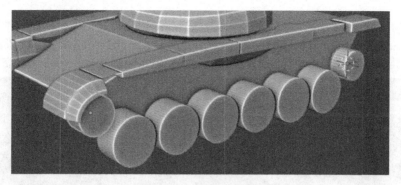

Figure 7.31 – Sprockets

4. Apply the **Array** modifier to the wheels.

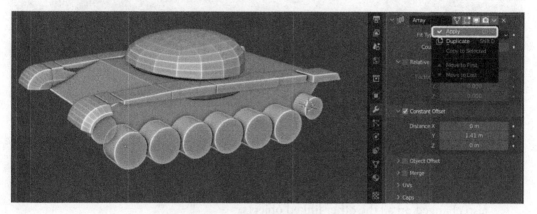

Figure 7.32 – Applying the Array modifier

5. Select all the wheels in **Edit Mode** and press *P* to separate them as **Loose Parts**.

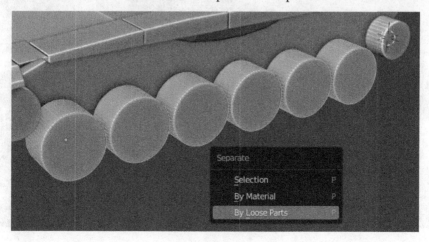

Figure 7.33 – Separating loose parts

6. After separating the wheels, select them all in **Object Mode**.

    In the **Object** menu at the top left, open the **Set Origin** submenu and select **Origin to Geometry**. This will place the origin of every wheel in the center of the object.

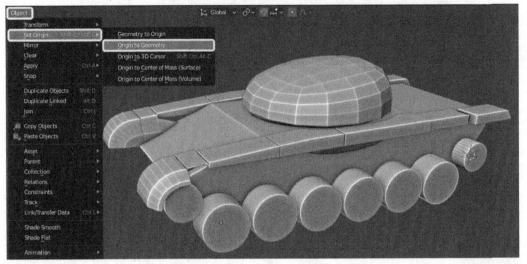

Figure 7.34 – Origin to Geometry

7. Select all the wheels and press *Ctrl + L*. In the **Link/Transfer Data** menu, select **Link Object Data**.

    This will make the objects share data so that when it is changed on one object, it is also changed on all the other linked objects.

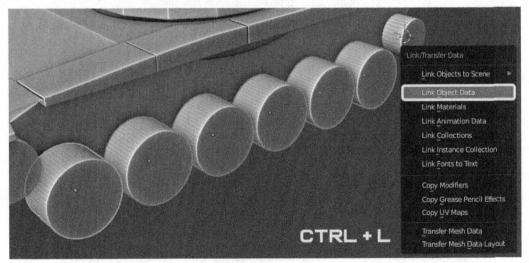

Figure 7.35 – Link Object Data

For example, changing the mesh of one wheel, as shown in *Figure 7.36*, will automatically change the shape of all the other wheels as well. This can save a lot of time because you only need to work on one wheel, since they are all identical:

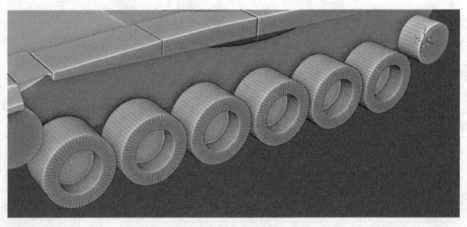

Figure 7.36 – Linked object data

8. Duplicate all the wheels, and scale them to *-1* on the *X* axis while the 3D Cursor is at the world origin to copy them to the other side of the tank.

   Remember to correct the normals on the inverted wheels by pressing *Shift + N* in **Edit Mode**.

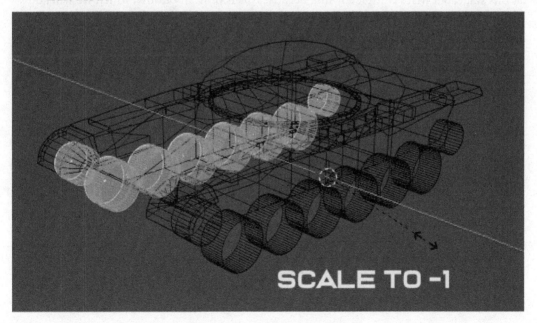

Figure 7.37 – Copying the wheels

The main gun is the final shape we need to add for now. *Figure 7.38* shows the basic shapes necessary for the T-72 tank:

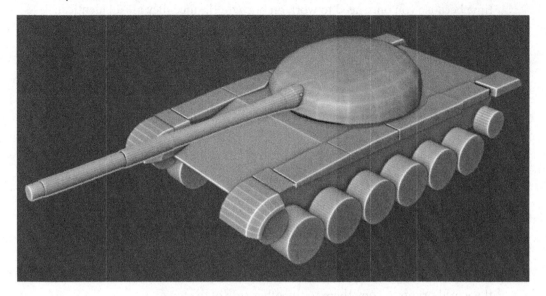

Figure 7.38 – Basic shapes

We now have a simple version of a T-72 tank. As usual, the model looks unimpressive at this stage, but that's completely fine because this is only an outline, which we will add more details to in the following chapters.

Summary

In this chapter, we created a simple version of a T-72 tank to serve as a foundation for creating the rest of the model. We used edge measurements to set the proportions correctly so that we don't have to worry about scale issues later. We also created cylinders as placeholders for the wheels to give us an idea of their size and placement. The object data is linked among the wheels to allow us to easily modify them all simultaneously later.

In the next chapter, we will separate the hull and finish it by adding more details and objects. This is the central part of the tank, which holds the turret and the tracks, so we will finish it before moving on to the other parts.

8
Modeling the T-72 Tank Hull

In this chapter, we will finish the hull of the T-72 tank. We are going to work on adding more objects and details to the front, sides, and rear of the tank to make it look realistic and complete. By the end of this chapter, not only will we have a very detailed tank hull, but we will have also learned several new detail creation techniques to help us create various objects in the future.

We will cover the following topics in this chapter:

- Completing the front end
- Detailing the lower plate
- Modeling the side armor
- Completing the hull front
- Modeling the skirt
- Creating exhaust grills with arrays
- Finishing the rear

Completing the front end

In this section, we will finish shaping the front of the tank and add some details to the lower plate. In the following few steps, we are shaping the top plate:

1. Press *G* twice to slide down the edges at the front of the hull, as shown in *Figure 8.1*. Remember to merge vertices with *Shift + W*.

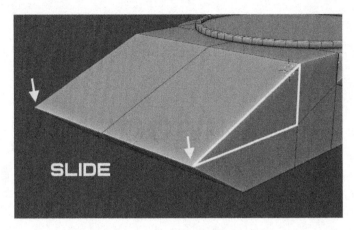

Figure 8.1 – A sliding edge

2. Extrude the upper face (called the **front plate**). Bevel the loop cut in the middle with *Ctrl + B* to turn it into two Edge Loops.

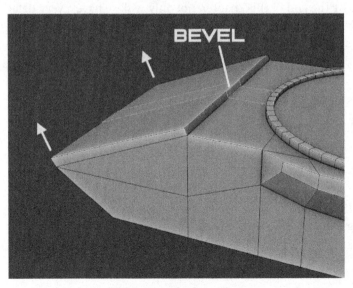

Figure 8.2 – The front plate

3. Select the top-middle edge on the top plate and bevel it. It should produce a shape as shown in *Figure 8.3* (right).

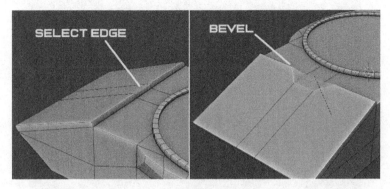

Figure 8.3 – The middle edge (left) and a beveled shape (right)

We now have the top plate correctly shaped. Next, we will work on the lower plate.

Detailing the lower plate

We will now add some new objects and details to the lower plate at the front of the tank. In the next few steps, we will create various new items using tools and techniques that we have already learned:

1. Create a plane and align it with the lower plate. You can do this by selecting the face and pressing *Shift + 7*, and then adjusting the alignment settings in the **Add Plane** menu.

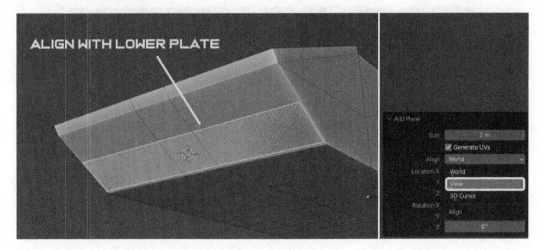

Figure 8.4 – Creating a plane (left) and aligning with View (right)

2. Add a loop cut to the middle of the shape and bevel it to create two edges from one.

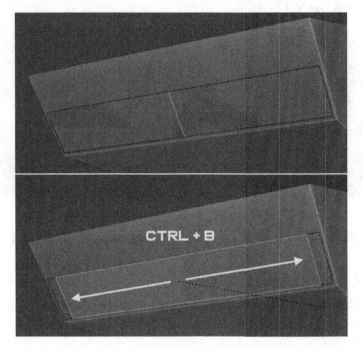

Figure 8.5 – The lower plate edge

3. Repeat *Step 2* to create more edges. The edges should create thin faces, arranged as shown in *Figure 8.6*. Place the 3D Cursor at the lower-middle edge.

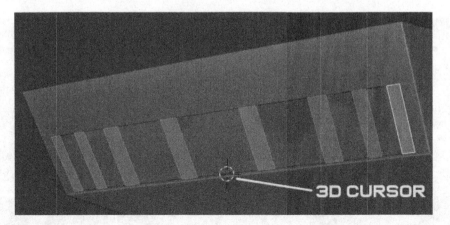

Figure 8.6 – Adding the edges

4.   Select the edges at the top of the faces, marked previously in *Figure 8.6*. Extrude the edges with *E*, and snap them back to their original place with the right mouse button.

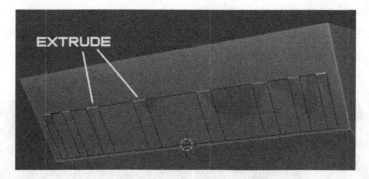

Figure 8.7 – Extruding the edges

5.   Scale the edges by pressing *S* and then *Shift + X*. The 3D Cursor is the pivot point.

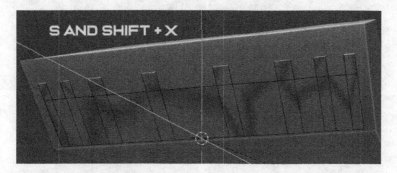

Figure 8.8 – Scaling

6.   Extrude the surface to make it thicker and bevel some of the inner edges, as shown in *Figure 8.9*.

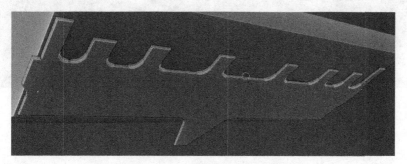

Figure 8.9 – Beveling the edges

Having completed this shape on the lower plate, we will now begin creating some smaller details on this part of the hull. The following is a four-step guide to creating a piston at the bottom of the lower plate.

7. Add a small cube with two loop cuts.

8. Delete the middle face loop and reshape the object with edge sliding and beveling.

9. Add some small details, such as a thin plate and a bolt, to the object.

10. Create the following piston using simple shapes.

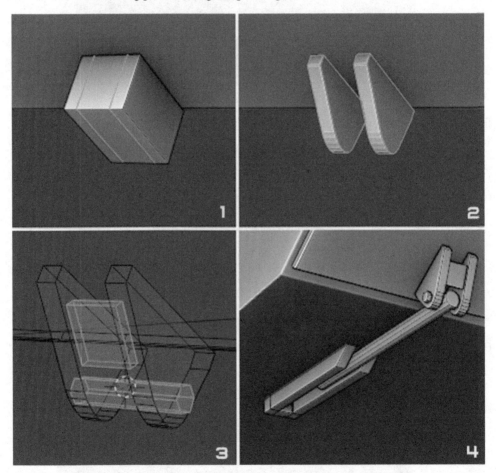

Figure 8.10 – A hydraulic piston

Figure 8.11 shows how to correctly place this detail on the tank.

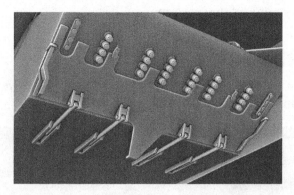

Figure 8.11 – Piston placement

Figure 8.12 shows some more details placed on the lower plate, such as the bolts gathered into sets of four. Here are a few steps for creating bolts like this.

11. Use a cylinder and a hexagon to form the basic shape of a bolt.

12. Add a circle to the bottom of the bolt.

13. Extrude the circle and bevel it so that it forms a ring at the bottom of the bolt.

14. Randomly move some of the vertices on the ring to make it appear messy.

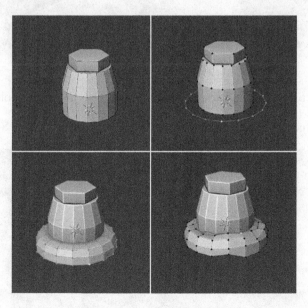

Figure 8.12 – Creating a bolt

You can now place this bolt on the lower plate (or other places), as we saw in *Figure 8.11*. Next, we will work on some of the side armor on the hull.

Modeling the side armor

We are now going to create the side armor and the fuel tanks. Here, we will focus on mudguards, side armor (also called the **skirt**), and some rear details.

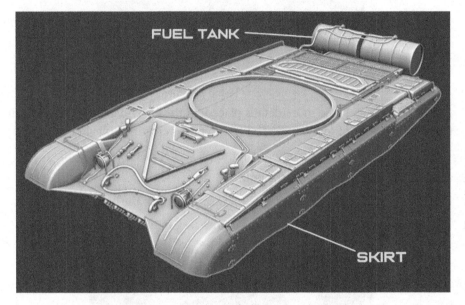

Figure 8.13 – A hull overview

In the next few steps, we will turn our basic shapes into more detailed objects:

1. Bevel the edges on the mudguard and solidify the surface with a **Solidify** modifier.

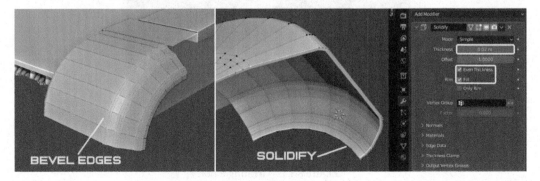

Figure 8.14 – The mudguard

When applying smooth shading to an object, we can manually mark which edges we want to shade sharply. We can then use a modifier to tell Blender how to shade the object.

2. Select the sharp edges and press *Ctrl + E*. In the menu, select **Mark Sharp**.

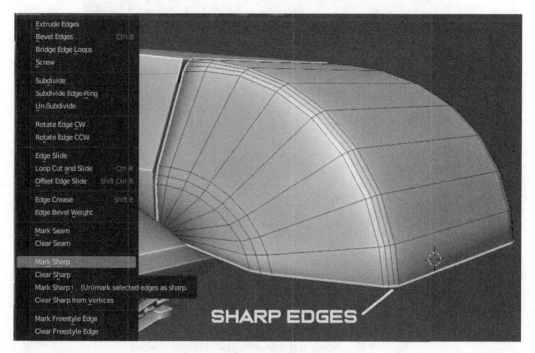

Figure 8.15 – Sharp edges

3. Add an **EdgeSplit** modifier. In the modifier, uncheck **Edge Angle** and check **Sharp Edges**.

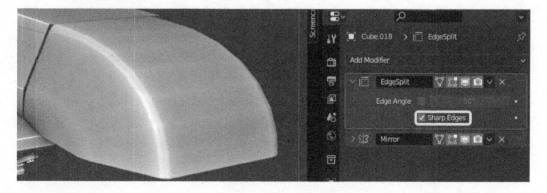

Figure 8.16 – EdgeSplit

4. Add some more details to the mudguard, such as bevels and hinges.

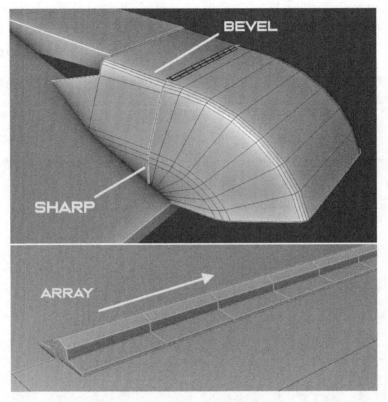

Figure 8.17 – Bevels and sharps (top) and hinges (bottom)

In another four-step breakdown of an important detail, we will create a box for the side skirt.

5. Create a flattened cube and bevel the edges.

6. Add a loop cut and slide the vertices at the front by double-pressing G to make that part of the bevel wider.

7. Create more loop cuts on the shape. These will be used to create a shape for extruding.

8. Shape and extrude a hole at the end.

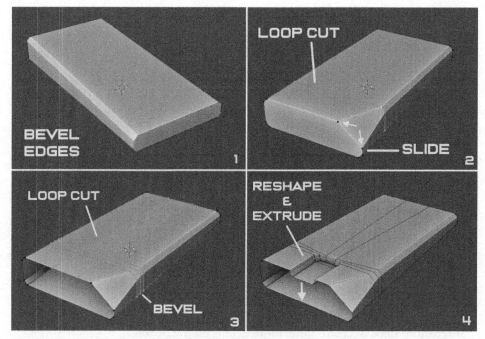

Figure 8.18 – Box creation

Let's continue adding more details to this shape in a few more steps.

9. Fill the hole with details and repeat on both sides of the box. We are using this box to replace the basic shapes that we created at the sides of the hull. *Figure 8.19* shows some detailed ideas that can be created here.

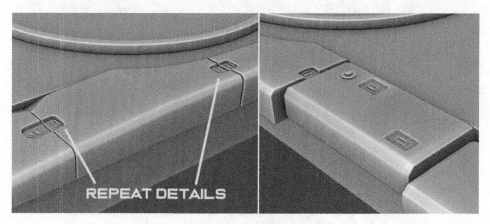

Figure 8.19 – Box details

10. Connect the boxes with a strap, as shown in *Figure 8.20*. This is a close-up image containing some more detailed ideas.

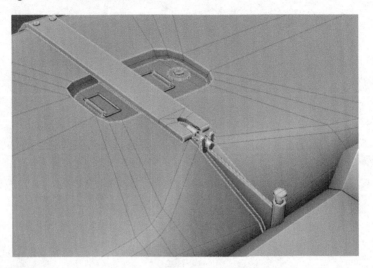

Figure 8.20 – A box strap

On the other side of the tank, we will make the boxes slightly different. Here are three more steps to create some more details on the boxes.

11. Add a plane and align it with the surface of the box at the front.

12. Extrude the plane slightly and bevel its edges.

13. Create some more straps on this shape to make it look more detailed.

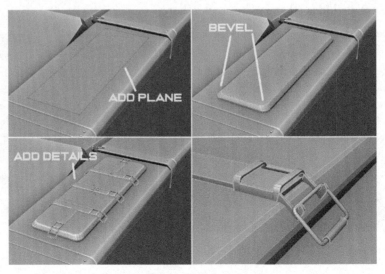

Figure 8.21 – More box details

Figure 8.22 shows the finished boxes on the sides of the tank.

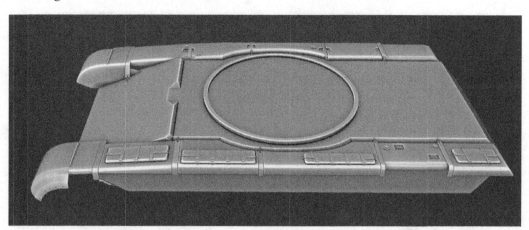

Figure 8.22 – The finished boxes

We now created some details on the side of the tank. We will return to this part later by adding some side armor. Next, we will focus on the front of the tank once again and add lots of details to finish it.

Completing the hull front

In this section, we will add some objects to the top plate at the front of the hull, such as windows, viewports, and hatches. In the following steps, we will be creating the driver viewport:

1. Create a plane and extrude its edges downward.
2. Bevel the edges and use loop cuts to create dents in the sides.
3. Solidify the shape with *Alt + S* and use the same technique to create a cover for it.

4. Add some small details to the shape.

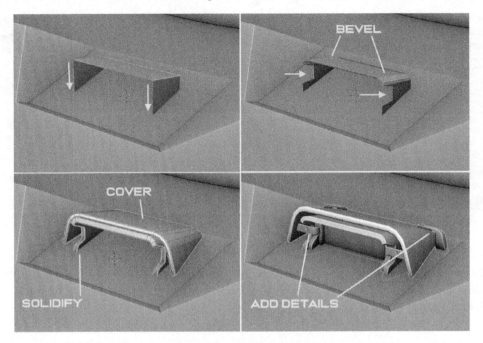

Figure 8.23 – The driver viewport

5. Use cubes with beveled edges to create some bars on the top plate, under the window.

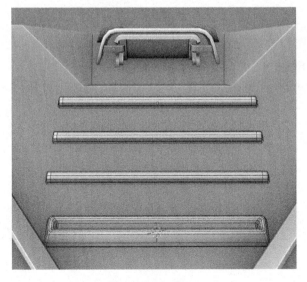

Figure 8.24 – Bars

Next, we will create some headlights for the tank in a few steps:

1. Add a cylinder and turn it to the side.

2. Bevel the Edge Loop at the back.

3. Inset and extrude a face at the front.

4. Add some details, such as screws and bevels.

Figure 8.25 shows the procedure for shaping the headlight.

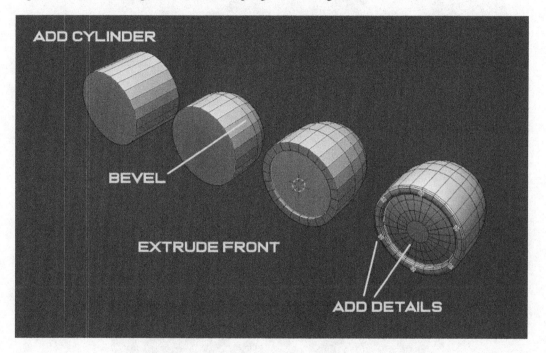

8.25 – The headlight shape

After creating the headlight, we will create some bars around the headlight:

1. Add a circle in front of the light that is larger than it.

2. Extrude the circle backward.

3. Solidify the circle with *Alt + S* to make it as thick as it is wide.

4.   Bevel the Edge Loops on the shape to make them look circular.

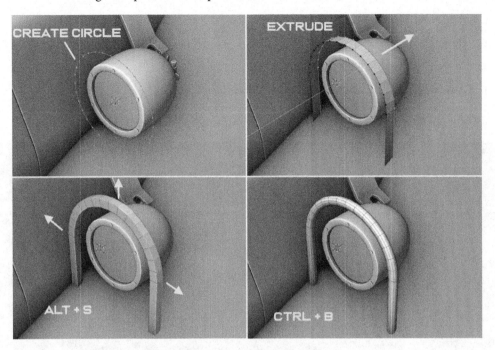

Figure 8.26 – The headlight

5.   Duplicate the bar, move it to the back, and connect it with some simple cylinders. Then, add some random details to the headlight.

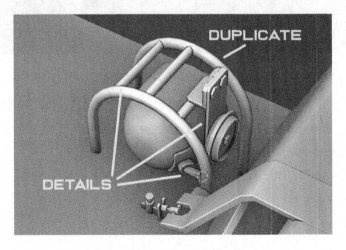

Figure 8.27 – Headlight details

Next, we will create a tow cable on the top plate, as shown in *Figure 8.28*.

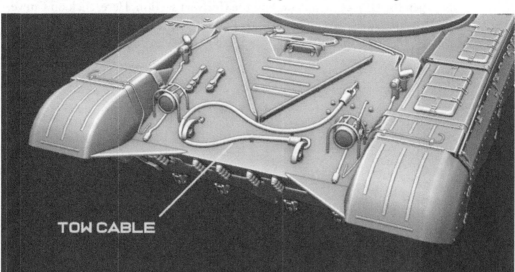

Figure 8.28 – The finished tow cable

6. Add a plane and collapse it. To do this, select the plane and press *X* to open the **Delete** menu, and then click on **Collapse Edges & Faces**.

7. Use the resulting vertex to extrude the rough shape of the cable, as shown in *Figure 8.29* (right).

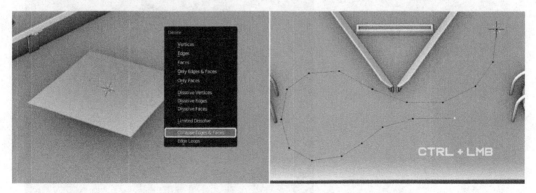

Figure 8.29 – Collapsing (left) and the cable shape (right)

8. Apply a **Subdivision Surface** modifier to the shape and convert it into a curve. To do this, open the **Object** menu and find the **Convert** section. Here, click on **Curve**.

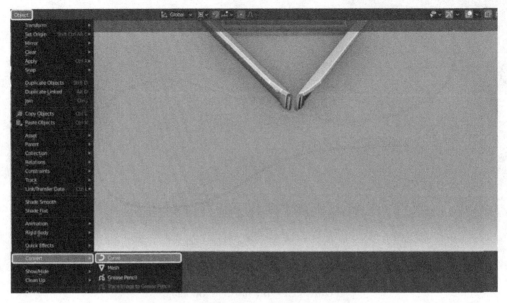

Figure 8.30 – Converting to a curve

9. At the beginning of the curve, create a small vertical cylinder array. The width of the cylinder will be the width of the cable. Delete the top and bottom faces of the cylinder.

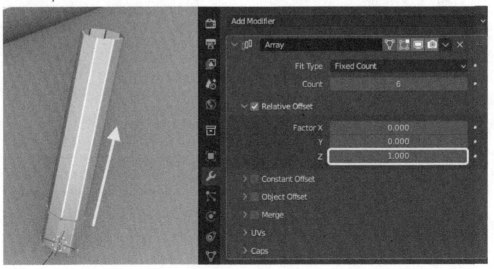

Figure 8.31 – The cylinder array

10. Add a **Curve** modifier to the cylinder array. In the **Curve Object** field, select the curve that we just created. You may need to adjust the **Deform Axis** factor until it fits correctly. Afterward, apply the **Curve** modifier.

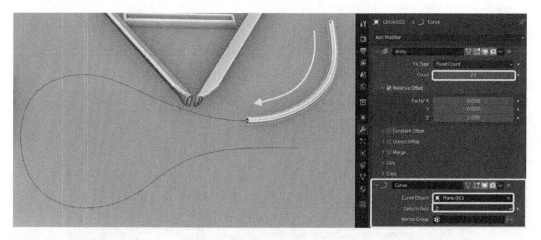

Figure 8.32 – The Curve modifier

11. Finish the cable by attaching the cable to the hull and adding some hooks to the ends.

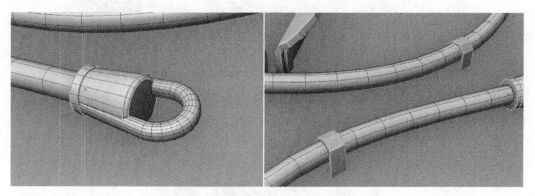

Figure 8.33 – The finished cable

Now, let's create another detail for the hull. In the following few steps, we will create a tow hook and place it on the top plate:

1. Create a circle and extrude it outward.

2. Reshape the circle and extrude parts of it to form a shape, as shown in *Figure 8.34*.

3. Extrude the shape and make it look smoother by adding loop cuts around it and solidifying the inner-face loop.

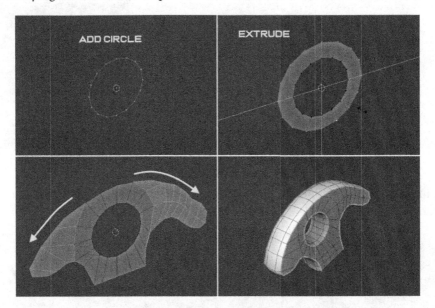

Figure 8.34 – The tow hook

4. Add some shapes to the back of the hook and connect it to the tow cable. Note how the hook looks welded to the hull. To do this, use the same technique we used for the bolts on the lower plate.

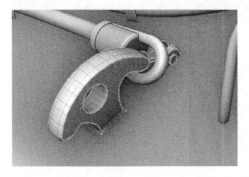

Figure 8.35 – The finished tow hook

The front of the tank is nearly finished. See *Figure 8.36* for some more details, which can be created using the same techniques we have already covered.

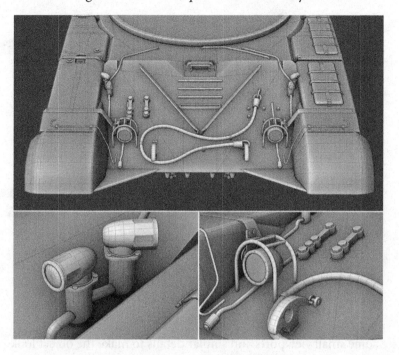

Figure 8.36 – Frontal details

Next, let's create a hatch behind the drivers' viewport in a few steps:

1. Create a circle behind the viewport and stretch it. By its side, create a smaller circle.

2. Delete some of the vertices on each circle and connect the circles together. You may want to move some vertices around to make the connection smooth.

3. Extrude this outline upward and use a **Boolean** modifier to cut out a shape in the object.

4. Use loop cuts to reshape the Boolean cut and use bevels to smooth the edges.

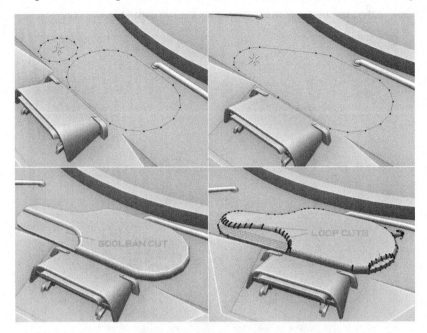

Figure 8.37 – The driver hatch

5. Create some small viewports and similar details to make the object look more complete.

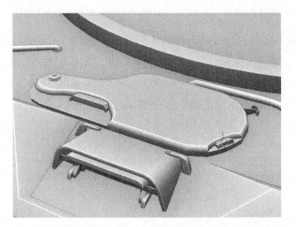

Figure 8.38 – The finished hatch

We learned how to create a hatch, and we will create more objects like it on other parts of the tank. Next, we will continue modeling the sides of the tank.

Modeling the skirt

Let's return to the sides of the hull and start creating some skirts. In the next few steps, we will add side armor and details:

1. Use planes to create some simple shapes on the sides of the boxes we created before. Extrude them downward to get a shape, as shown in *Figure 8.39*.

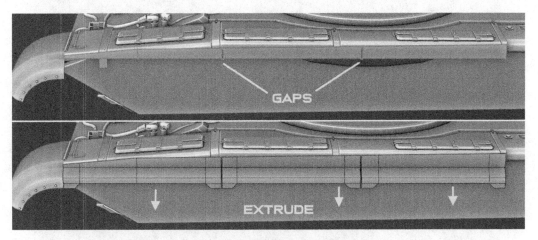

Figure 8.39 – Skirt basic shapes

2. Add thickness to the shapes that we just created on the sides with *Alt + S*. Adding some screws with the help of **Array** modifiers improves this part greatly.

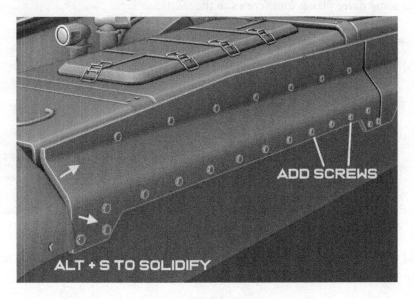

Figure 8.40 – Solidification and screws

3. Add some details, such as hinges and clamps, using tools and techniques that we have already learned.

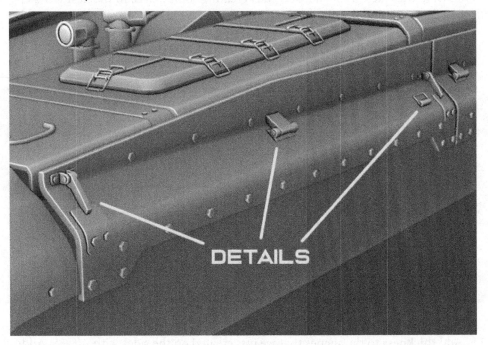

Figure 8.41 – Skirt details

4. Add some more planes and screws to the skirts.

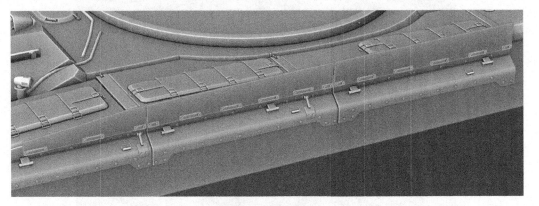

Figure 8.42 – Side planes

5. Add more shapes below the parts we created in *steps 1–3* and connect them with some hinges.

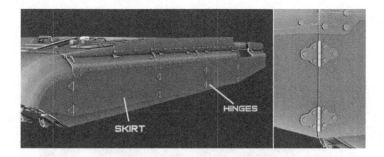

Figure 8.43 – Skirts (left) and hinges (right)

We have now finished the side armor, but we still need to add some more details to some parts, such as an exhaust pipe on the side of the tank.

Adding an exhaust pipe

We will now add an exhaust pipe to the left side of the tank in the next few steps:

1. Create a gap in the side armor near the back and add some wide cubes with bevels.

2. Using loop cuts and solidification, add some details to these shapes.

3. In the exhaust pipe, add some thin cubes as separators and some screws to the side.

4. Finish the object with some more details, such as thin covers and more screws.

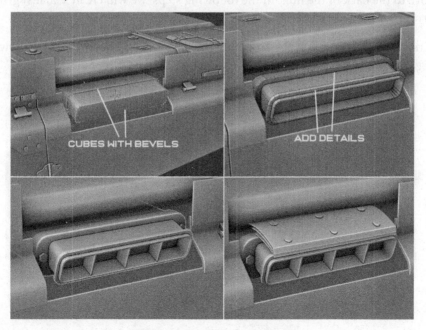

Figure 8.44 – An exhaust pipe

5.   Add some more metal sheets and screws below the exhaust pipe.

Figure 8.45 – Skirt sheets

We have added some more details to the sides of the tank. Next, we will continue by working on the back part of the tank.

Creating exhaust grills with arrays

Let's move to the back of the hull. In the following steps, we will create exhaust grills using arrays:

1.   Create a simple frame at the far end of the tank and add details to it, as shown in *Figure 8.46*.

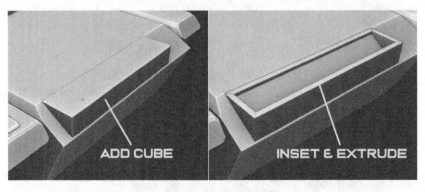

Figure 8.46 – Creating grills

2. Add some basic shapes (namely, reshaped cubes) to form some bars inside the frame.

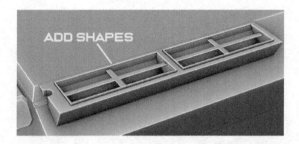

Figure 8.47 – The exhaust frame

3. Create a long and thin shape in the frame and add an array to create the grills. Set the **Relative Offset** factor to **2.000** (or **-2.000**, depending on the direction).

Figure 8.48 – The grill array

4. Repeat in the other direction to create a grid pattern.

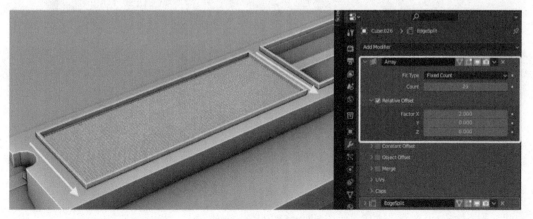

Figure 8.49 – The grid

5. Use the same technique to create some larger exhausts on the hull.

Figure 8.50 – Exhaust grills

The back of our hull now has exhaust grills. We will now continue adding details to this part of the hull. Here are a few steps to create another hatch.

6. In front of the large grills, add a thin panel with beveled edges.

Figure 8.51 – A panel

7. Add another panel to cover the previous one.

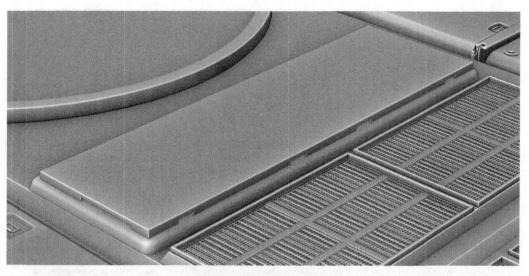

Figure 8.52 – A panel cover

8. Create an outline, as shown in *Figure 8.53*, on top of the panel. You can do this by creating the shape using a plane, insetting faces, and deleting the inner faces.

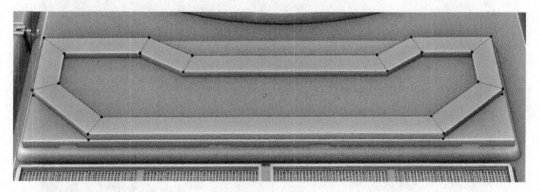

Figure 8.53 – An outline

9.   Bevel the Edge Loops on this shape and add some bars to the inside.

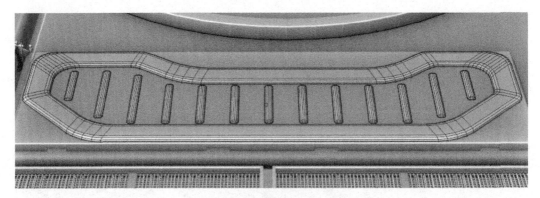

Figure 8.54 – The finished panel

10. Continue adding more details using tools and techniques that we have already covered. *Figure 8.55* shows the back end of the skirt.

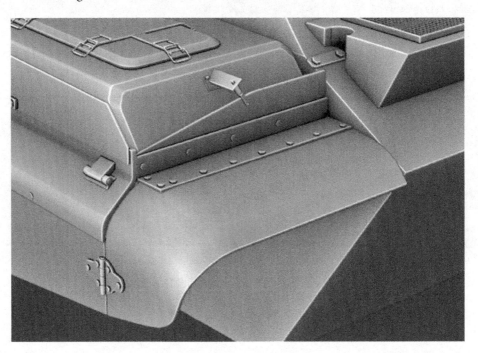

Figure 8.55 – The skirt back end

Here are a few more item and object ideas that can be added to the back of the hull. *Figure 8.56* shows various fine details, such as screws, bolts, and bars.

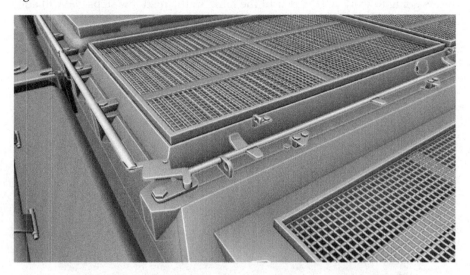

Figure 8.56 – Fine details

Figure 8.57 shows another angle, with a smaller exhaust grill and some more fine details.

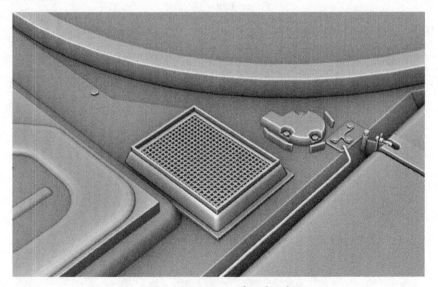

Figure 8.57 – More fine details

Next, we will visit the rear end of the hull and add some more objects to it.

Finishing the rear end of the hull

We are now going to work on the rear of the tank. In the next few steps, we will add some objects and details to the rear, which will give us a finished hull:

1. Add some more details around the exhaust grills, such as the ones we already learned to create on other parts of the tank.

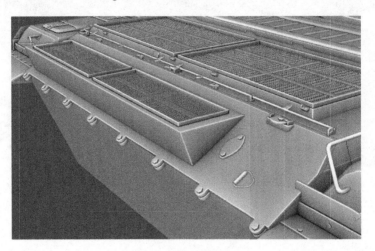

Figure 8.58 – The rear

2. At the bottom of the rear, create a long cube with two loop cuts.

Figure 8.59 – A cube with loop cuts

3. Scale the two outer-face loops to make them wider than the middle. You can also expand them with *Alt + S*.

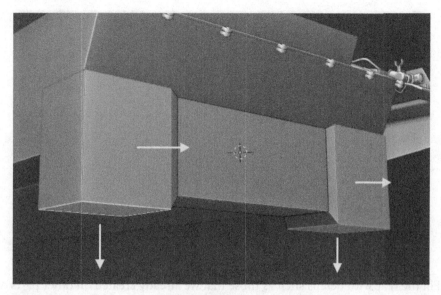

Figure 8.60 – Scaling the face loops

4. Bevel some of the edges to create a shape like the one shown in *Figure 8.61*.

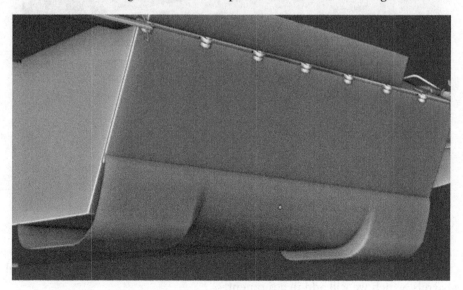

Figure 8.61 – A beveled shape

5. Add a plane and reshape it to cover the rear of the tank. It should look something like *Figure 8.62*. Feel free to add some details, such as hatches and bolts.

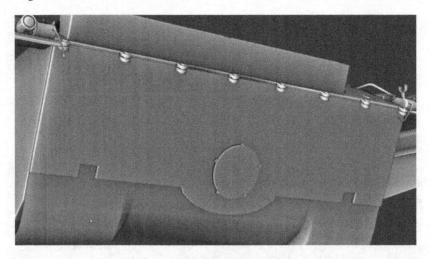

Figure 8.62 – The rear cover

6. Fill the rear with details such as those that we already created on other parts of the hull. Note that we copied the same tow hooks from the top plate at the front.

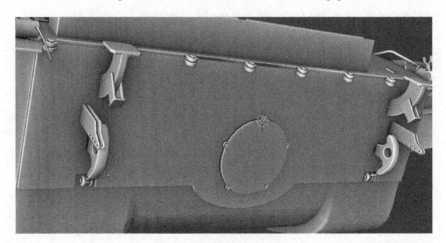

Figure 8.63 – Rear details

7. Add a long cylinder, along with a few details that will make it look like it's tied to this part of the tank. We are also adding some objects that will support the fuel barrels, which we will add in a moment.

This log is often used to help tanks regain mobility after getting stuck in the mud.

Figure 8.64 – More rear details

Here are a few steps to create the fuel barrels at the back of the tank:

I.   Add a long cylinder on top of the barrel holders we created a moment ago.

II. Modify the shape using simple extrusion, loop cuts, and solidification to make it look more like a barrel.

III. Add some disconnected rings around the barrel.

IV. Connect the rings with a screw.

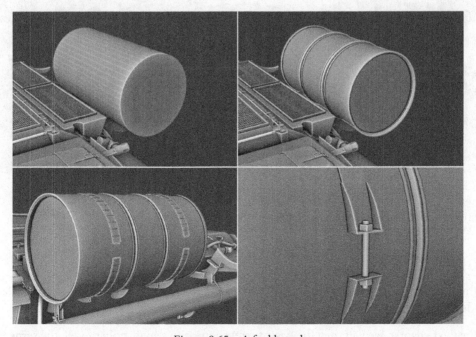

Figure 8.65 – A fuel barrel

V. Finish the fuel barrels by connecting them to the hull with some pipes. You can do this using the **Array** and **Curve** modifier technique that we learned earlier.

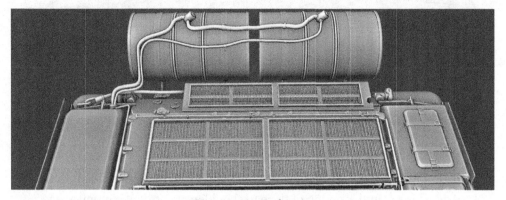

Figure 8.66 – Fuel pipes

Figure 8.67 shows the finished T-72 hull.

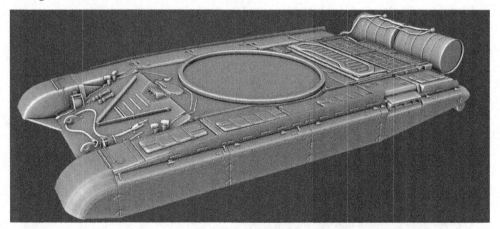

Figure 8.67 – The finished hull

We have now completed the T-72 hull by filling it with lots of new details.

Summary

In this chapter, we learned new tools and techniques to create fine details on a hard-surface model. With our hull ready, we can now continue adding more parts to the tank.

In the next chapter, we will turn the basic turret shape into a high-poly model, the same way we did with the hull in this chapter.

9
Modeling the T-72 Tank Turret

In this chapter, we will create a high-poly turret for our T-72 tank. We will use advanced modeling techniques and we will learn a few new tricks to achieve the highest level of quality and detail. By the end of this chapter, the bulk of our tank will be complete, and we will be ready to move on to the wheels and tracks.

This chapter covers the following topics:

- Modeling the commander's hatch
- Creating more turret details
- Finishing the gun

Modeling the commander's hatch

Figure 9.1 shows the current basic shape of the turret. The left picture shows the subdivided mesh, while the right picture shows the wireframe view of the base mesh:

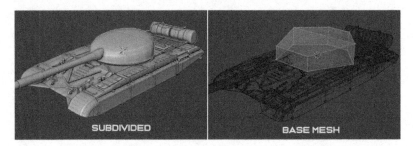

Figure 9.1 – Subdivided mesh (left) and base mesh (right)

We will now begin adding more objects and details to this turret, starting with the commander hatch:

1. Add a circle above the turret shape. We will use this to create the commander hatch:

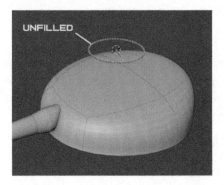

Figure 9.2 – Unfilled circle

2. Press *F2* while the turret is selected and rename the turret to a recognizable name:

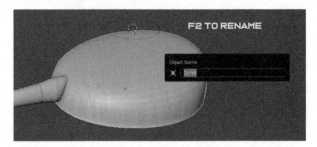

Figure 9.3 – Renaming the turret

3.   Add a **Shrinkwrap** modifier to the empty circle we added in *Step 1*:

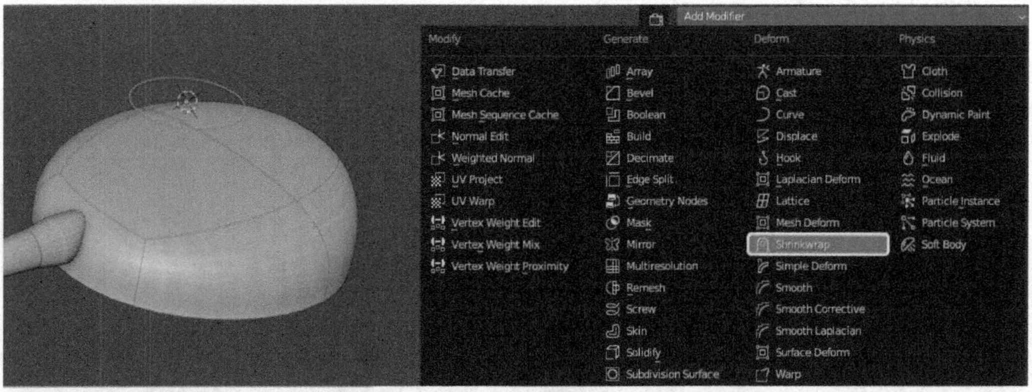

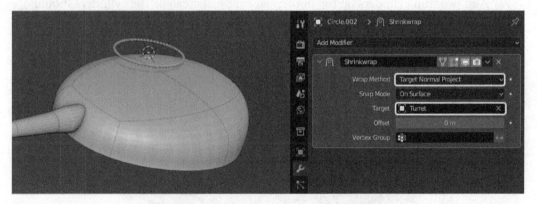

Figure 9.4 – Shrinkwrap modifier

4.   In the **Shrinkwrap** modifier, set **Wrap Method** to **Target Normal Project** and set **Turret** as the **Target** object:

Figure 9.5 – Shrinkwrap settings

5.   Apply the modifier and extrude the circle upward. The circle now has the shape of the surface below it:

Figure 9.6 – Extruding the circle

6. Select the top Edge Loop and press *W*. In the **LoopTools** menu, select **Circle** to turn the loop into a perfect circle:

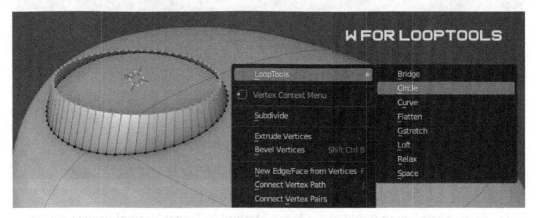

Figure 9.7 – LoopTools

7. Add two thin cylinders on top of the shape we just created. The cylinders should have 48 vertices or edges:

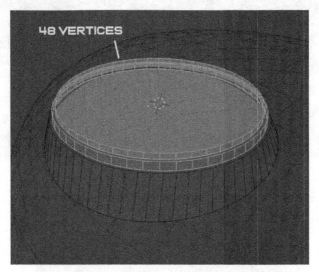

Figure 9.8 – Adding two cylinders

8. Separate the top cylinder into a new object and select six consecutive faces on the side. Then, press *Ctrl + I* to inverse the selection (select all unselected faces and deselect all selected faces) and delete all the remaining faces including the top and the bottom. This will leave us with only a segment of the cylinder.

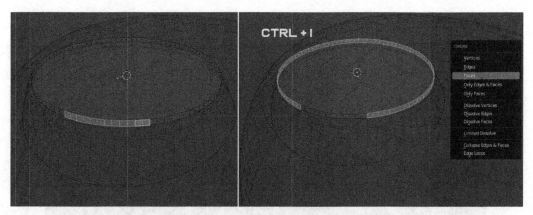

Figure 9.9 – Selecting faces (left) and deleting faces (right)

9. Use loop cuts (*Ctrl + R*) and bevels (*Ctrl + B*) to create a dent in one of the remaining faces:

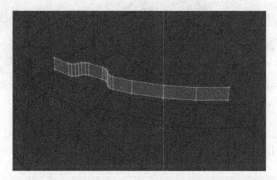

Figure 9.10 – Cylinder segment

10. Select the segment, duplicate it, and rotate it around the center of the circle by 45 degrees:

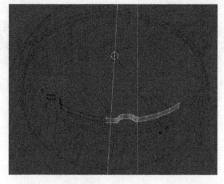

Figure 9.11 – Rotating the segment

11. Repeat *Step 8* until the circle is complete:

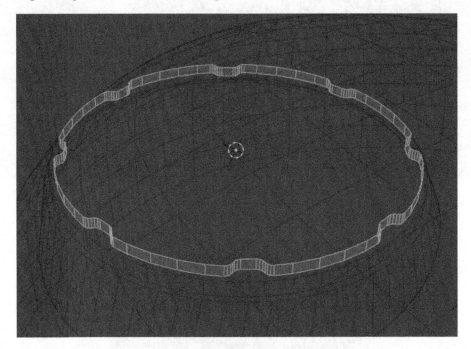

Figure 9.12 – Full circle

12. Fill the top face and add some screws into the dents. Then, add another layer using the same technique from *steps 8-11*.

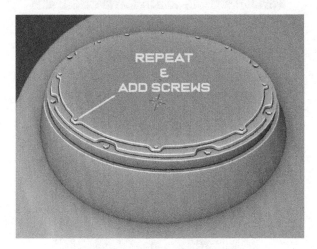

Figure 9.13 – Second layer

13. Create a dome on top of the hatch and use half of an octagon to create a shape, as in *Figure 9.14*:

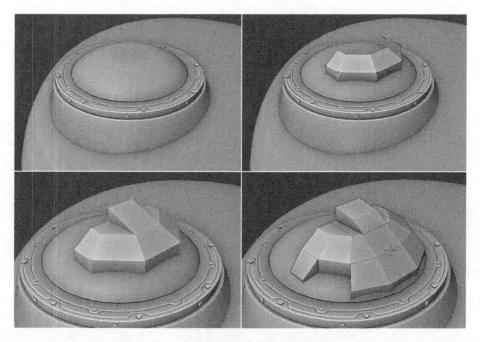

Figure 9.14 – Hatch shape

14. Use a **Subdivision Surface** modifier to turn this shape into a smoother object:

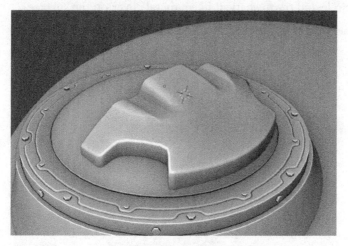

Figure 9.15 – Subdivision Surface

15. Fill the hatch with various smaller objects as shown in *Figure 9.16*:

Figure 9.16 – Adding hatch details

We have now finished the commander hatch; we will create another hatch next to this one and we will add a few more similar objects to the top of the turret.

Creating more turret details

There are a few more objects and hatches on the top of the turret around the commander's hatch. In the following four steps, we will create a second hatch using a similar method:

1. Create a circle above the turret surface.

2. Move a vertex backward with **Proportional Editing** to flatten this part of the circle.

3. Fill the circle and try to shape it like a metal cover on the surface.

4. Add some more items to the hatch like handles, hinges and so on.

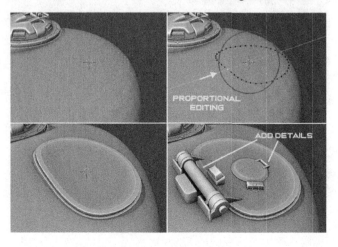

Figure 9.17 – Second hatch

Let's create another viewport on the turret in a few steps:

I.   Create two basic shapes: a cylindrical base and a cube with beveled edges.

II. Extrude the front of the top shape and create a circular window inside.

III. Model a simple cover using a plane and loop cuts.

IV. Add some smaller items to increase the detail level.

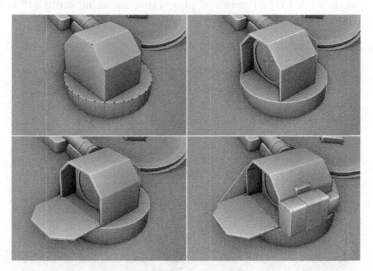

Figure 9.18 – Viewport

5.   Attach a light to this shape, like the one we created at the front of the hull:

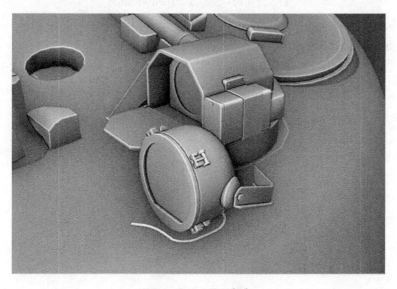

Figure 9.19 – Top light

Here are a few more steps for creating the smoke discharging tubes at the sides of the turret:

I. Create a cable on the side of the turret using the array and curve method, which we learned in *Chapter 8, Modeling the T-72 Tank Hull*.

II. Use a cylinder to shape a tube.

III.Connect the tube to the turret and plug it into the cable using a thin wire, using the same curve method.

IV. Repeat until there are seven tubes:

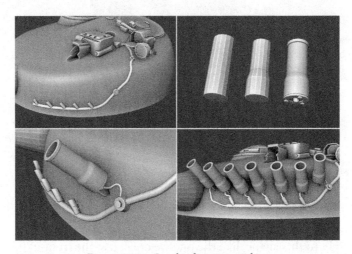

Figure 9.20 – Smoke dispenser tubes

Next, we will create a box on the side of the turret in a few easy steps.

6.   Create a cuboid on which the outer edges are beveled:

Figure 9.21 – Box

7. Add loop cuts to the cuboid with *Ctrl + R* and adjust the inner edges so that the box fits the turret shape:

Figure 9.22 – Fitting to the turret

8. Modify the shape of the box and add some bevels to its edges:

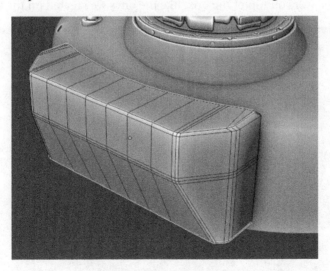

Figure 9.23 – Bevelled box

We need to attach the box to the turret. Here are three steps to create a clamp:

I.   Create two faces that are at a 90-degree angle.

II. Add some loop cuts to make its edges rounder.

III. Solidify the shape and add some screws to it:

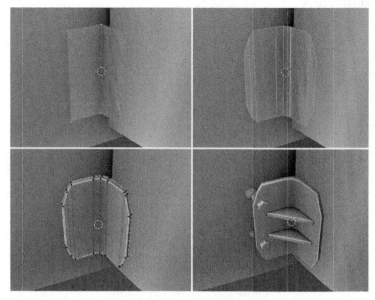

Figure 9.24 – Clamp

9.   Add some covers on top of the box, like the ones we created on the skirts:

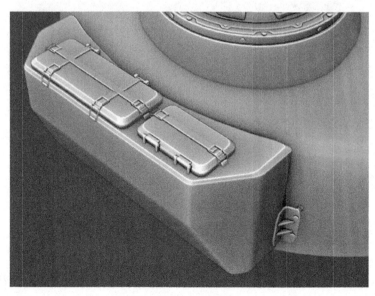

Figure 9.25 – Box covers

10. Repeat the same process to add another similar box at the back of the turret:

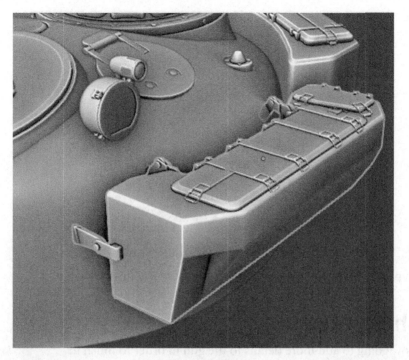

Figure 9.26 – Second box

Here is an example of some smaller boxes that can be added to the side of the turret:

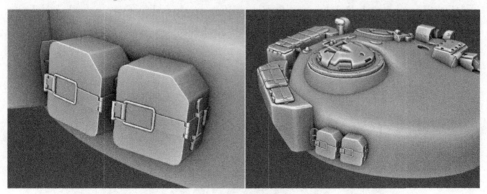

Figure 9.27 – Smaller boxes

We will also create some more smoke dispensers on the other side of the turret:

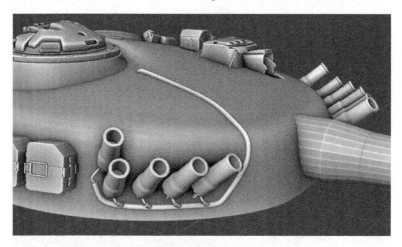

Figure 9.28 – More smoke dispenser tubes

The main part of the turret is now finished. Next, we will finish the gun.

Finishing the gun

We are now going to add more details to the gun in order to finish it:

1.   First, make an indentation in the turret at the base of the gun.

     We still have a **Subdivision Surface** modifier on this object, so we only need to extrude a few faces inward to achieve this shape.

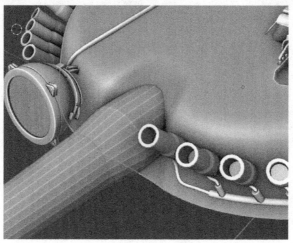

Figure 9.29 – Gun mantlet

2. Next, add an octagonal cylinder to the gun base and try to shape it so it fits the turret:

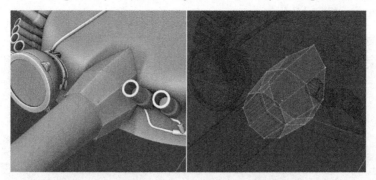

Figure 9.30 – Mantlet cover

3. Activate **Proportional Editing** by pressing *O*, and shape the back end of the cylinder like a square:

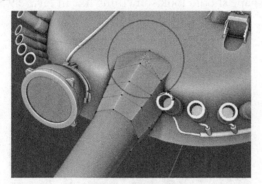

Figure 9.31 – Square base

4. Also fit the shape to the turret at the bottom of the gun, as shown in *Figure 9.32*:

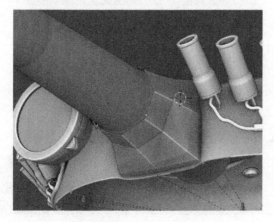

Figure 9.32 – Mantlet bottom

5. Apply a **Subdivision Surface** modifier to the shape. Then, modify the shape further with **Proportional Editing**.

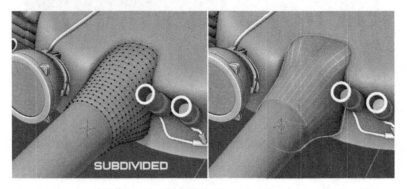

Figure 9.33 – Subdivided gun mantlet

In the end, this shape should look something like in *Figure 9.34*, before adding smooth shading:

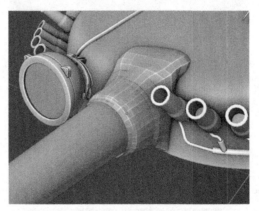

Figure 9.34 – Finished mantlet cover

Next, add a ring to keep the mantlet cover in place and place some screws on it using the 3D Cursor:

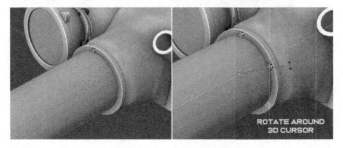

Figure 9.35 – Mantlet ring

6. Add a horseshoe shape around the gun and connect it with some clamps:

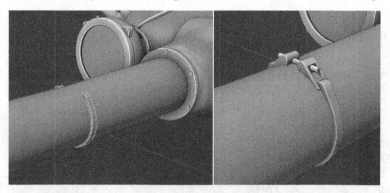

Figure 9.36 – Gun rings

7. Duplicate the ring to other parts of the gun barrel:

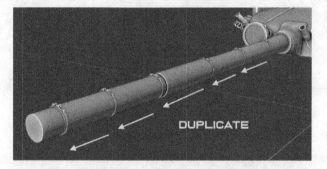

Figure 9.37 – Duplicating gun rings

8. Inset a face with *I* and extrude it inward with *E* at the end of the barrel. Feel free to add some more details on top of the gun, as shown in *Figure 9.38*:

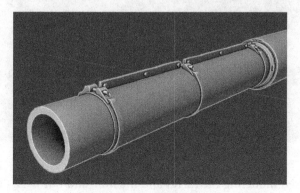

Figure 9.38 – Finished gun

Figure 9.39 shows the completed turret from three different angles:

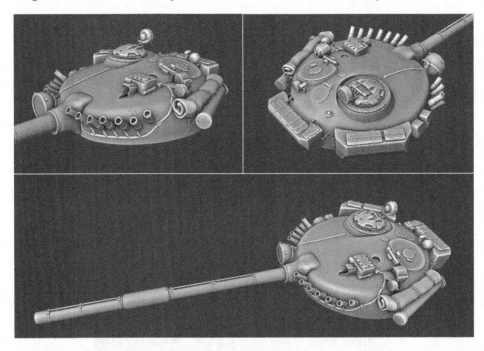

Figure 9.39 – Turret

Figure 9.40 shows the turret attached to the hull:

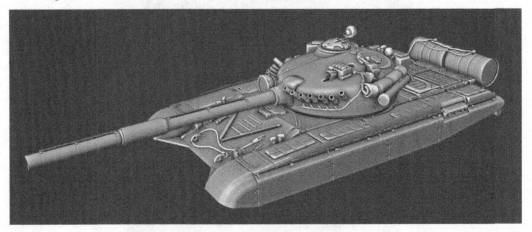

Figure 9.40 – T-72 turret and hull

We have now finished modeling the turret and the hull, and our T-72 tank is almost finished. Now, our model is only missing its wheels and tracks.

Summary

In this chapter, we created a high-poly turret for our T-72 tank and attached it to the hull that we created in *Chapter 8, Modeling the T-72 Tank Hull*. This leaves us with only one more modeling chapter, in which we will create the wheels and tracks.

In the next chapter, we will create the wheels and tracks for our T-72. This will complete our model, and we will later use these tracks to rig the tank, which will make it possible to animate the tank.

10
Modeling Tank Tracks

In this chapter, we will model the wheels, tracks, suspension, and sprockets for the T-72 tank. We will model the wheels from the basic shapes that we created in *Chapter 7, Modeling the T-72 Tank: Basic Shapes*, and we will create the tracks using **Array** and **Curve** modifier techniques, which we have already learned about.

By the end of this chapter, our T-72 tank model will be complete and ready for rigging and texturing.

We will cover the following topics in this chapter:

- Creating the suspension and wheels
- Modeling a sprocket
- Creating the tracks
- Finishing the tracks

Creating the suspension and wheels

In this section, we will create the wheels and suspension to attach them to the hull, using the basic shapes that we created before:

1.   Select all the wheel cylinders:

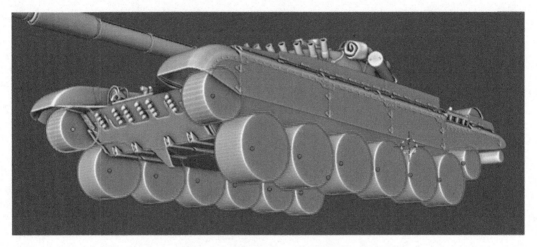

Figure 10.1 – Selecting the basic shapes

2.   Set **Pivot Point** to **Individual Origins** and scale all the shapes by a factor of 0.2.

This will make it easier for us to work on this area while keeping the wheels as placeholders.

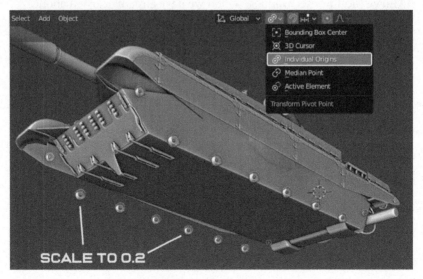

Figure 10.2 – Scaling the wheels

3. Create a cylinder with extruded and rounded edges on four sides as shown in the following screenshot:

Figure 10.3 – Wheelbase

4. Place this shape in front of the first wheel. This will be the base of the suspension arm:

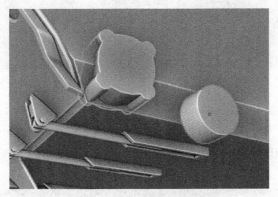

Figure 10.4 – Wheelbase placement

5. Use simple shapes created by circles and cylinders to model the suspension arm and add some screws:

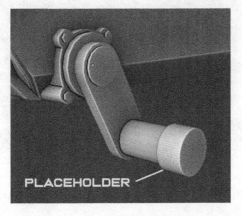

Figure 10.5 – Suspension arm

6. Join the suspension arm with the first wheel placeholder. Do this by selecting the suspension first, then selecting the wheel and pressing *Ctrl + J* to join them into one object.

    We linked the object data for the wheels in *Chapter 7*, *Modeling the T-72 Tank: Basic Shapes*. This will cause the suspension to be copied to all the other wheels. If you have not done this, you can do it by selecting all the wheels, then selecting the front wheel last, pressing *Ctrl + L*, and linking object data:

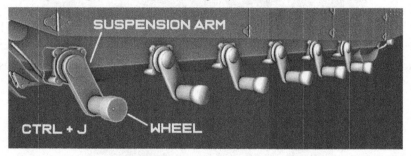

Figure 10.6 – Joining objects

7. Select all the wheels and suspensions, having selected the front one last. Then, press *Ctrl + L* again and select **Copy Modifiers**.

    This will copy the **Edge Split** modifier to all the other objects, which will produce better shading:

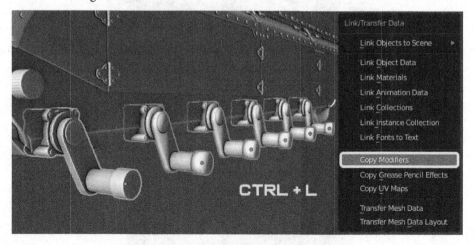

Figure 10.7 – Copying modifiers

The suspension is now complete, and we can begin attaching wheels to it.

Modeling the wheels

We will now create the first set of wheels for the tank. In the following steps, we will turn the cylinders into complex wheels:

1. In **Edit Mode**, enlarge the wheel placeholder by selecting it and scaling it by a factor of 5.

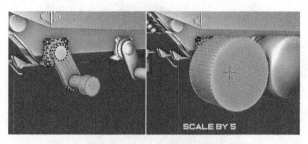

Figure 10.8 – Scaling the wheel

2. Create two loop cuts in the cylinder and extrude them inward by pressing *Alt + S* to create a gap:

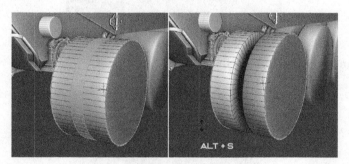

Figure 10.9 – Wheel gap

3. Extrude a hole at the front of the wheel:

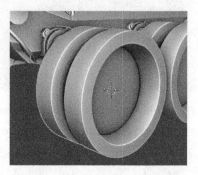

Figure 10.10 – Extruding the front of the wheel

4. Create a hollow circle with `16` edges in the middle of the wheel. Extrude every other edge on this circle and scale them down slightly.

5. To do this, select every other edge, extrude it with *E*, and snap it back into place with the right mouse button. Then, scale the extruded edges down on two axes towards the middle of the circle:

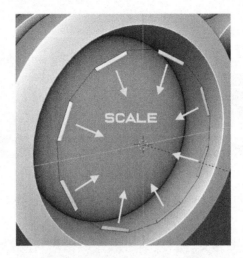

Figure 10.11 – Inward extrusion

6. Repeat and extrude closer to the middle:

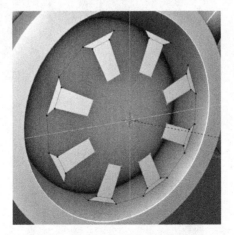

Figure 10.12 – Further inward extrusion

Here are a few steps to turn this shape into a rim for the wheel:

I. Extrude the outer circle outward to create a thicker edge.

II. Loop-select the inner edges by pressing *Alt* + right mouse button.

III. Extrude the inner edges, push them backward, and resize them by pressing *Alt + S*.

IV. Fill the gap between two ends and round it with loop cuts.

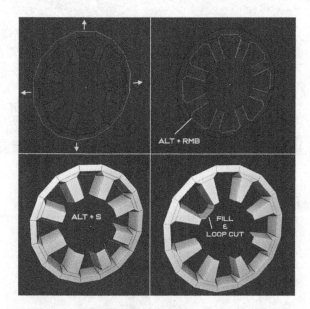

Figure 10.13 – Creating the rim

5. Duplicate the bridge between the two ends and rotate it by 45 degrees to copy it to the other gap. After completing the circle, press *Shift + W* to merge double vertices and weld the shapes:

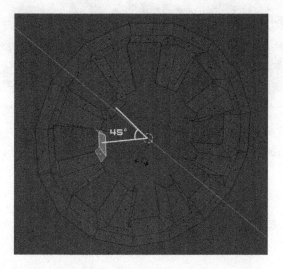

Figure 10.14 – Copying the bridge

6. Fill in the shape and extrude some circles in the middle of the rim:

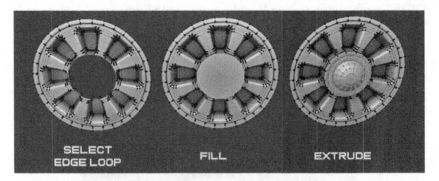

Figure 10.15 – Rim center

You can then place this shape into the hole of the wheel to complete it:

Figure 10.16 – Completed wheel

The main set of wheels is now complete. Next, we will create the three other types of wheel needed for this tank.

Modeling the rear sprocket

In this section, we will create the rear sprocket. This is the last wheel on the back of the tank, which turns the tracks:

1. Create a circle with 48 vertices:

Figure 10.17 – A 48-vertex circle

2. Create a cube at the top of the circle and shape it like a sprocket tooth. The cube should be as wide as two faces on the circle as shown in the following screenshot:

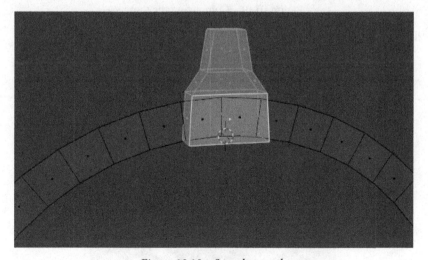

Figure 10.18 – Sprocket tooth

3. Delete the front, back, and bottom faces of the tooth.
4. Make the outline wider with *Alt + S*.

5. Move the edge loops down and bevel them:

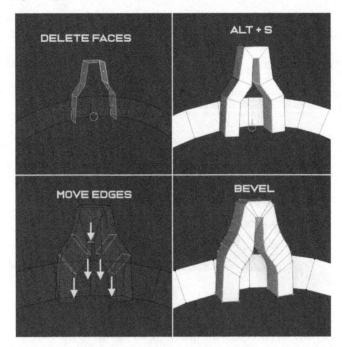

Figure 10.19 – Completing the tooth

6. Copy the tooth and rotate it by 30 degrees:

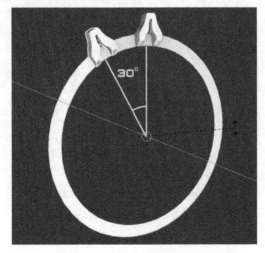

Figure 10.20 – Rotating the tooth

7. Extrude some faces at the back of the teeth:

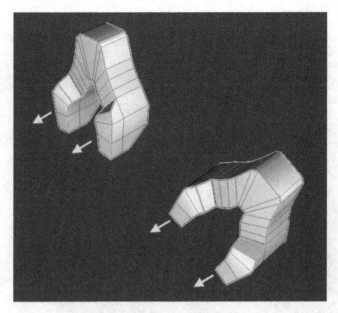

Figure 10.21 – Extruding faces

8. Delete the faces on the sides of the extruded shapes:

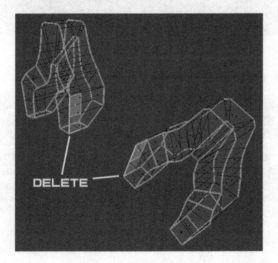

Figure 10.22 – Deleting faces

9. Select the edge loops around the holes, then press *W*, and select **Bridge Edge Loops**.

Ensure that the two teeth are part of the same object to allow this. If they are not, select them both and join them with *Ctrl + J*.

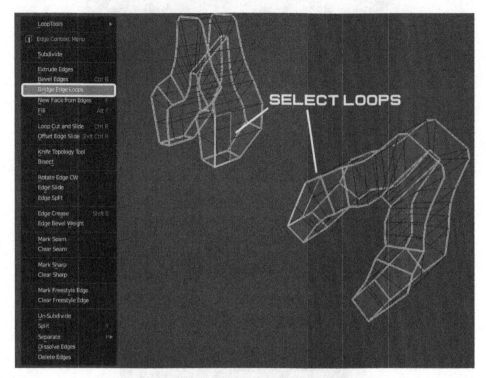

Figure 10.23 – Bridging edge loops

10. Round the bridge using edge loops and bevels:

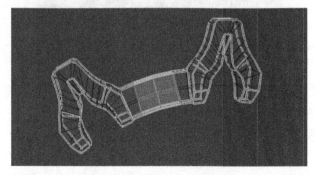

Figure 10.24 – Rounding the bridge

11. Duplicate one of the teeth and the bridge and rotate it by 30 degrees.

Ensure that the faces on the outer sides of the teeth are also deleted so that they can have a bridge connected to them.

12. Repeat this until the outer sprocket is complete:

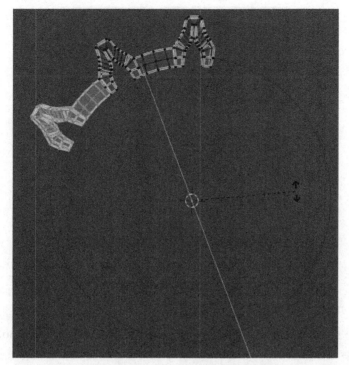

Figure 10.25 – Duplicating the tooth

After completing the outer part of the sprocket, we will move on to the inner part.

13. Add a cylinder in the middle of the circle and create a shape to connect it to the outer sprocket:

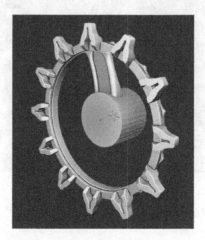

Figure 10.26 – Sprocket center

14. Add some details to the sprocket, such as screws in the teeth and in the center:

Figure 10.27 – Adding details

15. Using the same techniques that we used to create the sprocket so far, try to create a few more layers behind the sprocket.

Remember that the back of the sprocket should also have teeth for pulling the tracks.

Figure 10.28 – Completed sprocket

16. Place the sprocket at the back of the tank:

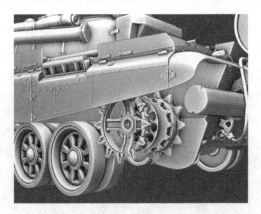

Figure 10.29 – Sprocket placement

We have now finished the rear sprocket. There are still two types of wheels that we must create, and we will do that next.

Modeling the front sprocket

We will now create the front sprocket using similar tools and methods:

1. Create a circle with 50 vertices and select five of the edges equally apart.

   To ensure equal distance, create another circle with five vertices in the middle. We will use this five-sided shape to accurately measure the equal distance between selected edges.

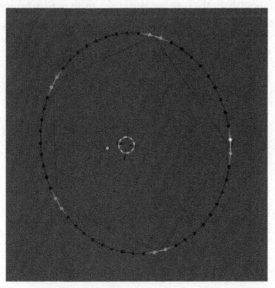

Figure 10.30 – Selecting five edges

2. Activate proportional editing by pressing *O*, and set the mode to **Sharp**. Then, move the five edges forward to turn them into spikes:

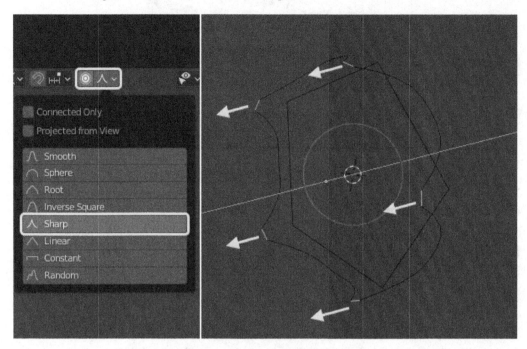

Figure 10.31 – Proportional editing

3. Extrude the circle with *E*, then press the right mouse button to snap the extruded shape back to its original place. Then, scale the shape up to add some width:

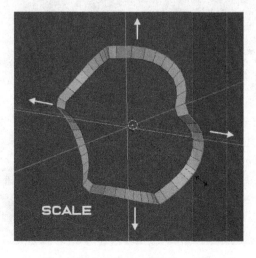

Figure 10.32 – Extruding the circle

Here are a few steps to turn this shape into our second sprocket:

I.   Extrude the shape backward and flatten it in the back by scaling it to 0 on the appropriate axis.

II. Duplicate the shape and mirror it by scaling it to -1. Remember to correct the normals.

III. Add a rim the same way we did on the previous sprocket, that is, by creating one arm and then duplicating and rotating it around the center.

IV. Add some screws and general details to the object:

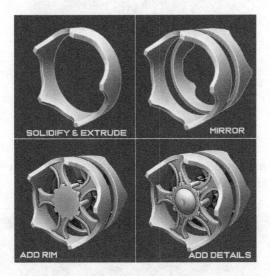

Figure 10.33 – Completing the front wheel

5.   Attach the front wheel to the front of the tank by creating a simple shape to hold it to the hull:

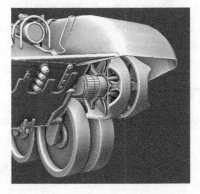

Figure 10.34 – Attaching the wheel

The front and rear sprockets are complete. We need one more final type of wheel on our tank.

6. Create a small and simple wheel above the main wheels we created earlier. This is used to keep the tension in the tracks:

Figure 10.35 – Tension wheel

7. Duplicate the tension wheel and place it in three locations: between wheels *1* and *2*, wheels *3* and *4*, and wheels *5* and *6*:

Figure 10.36 – Tension wheels

We have now created all the wheels for the tank. Next, we will create the tracks and place them around the wheels.

Creating the tracks

In this section, we will model a single track, duplicate it with an **Array** modifier, and wrap the tracks around the wheels using a curve:

1. Add a thin plate, just long enough to fit in between the teeth of the sprocket:

Figure 10.37 – Track plate

2. Add a cylinder with four loop cuts along the side of this shape. This will act as a hinge to connect the tracks:

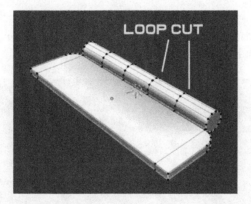

Figure 10.38 – Cylinder with loop cuts

3. Duplicate two of the face loops and mirror them to the other side of the track with the 3D Cursor:

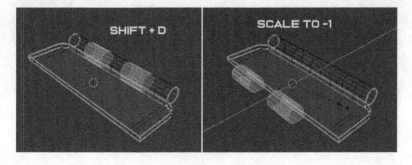

Figure 10.39 – Mirroring face loops

4. Delete some face loops to create an interrupted cylinder, like in *Figure 10.40*. This is the basic shape of the track:

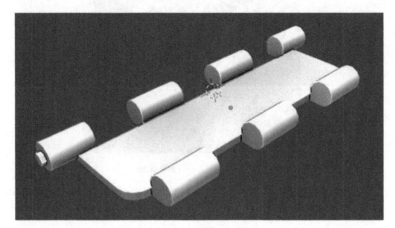

Figure 10.40 – Basic track shape

5. Use a plane to create some borders around this shape. When solidified, this will be the tank-track equivalent of tire tread on a car's wheel:

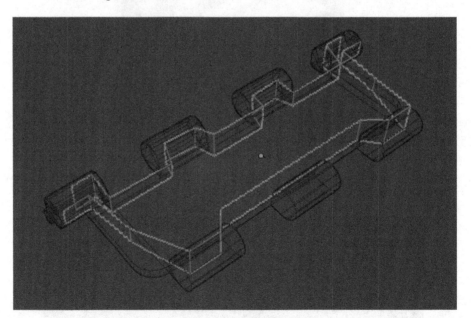

Figure 10.41 – Track tread

6. Solidify the shape and bevel its edges:

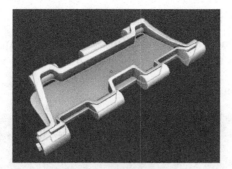

Figure 10.42 – Solidified track tread

7. Connect the two sides with some more bars:

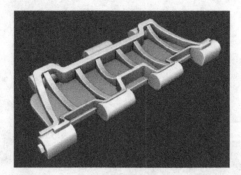

Figure 10.43 – Completed track

Adding an **Array** modifier to the track will show that multiple tracks can connect perfectly:

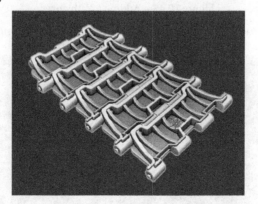

Figure 10.44 – Arraying the tracks

We have now modeled a single track and copied it with an **Array** modifier. Next, we will place the tracks around the wheels and sprockets.

Finishing the tracks

In this section, we will wrap the tracks around the wheels and sprockets using a curve with a **Curve** modifier. In the next few steps, we will create a curve around the wheels:

1. Add a **Path** curve beneath the wheels:

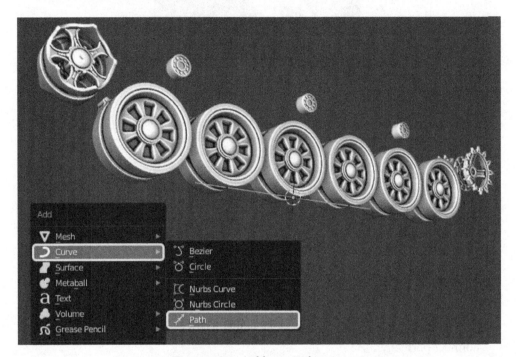

Figure 10.45 – Adding a Path curve

2. In side view, extrude the curve vertices around the wheels and sprockets:

Figure 10.46 – Extruding the curve

3. Connect the end of the curve back to the beginning by selecting the first and last vertices of the curve and filling by pressing *F*:

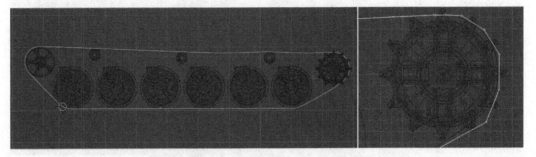

Figure 10.47 – Completing the curve loop

4. Place the tracks on the curve and ensure that the origin of the curve and the origin of the track are roughly in the same place.

Remember that the origin can be set to the 3D Cursor in the **Object** menu.

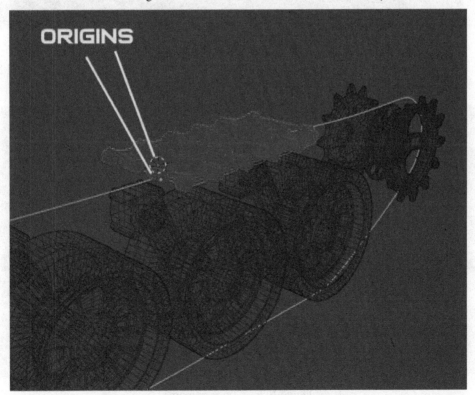

Figure 10.48 – Setting origins

5. Add a **Curve** modifier to the tracks and select the path curve for **Curve Object**:

Figure 10.49 – Curve Object

When setting the curve object, the tracks often snap to a different place at an odd orientation, like in *Figure 10.50*:

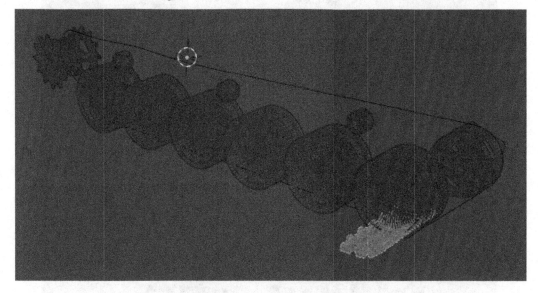

Figure 10.50 – Track snapping

6. To correctly place the tracks, adjust **Deform Axis** in the **Curve** modifier menu. The correct axis can vary, so try all options to see which one works best:

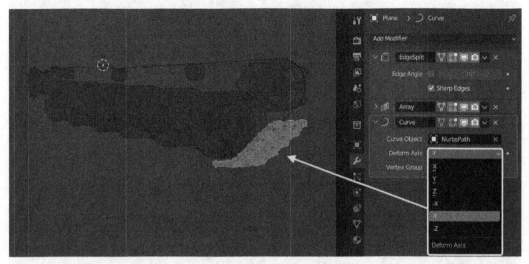

Figure 10.51 – Deform Axis

7. Increase the count in the **Array** modifier to complete the tracks:

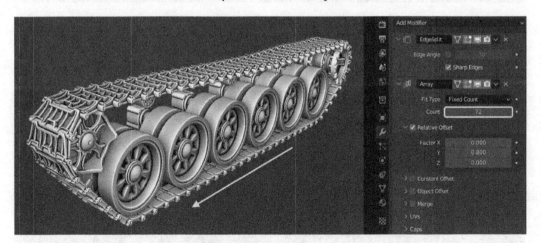

Figure 10.52 – Array count

Sometimes, the connecting track will not be aligned correctly, like in *Figure 10.53*:

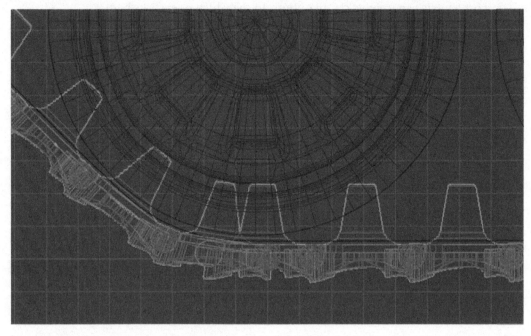

Figure 10.53 – Unaligned tracks

8. To correctly align the tracks, slightly adjust the offset **Factor** value in the **Array** modifier menu:

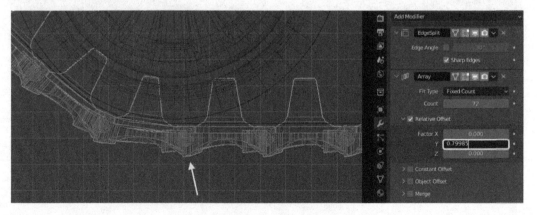

Figure 10.54 – Offset Factor

9. Finally, duplicate all the wheels, sprockets, and tracks and copy them to the other side of the tank:

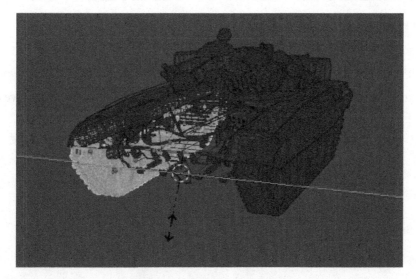

Figure 10.55 – Mirroring the tracks

Figure 10.56 shows the completed T-72 model:

Figure 10.56 – T-72 tank

We now have a completed high-poly T-72 tank model with tracks ready for rigging.

Summary

In this chapter, we created wheels, sprockets, and tracks and so completed the T-72 tank model. This is the last modeling chapter of this book.

In the next chapter, we will use constraints to rig the tracks and wheels so that we can put the tank into motion and enable it for animation.

11
Rigging Tank Tracks

In this chapter, we will go beyond modeling and explore Blender's **Constraint** features. Constraints are functions used to form relationships between objects, so that one object change depending on the behavior of another object. In our case, we will form a relationship between the movement of the tank and the rotation of the wheels and tracks, which will automatically turn them as the tank moves.

By the end of this chapter, you will have a solid understanding of the **Transformation** constraint, and a fully rigged tank. The skills learned in this chapter can also be used to rig a bicycle chain, chainsaw, gears, and many other things with similarly related mechanical behavior.

We will cover the following topics in this chapter:

- Adjusting the tracks
- Rigging with constraints
- Rigging the wheels and sprockets
- Parenting the tracks

Adjusting the tracks

In this section, we will make some adjustments to the tracks that we created in *Chapter 10, Modeling Tank Tracks*. Namely, we will fix some alignment issues, which will allow us to create a more realistic rig.

Figure 11.1 shows that the tracks are not correctly aligned with the sprocket. We can see this because parts of the tracks are clipping through the sprocket teeth. There are also visible scaling issues, as the tracks are wider than the gaps between the sprocket teeth:

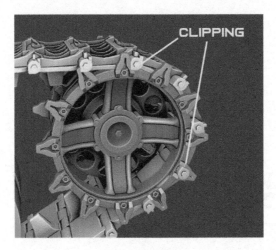

Figure 11.1 – Clipping

In the following few steps, we will adjust the curve and the scale of the tracks to make them fit the sprocket correctly:

1. Scale the track down in **Edit Mode**, but make sure its length still fits the width of the sprocket. To ensure the length stays the same, scale only on two axes (the *Z* and *Y* axes):

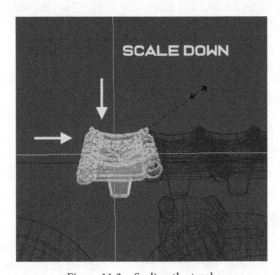

Figure 11.2 – Scaling the track

Now, the distance between each track is the same as the distance between the teeth:

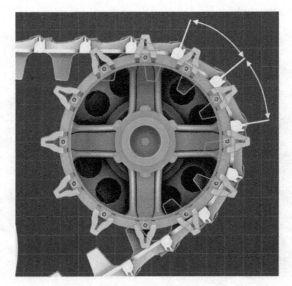

Figure 11.3 – Track distance

2.   Move the tracks so that the track knots are exactly in the middle of the tooth gaps:

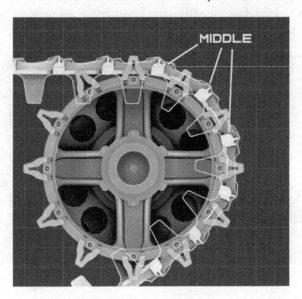

Figure 11.4 – Track knots

3. Bring the vertices of the curve closer to the sprocket to close any gaps between the tracks and the sprocket:

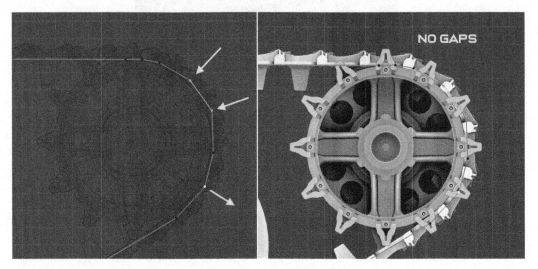

Figure 11.5 – Curve alignment

4. Correct the **Count** and Offset **Factor** values in the **Array** modifier so that the tracks connect again. We scaled the tracks down, so we need more tracks to complete the loop:

Figure 11.6 – Array modifier

Our tracks are now correctly aligned and technically more realistic. Next, we will begin rigging the tracks and wheels.

Rigging with constraints

In this section, we will use empty objects and constraints to rig the tracks and wheels. In the following steps, we will bind the movement of the tracks to the rotation of an empty sphere using constraints:

1. Create an **empty sphere**. To do so, press *Shift + A*, and find **Sphere** in the **Empty** menu.

    An empty object is an object that exists but is not visible in renders. It is commonly used as a placeholder, reference, or rigging object.

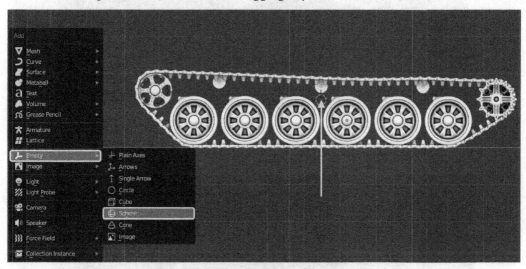

Figure 11.7 – Empty sphere

2. Press *F2* to rename the object as Sphere:

Figure 11.8 – Renaming

3. Select the tracks and find the **Object Constraint Properties** tab. Then, open the **Add Object Constraint** menu:

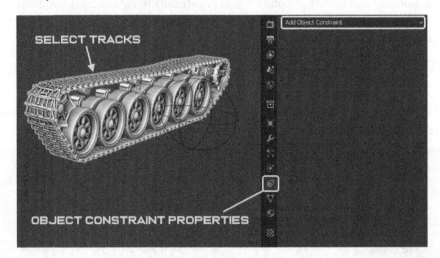

Figure 11.9 – Object Constraint

4. Add a **Transformation** constraint:

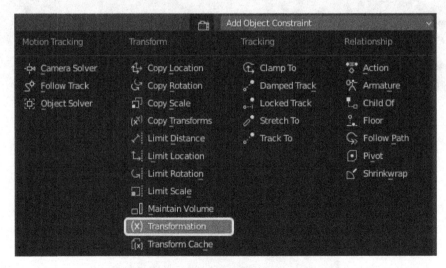

Figure 11.10 – Transformation constraint

This will create a menu in the **Object Constraints** tab, much like a modifier. *Figure 11.11 (left)* shows the default **Transformation** constraint menu.

5. Check the **Extrapolate** checkbox and set **Owner** to **Local Space**, as shown in *Figure 11.11* (right):

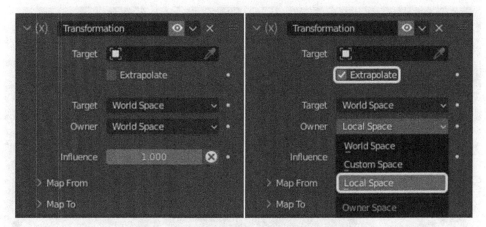

Figure 11.11 – Transformation constraint (left) and constraint settings (right)

6. In the **Target** menu, find the empty sphere named **Sphere**:

Figure 11.12 – Target

7. Expand the **Map From** and **Map To** menus. Select **Rotation** in the former and **Location** in the latter.

    By doing this, we are translating the rotation of the sphere into the movement of the tracks. In other words, when the sphere rotates, the tracks move.

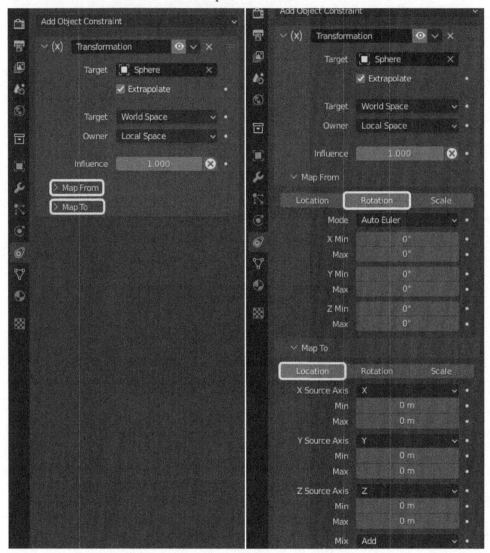

Figure 11.13 – Rotation to Location

8. In the **Map From** menu, set **X Max** to 1 degree. In the **Map To** menu, set **Y Source Axis** to X:

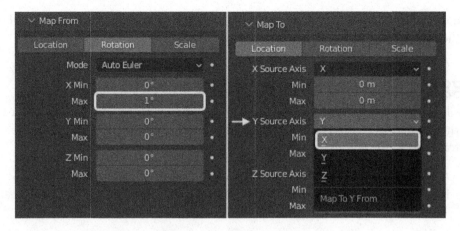

Figure 11.14 – Axes settings

9. In the **Map To** menu, set **Y Source Axis Max** to -1 m.

For every one degree by which the empty sphere rotates around the *X* axis, the tracks will move by one meter in the negative direction along the *Y* axis.

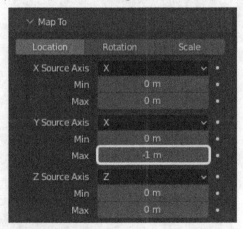

Figure 11.15 – Map To

Rotating the empty sphere will now cause the tracks to move:

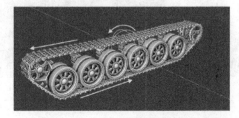

Figure 11.16 – Track movement

The tracks now move with the sphere, but the wheels do not yet rotate. Next, we will also link the wheels to the empty sphere.

Rigging the wheels and sprockets

We will now map the rotation of the sphere to the rotation of the wheels. This will make the wheels rotate in relation to the empty sphere. In the following steps, we will add constraints to all the wheels and sprockets:

1. Add a **Transformation** constraint to the sprocket, and map from **Rotation** to **Rotation**. Set **X Max** to 1° in the **Map From** menu, and to 100° in the **Map To** menu.

   Remember to set the same settings as before at the top of the constraint menu:

Figure 11.17 – Sprocket constraint

For every one degree that the empty sphere rotates, the sprocket will now rotate 100 degrees. The problem now is that the sprocket is not turning quickly enough in relation to the tracks, which causes the tracks to clip through the sprocket as they are rotating:

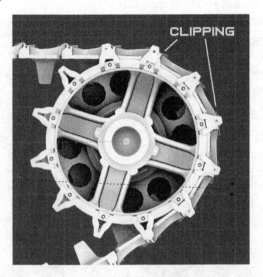

Figure 11.18 – Sprocket clipping

2. Tweak the **X Max** value in the **Map To** menu until you find a value that works well.

Keep in mind that your number will likely by different from mine, as our wheels have a slightly different radius.

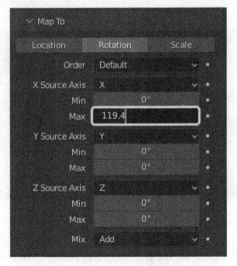

Figure 11.19 – Value tweaking

3. Create the same constraint for the wheels.

    It is easier to only create it on one wheel, and then duplicate the rigged wheel. This wheel has a different rotation value because it does not have the same radius as the sprocket, so it does not rotate at the same rate:

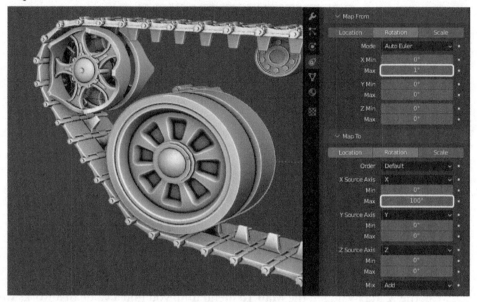

Figure 11.20 – Wheel constraint

4. Create the same constraint on all the other wheels, including the front sprocket and the tension wheels:

Figure 11.21 – Rigged wheels

We have now mapped the movement and rotation of the tracks and wheels to the rotation of the empty sphere. Next, we will map the rotation of the sphere to the movement of the tank.

Parenting the tracks

We will now parent the tracks to the tank and translate tank movement into track rotation. This way, movement of the hull will result in rotation of the empty sphere, which will in turn cause all the wheels and tracks to move. In the next few steps, we will bind the tracks to the rest of the tank using constraints:

1. Create an empty cube and scale it so that it completely contains the tracks:

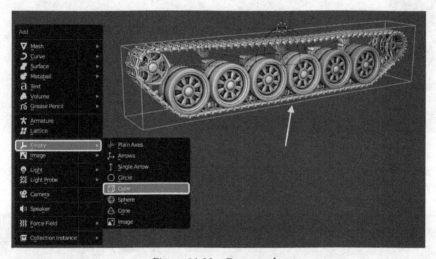

Figure 11.22 – Empty cube

2. Parent all the objects, including the empty sphere and the track curve, to the empty cube:

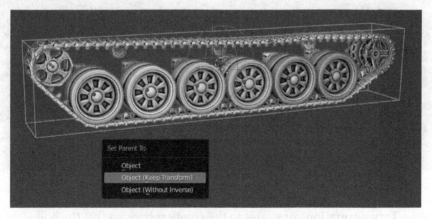

Figure 11.23 – Parenting to the empty cube

3.   Rename the hull of the tank as `Hull`:

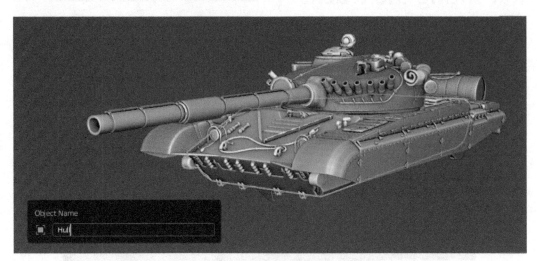

Figure 11.24 – Renaming the hull

4.   Parent the empty cube to the hull by selecting the cube, then the hull, and pressing *Ctrl + P*:

Figure 11.25 – Parenting to the hull

5.   Add a **Transformation** constraint to the empty sphere, so that the hull location is mapped to sphere rotation. To do this, copy the configuration shown in *Figure 11.26*:

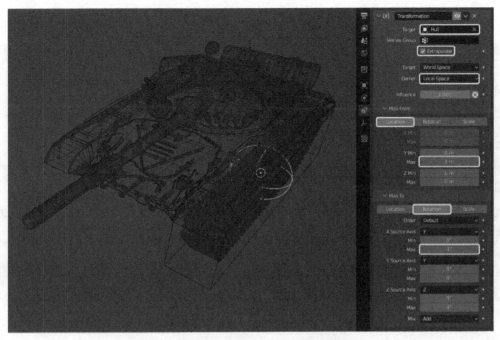

Figure 11.26 – Empty sphere constraint

6. Duplicate the wheels, tracks, and empties and mirror them to the other side of the tank. Remember to correct the normals:

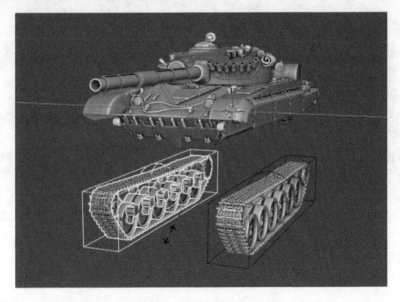

Figure 11.27 – Mirroring

Moving the tank back and forth will now rotate the wheels and tracks accordingly:

Figure 11.28 – Rotating tracks and wheels

7. Collapse the **Transformation** constraint menu of the empty sphere object using the arrow in the top-left corner of the menu:

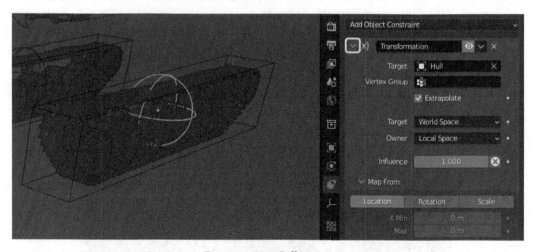

Figure 11.29 – Collapsing

8. Add a second **Transformation** constraint so that we now have two of them.

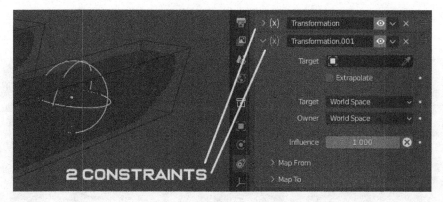

Figure 11.30 – Two constraints

9. Set **Hull** as the target object, and map from **Rotation** to **Rotation**.

In the **Map From** menu, set **Z Max** to 1°. In the **Map To** menu, set **X Source Axis** to Z and set **Z Max** to approximately -0.055°:

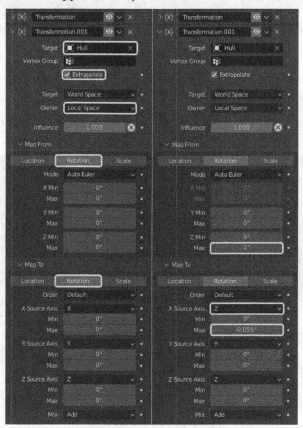

Figure 10.31 – Second constraint

Now, rotating the tank around the *Z* axis will cause the tracks and wheels to rotate accordingly:

Figure 10.32 – Tank rotation

10. Repeat *steps 7-9* on the other empty sphere. This time, set **X Max** to 0.055° (positive, as opposed to negative).

This will cause the tracks on the other side of the tank to rotate in the other direction, in relation to the ones on the other side, when the tank turns:

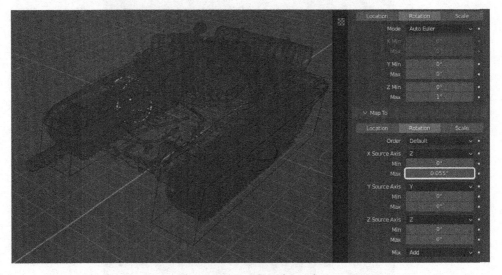

Figure 10.33 – The other side

When the tank moves or turns, the tracks will now rotate accordingly:

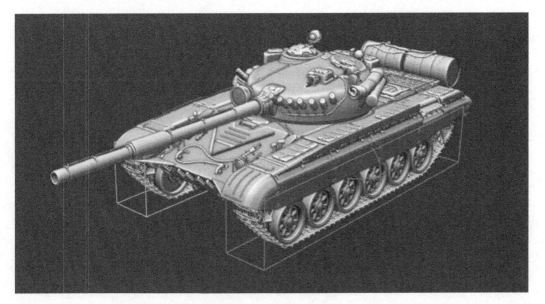

Figure 10.34 – Rigged tank

Our tank is now fully rigged with constraints and prepared for animation.

Summary

In this chapter, we learned how to use transformation constraints to convert the movement or rotation of one object into the movement or rotation of another. We translated the movement of the tank into the rotation of the tracks so that the tracks and wheels will animate when the tank moves around.

In the next chapter, we will apply the techniques that we have already learned to create some materials and textures for the tank and finish the project.

12
Texturing the Tank

In this chapter, we will create materials and textures for the T-72 tank using tools and techniques that we learned previously. By the end of this chapter, the tank will be complete.

We will cover the following topics in this chapter:

- Texturing the turret
- Combining nodes
- Texturing the tracks

Texturing the turret

We will now create a texture for the turret using UV unwrapping and an Edge Mask:

1. Create a simple green material for the body of the turret.

    The gun and turret details are left out because they are much more intricate than the turret, and they will have different material settings:

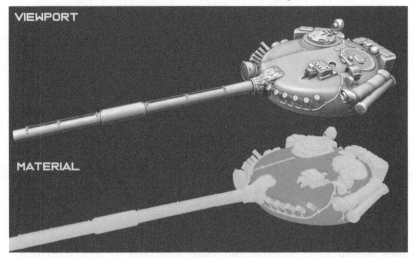

Figure 12.1 – Turret material

2. With the mesh selected in **Edit Mode**, select **Smart UV Project** in the **UV Mapping** menu:

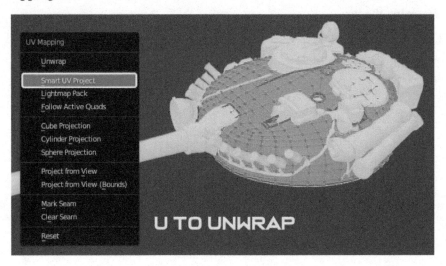

Figure 12.2 – Smart UV Project

3. On the **Shading** screen, create a new image with an **Image Texture** node. Name this image UV_TEST and set **Generated Type** to **UV Grid**:

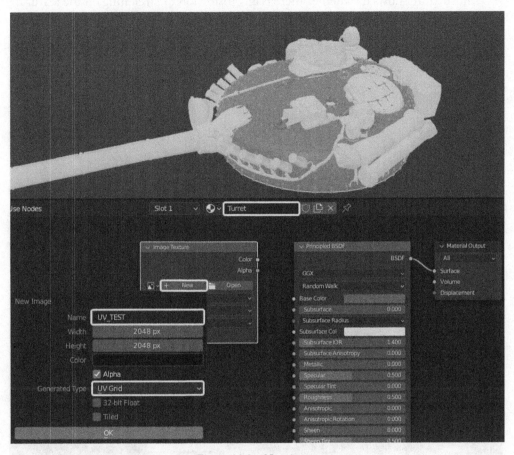

Figure 12.3 – New image

4. Plug this image into the base color to project it on the surface of the turret.

    This texture shows us whether there is any distortion or stretching on the texture resulting from bad UV unwrapping. In this case, the projection is good:

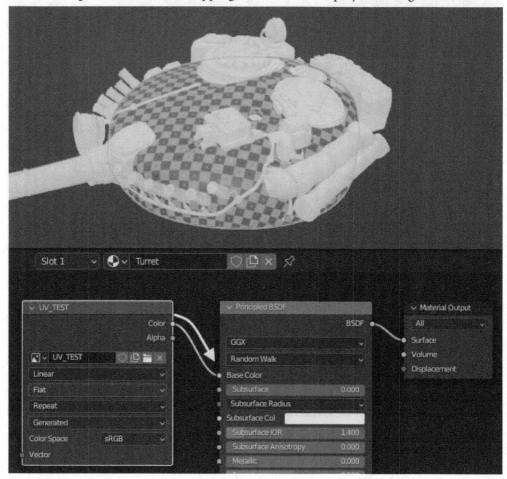

Figure 12.4 – UV_TEST

5. Copy the nodes from *Figure 12.5* to generate an Edge Mask. Delete all the other nodes:

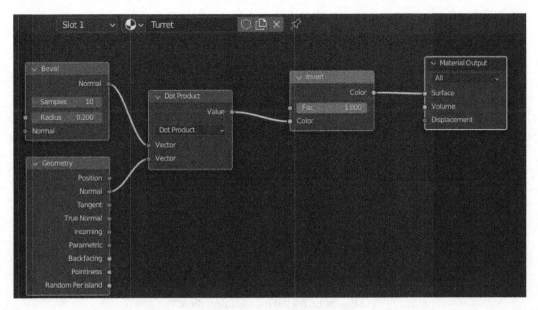

Figure 12.5 – Edge mask nodes

6. Create a new image in an **Image Texture** node and name it Turret_Mask. We will use this image to bake the Edge Mask for this object:

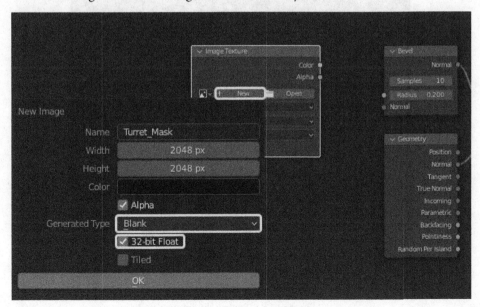

Figure 12.6 – Edge mask image

7. In the **Render settings** tab, set **Bake Type** to **Emit** and bake the Edge Mask. Remember that this will only work in cycles.

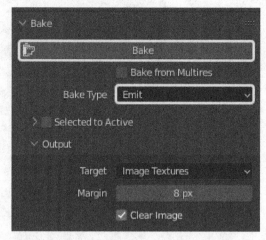

Figure 12.7 – Baking the Edge Mask

8. Save the baked Edge Mask:

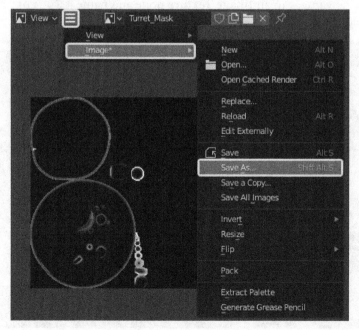

Figure 12.8 – Saving the image

We have now generated an Edge Mask that we can use to create edge wear on the turret. Next, we will combine the Edge Mask with some nodes to create a realistic texture.

Combining nodes

We will now use some nodes to turn the Edge Mask image into a realistic texture:

1. Use a **Mix RGB** node to control the colors of the Edge Mask:

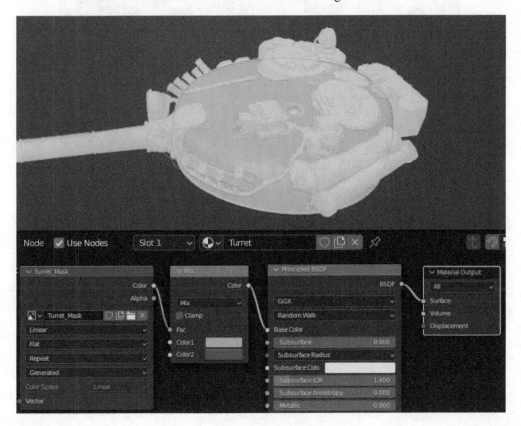

Figure 12.9 – Mix RGB

2. Set the **Math** node to **Power** to amplify the intensity of the edge wear effect:

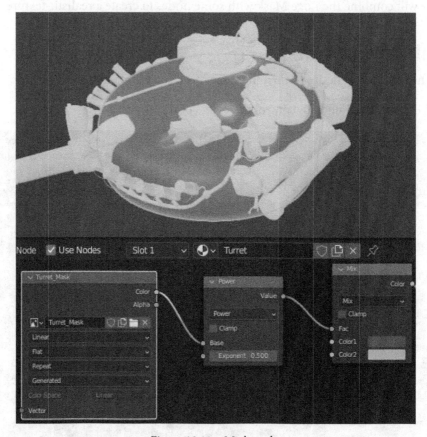

Figure 12.10 – Math node

3. Control the **Exponent** value of the **Power** node with a **Noise Texture** node and a **ColorRamp** node.

    This will make the surface appear worn and scratched:

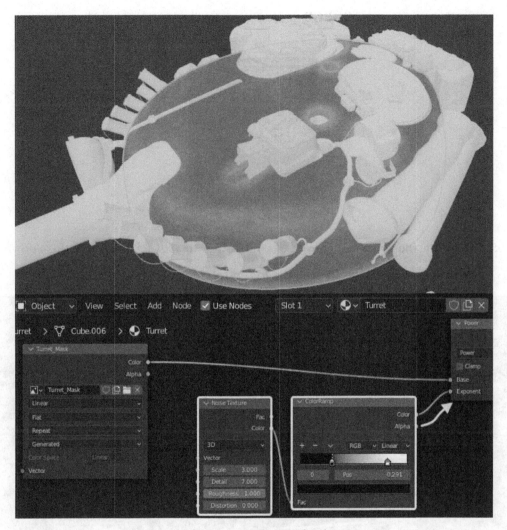

Figure 12.11 – Noise Texture and ColorRamp

4. Set the colors in the **Mix RGB** node to green for the paint and light brown or gray for the wear:

Figure 12.12 – Mix RGB colors

5. Duplicate the nodes from the base color input with *Shift + D* and move them down.

    We will use this second set of nodes to control the roughness of the texture:

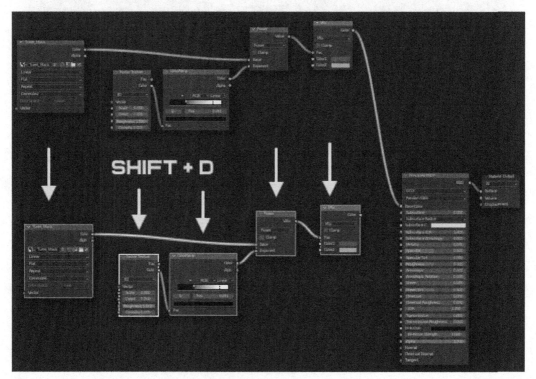

Figure 12.13 – Duplicating nodes

6. Set the colors of the second **Mix RGB** node to white and black. Remember that, on a roughness map, black equals shiny while white equals not shiny.

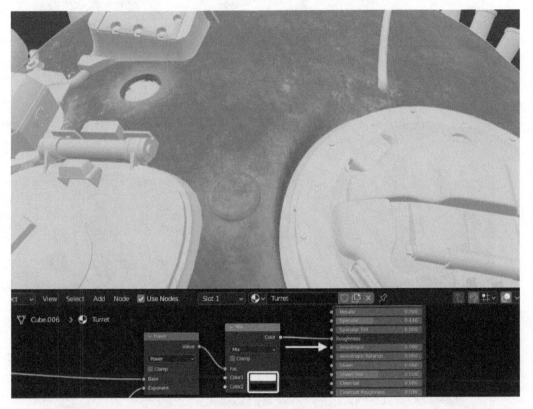

Figure 12.14 – Roughness

7. Add a **Noise Texture** node and a **Bump** node with settings like in *Figure 12.15*, and plug them into the **Normal** input of the **Principled BSDF** node.

This will make the surface of the turret appear slightly bumpy:

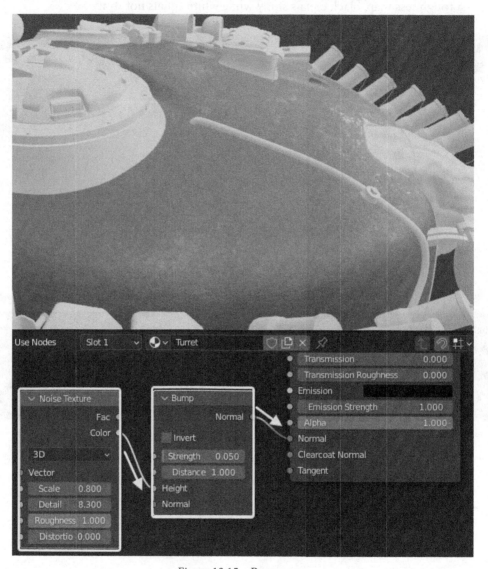

Figure 12.15 – Bump map

8. Repeat the same process on the other parts of the turret. Notice how there are a few new simple materials, such as dark glass or green fabrics.

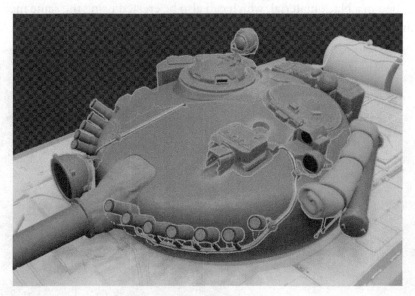

Figure 12.16 – Textured turret

9. Use the same method to texture the rest of the tank.

There is another new material on the skirts, which should appear to be made of rubber. This can be achieved by copying and assigning the same material here but changing the colors:

Figure 12.17 – Textured hull

The same technique can also be used to texture the wheels and sprockets since they appear to be made of the same material as the rest of the tank. The wheels are wrapped in a black material, which can also be created using the same method but with different colors:

Figure 12.18 – Textured wheels

We have now textured the turret, hull, wheels, and sprockets with similar materials. Next, we will texture the tracks.

Texturing the tracks

We will now create a texture for the tracks using a slightly different node setup:

1. First, create an Edge Mask for the track object:

3. Plug a **Noise Texture** node and a **ColorRamp** node into the **Mix RGB** node:

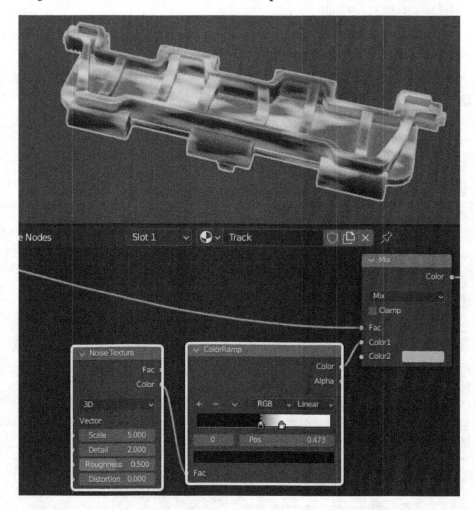

Figure 12.21 – Track texture

4. Add a **Node Wrangler** to the **Noise Texture** node by selecting it, pressing *Ctrl* + *T*, and using the UV output.

This will correct the projection of the noise texture. Note that we have also adjusted the settings in the **Noise Texture** node:

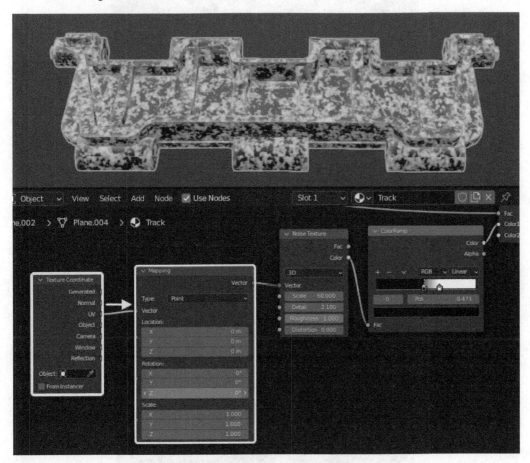

Figure 12.22 – Node Wrangler

5. Use the plus button to add a new marker in the **ColorRamp** node. This will create a multi-colored texture on the track:

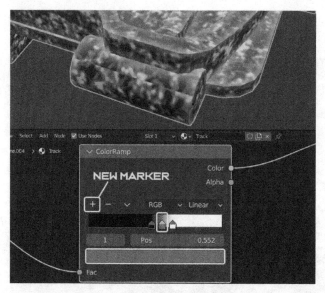

Figure 12.23 – ColorRamp texture

6. Create a mix of dark brown colors in the **ColorRamp** node to create a dark rusty texture:

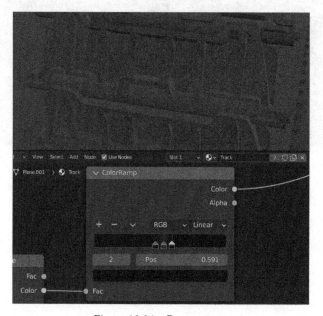

Figure 12.24 – Rust texture

7. Create another bump map with a **Noise Texture** node and a **Bump** node, but also add a **ColorRamp** node in between. Use multiple shades of gray in the **ColorRamp** node to create a bumpy surface:

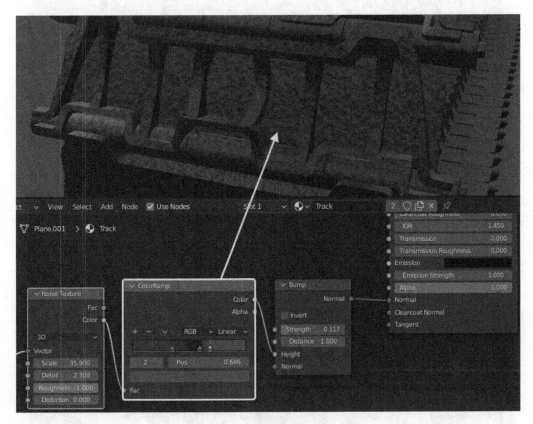

Figure 12.25 – ColorRamp bump map

8. Use a **Math** node to amplify the Edge Mask and set the edge color:

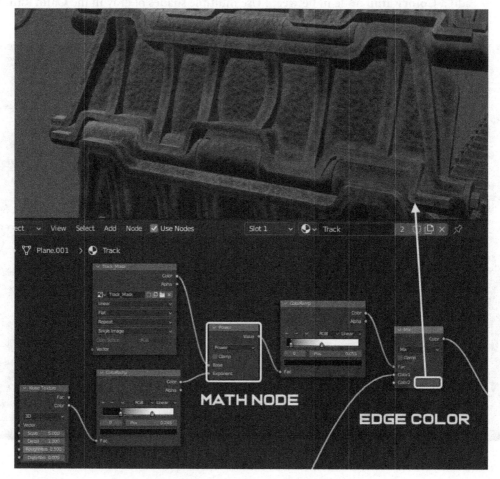

Figure 12.26 – Track edge wear

9. Place the tracks back onto the tank:

Figure 12.27 – Textured tracks

Figure 12.28 shows the final render of the T-72 tank:

Figure 12.28 – T-72 final render

The T-72 model is now fully textured. You can now prepare the lighting and camera settings to render the tank.

Summary

In this chapter, we used material and geometry nodes to bake Edge Masks for the various parts of the model. We then created textures, edge wear, roughness maps, and normal maps. Texturing the T-72 tank model completes the final project of this book.

We have now covered all the essential tools and techniques for modeling, texturing, and rigging in Blender. Having seen the procedures and workflows for creating advanced high-poly models, you are now ready to take on new projects by applying some of the skills you have learned from this book. Regardless of what your next project is going to be, the methods used will remain similar, and you can always revisit previous chapters to sharpen your abilities.

Index

Symbols

3D Cursor 34, 60, 61

A

Array modifier
  used, for completing rails 78-84

B

bevel 8
Blender
  hard-surface objects, defining 7

C

clipping 62
commander's hatch, T-72 Tank turret
  modeling 274-280
constraints
  rigging with 325-330

D

decals
  painting 206

E

edge loop 30
Edge Mask
  generating 109
edge wear
  creating 119-126
exhaust grills
  creating, with arrays for
      T-72 tank 262-267
exhaust pipe
  adding, to T-72 tank 261, 262

F

FN SCAR assault rifle
  attachment rails, creating 44-47
  barrel, detailing 93-99
  barrel shape, creating 48-50
  handgrip shape, adding 43
  iron sights, modeling 93-99
  lower receiver, modeling 28, 30
  Mirror modifier, applying 53
  parts, separating 27
  rails, completing with Array
      modifier 78-84
  references, preparing 24-27

simple magazine, adding 54-57
stock, creating 40-42
upper receiver, modeling 34-40
FN SCAR, materials
multiple materials, adding 106-109
FN SCAR project
Edge Mask, generating 109
edge wear, creating 119-126
lighting 132
materials, creating 102
rendering 132
reviewing 18
scene, lighting 132-136
scene, rendering 136-140
FN SCAR project, Edge Mask
edge map, baking 116-119
edges, detecting 109-115
FN SCAR project, edge wear
materials, separating 126-129
nodes, copying to other
materials 129-131
FN SCAR project, materials
Material Nodes, using 102-105
nodes, combining 105, 106
front end
designing, for T-72 tank 238, 239
front plate 238
front sprocket
modeling 307-310

H

handgrip, FN SCAR assault rifle
modeling 61-66
hard-surface modeling
about 4, 5
organic modeling 5

hard-surface modeling workflow
Block-Out Model, creating 16
creating 14
detail, increasing 16, 17
parts, separating 15
references, gathering 14
hard-surface models
Edge Loop 11, 12
edges 8, 9
loose parts 13, 14
surfaces 9-11
hard-surface objects
defining, in Blender 7
hue, saturation, value (HSV) 104
hull front
designing, for T-72 tank 249-258

L

loop cutting 30
loose parts 13, 14
lower plate
designing, for T-72 tank 239-244
lower receiver, FN SCAR assault rifle
loop cutting 30-32
modeling 28, 30
viewport, shading 32, 34

M

Material Capture (MatCap)
about 173
applying 174, 175
Material Nodes 102-105
materials
creating 102
nodes, copying to other 129-131
separating 126-129

Mirror modifier
  about 50
  object, mirroring with 50-53

N

N-gont 39
nodes
  combining 105, 106
  combining, with Edge Mask 347-354

O

object
  mirroring, with Mirror modifier 50-53
organic modeling 5-7
origin 50
orthographic projection 25

P

Proportional Editing 10

R

rear end
  designing, for T-72 tank 268-272
rear sprocket
  modeling 301-07
receiver, FN SCAR assault rifle
  detail creation, simplifying 73-75
  detailing 67-72
  screws, modeling 75-78
references
  about 24
  preparing, for FN SCAR
    assault rifle 24-27

S

scene
  lighting 132-136
  rendering 136-140
sci-fi race ship
  armor panels, texture painting 193-203
  bevel map, baking 189-192
  decals, painting 204-214
  normal decals, baking 207-211
  normal decals, painting 207
  normal map, baking 178-184
  UV unwrapping 184-188
Sci-Fi Race Ship
  armor panels, modeling 157-161
  basic shapes, attaching 146-149
  basic shapes, modeling 144-146
  details, adding to basic shapes 150-156
  final details, adding 171-173
  MatCap, applying 173-175
  rear part of ship, adding 168-171
  wings, adding 162-167
Sci-fi race ship project
  reviewing 18
Shear tool 156
side armor
  modeling, for T-72 tank 244-249
skirt
  about 244
  modeling, for T-72 tank 259-261
solidification technique 49
sprockets
  rigging with 330-332
stock
  finishing 85-92
suspension
  creating, for T-72 tank 294-296

T

T-72 tank
  exhaust grills, creating with
      arrays 262-267
  exhaust pipe, adding 261, 262
  front end, designing 238, 239
  hull front, designing 249-258
  hull, modeling 220-226
  lower plate, designing 239-244
  nodes, combining 347-354
  rear end, designing 268-272
  side armor, modeling 244-249
  simple turret, adding 230, 231
  skirt, creating 226-230
  skirt, modeling 259-261
  suspension, creating 294-296
  tracks, adjusting 321-324
  tracks, creating 310-313
  tracks, parenting 333-339
  tracks, texturing 354-361
  tracks, wrapping 314-319
  turret, texturing 342-347
  wheels, adding 232-236
  wheels, creating 294-296
  wheels, modeling 297-300

T-72 tank project
  reviewing 19
T-72 Tank turret
  commander's hatch, modeling 274
  details, adding for completion 286-290
  details, creating 280-286
tracks
  adjusting, for T-72 tank 321-324
  creating, for T-72 tank 310-313
  parenting, for T-72 tank 333-339
  texturing 354-361
  wrapping, for T-72 tank 314-319
transformations 61
turret 230

W

wheels
  creating, for T-72 tank 294-296
  front sprocket, modeling 307-310
  modeling, for T-72 tank 297-300
  rear sprocket, modeling 301-307
  rigging with 330-332

Other Books You May Enjoy

If you enjoyed this book, you may be interested in these other books by Packt:

Shading, Lighting, and Rendering with Blender EEVEE

Samantha Crowder

ISBN: 9781803230962

- Explore EEVEE Render Properties for optimal outcomes.

- Focus on shading processes, including those that are both traditional and more cutting-edge.

- Understand composition and create effective concept art inside Blender.

- Discover procedural workflows to shorten the artistic process instead of getting mired in details.

Taking Blender to the Next Level

Ruan Lotter

ISBN: 9781803233567

- Use geometry nodes to quickly create complex 3D scenes and motion graphics renders.

- Create realistic textures using physically based rendering materials.

- 3D scan real-life objects using a normal camera and clean up the model using Blender.

- Use rigid body simulations to create dynamic scenes.

- Understand how to perform 3D tracking within Blender.

Packt is searching for authors like you

If you're interested in becoming an author for Packt, please visit `authors.packtpub.com` and apply today. We have worked with thousands of developers and tech professionals, just like you, to help them share their insight with the global tech community. You can make a general application, apply for a specific hot topic that we are recruiting an author for, or submit your own idea.

Share Your Thoughts

Now you've finished *Blender 3D Incredible Machines*, we'd love to hear your thoughts! Scan the QR code below to go straight to the Amazon review page for this book and share your feedback or leave a review on the site that you purchased it from.

`https://packt.link/r/1801817812`

Your review is important to us and the tech community and will help us make sure we're delivering excellent quality content.

Made in the USA
Coppell, TX
26 November 2023

24671808R00214